FIGHTER  ACES

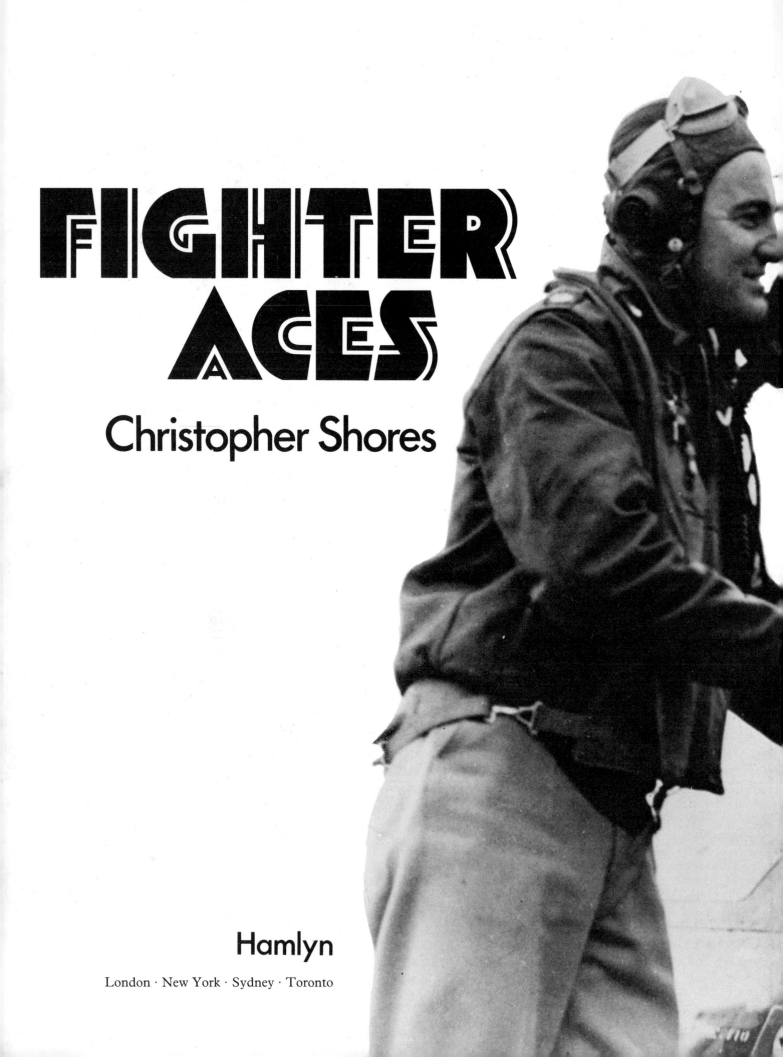

FIGHTER ACES

Christopher Shores

Hamlyn

London · New York · Sydney · Toronto

Published by
The Hamlyn Publishing Group Limited 1975
London · New York · Sydney · Toronto
Astronaut House, Hounslow Road,
Feltham, Middlesex, England

© Copyright
The Hamlyn Publishing Group Limited 1975

ISBN 0 600 30230 X

Printed in Great Britain by
Jarrold and Sons Limited, Norwich

Endpapers
Some of the striking talismans and identification symbols
which adorned the aircraft of German, Italian, French,
American and Japanese fighter pilots during the First and
Second World Wars.

page 1
Ritter von Schleich, the 'Black Knight', German ace of the
First World War.

pages 2–3
Major Francis Gabreski (right), an American ace in both
the Second World War and the Korean conflict, is
congratulated on return from a successful mission.

page 5
Captain Albert Ball, British ace of the First World War.

CONTENTS

INTRODUCTION

In every field of human endeavour a small number of men always rise head and shoulders above their fellows. This is certainly true in the field of aerial combat, and here the outstanding successes have often become national heroes and household names. These men are the fighter aces.

The story of the fighter ace is virtually the story of air combat. Nowhere has fighting between rival air forces continued for long before individual pilots have emerged who have enjoyed exceptional success in shooting down numbers of opposing aircraft. Again and again experience has proved that a small percentage of the pilots involved in air fighting will achieve the lion's share of the measurable results. This is not to decry the efforts and achievements of the less fortunate majority, whose presence and performance go far to create the conditions where the select bands of experts can function to the greatest advantage of all concerned.

The factors which combine to make a fighter ace are not easy to pin down. Some say strength is necessary to throw around a heavy fighter, yet exceptions to this rule frequently throw this argument into doubt. Brilliant piloting does not seem to feature often as a major factor, though doubtless it helps; many of the greatest aces were no more than adequate pilots. Good eyesight and quick reflexes are without question two of the greatest attributes, while the ability to shoot accurately and with economy of ammunition is of the greatest value—particularly for those who have mastered the difficult art of deflection shooting (i.e. firing at an opponent approaching or departing on a different line of flight to that followed by the attacker, rather than from directly astern or ahead).

Naked aggression may sometimes lead to the rapid building-up of a big score, but also almost always results in an early death as this can lead to headstrong and ill-conceived actions. The truly successful aces have usually enjoyed a modicum of aggression tempered by a wary self-control, which has governed when it is, or is not, prudent to attack. Training, experience and morale are all factors of great importance, while equipment is also a factor, though not quite such a vital one as it is often thought to be. A good, experienced pilot in a mediocre aircraft can almost always devise tactics which will allow him to outfight a less experienced or well-trained adversary in an excellent machine. Position and type of armament is also of far more importance than is generally realized. A good marksman, with a single cannon mounted in the fuselage along the centre-line of flight, will invariably obtain better results than a pilot with two such guns mounted in the wings. If his single gun carries 600 rounds of ammunition and his wing guns 300 rounds each, he will

frequently achieve double or more the number of successes for rounds fired with the former arrangement than with the latter.

The final factors—and probably the most important of all—are luck and circumstance. The sky is a big place, and the finest marksman and pilot in the world may simply never find himself in the right place at the right time, so that he goes for months without even seeing an opposing aircraft in the air. A fellow-pilot of equal ability may be more fortunate, and engage in combat on almost every flight. Clearly, a pilot in an air force which enjoys aerial superiority may seldom see the numerically weaker enemy, and consequently have little opportunity to build up a personal score. Conversely, the good pilot in the weaker air force will meet his numerically superior foes with much greater frequency, and as a result will have more opportunity to increase both his score and his expertise. Great aces do not therefore always reflect national success. Indeed, frequently the reverse is the case, their very level of success indicating that their backs are to the wall.

An attempt has been made here to provide a history of the fighter ace throughout the world, indicating where and when these men have appeared, what they have achieved, how many there have been, and what kind of men they were. It is felt that the reader will come to realize before he reaches the end of this book that this is a vast subject with many aspects. While the author has tried to provide as comprehensive an overall picture as possible, it has obviously been possible to touch only on some of the highlights and salient points. However, if what is written here encourages the reader to dig more deeply into any elements of this subject, then it will have more than served its purpose.

Not surprisingly in compiling so wide a variety of material, many people have aided the author either directly or indirectly, and a great debt of gratitude is due to them for making this book possible. At the top of the list must come Don Chalif, whose assistance with some of the smaller air forces – and particularly with the Chinese—was of critical importance. Many thanks are due also to Don's fellow-Americans Bill Hess, Frank Bailey, Wayne Braby, Dennis Connell, Kenn Rust, Edward Sims and Ray Toliver; in this country to Norman Franks, Clive Williams, Jean Alexander, Eddie Baker, and Brian Bridgeman; to Harry Creagen and Raymond Collishaw in Canada; to Eino Ritaranta and Kalevi Keskinen in Finland; Chris Ehrengardt in France; Fred Dierickx in Belgium; Corrado.Ricci in Italy; Hans Ring in Germany; Yasuho Izawa in Japan; Julius Gaal in Australia; and last but by no means least, to Michael Schoeman in South Africa.

7

THE FIRST WORLD WAR

The First World War
THE BACKGROUND

previous page
Pilots and other personnel of
No. 1 Squadron, RAF, with
their SE 5A fighters at
Clairmarais airfield, near St
Olmer, France, on 3 July 1918.

Fighter Ace! The very words are evocative of modern knights in the sky, the Red Baron, carefree young men rushing to their aircraft for another scramble, gaudily decorated fighters, dawn patrols and the Battle of Britain. But what is the truth that lies behind these romantic images? Who were the fighter aces?

Some of these questions can be easily answered, others cannot. Of one thing there is little doubt; it was the French, with their ready appreciation of the hero and their flair for the dramatic, who first coined the term 'Ace' – top of the pack. For the publicists and journalists the ace could not have appeared at a more opportune moment. 1915, the second year of the First World War, saw vast, anonymous armies stuck fast in the deadlock of trench warfare. The darling of the public, the cavalryman, was virtually unemployed, his role made redundant by the ugly reality of the trench and the machine-gun. The public and the press were aching for heroes when, for the first time, men began to fight each other in the sky.

In 1914 the aircraft of both sides began coming into contact with each other. At first each side was involved only in reconnaissance for the army, but it was not long before the more aggressively inclined were shooting at each other. Initially they used revolvers, rifles or carbines, but then some began taking machine-guns up with them, and before long each side had shot down some of the other's aircraft.

While official interest in these activities remained minimal, individual invention was soon to develop this haphazard exchange of fire into a more cold-blooded and determined business. During the spring of 1915 a Frenchman, Roland Garros, began flying over the front in a Morane monoplane scout with a Hotchkiss machine-gun fitted to fire directly forward over the nose of his aircraft. The scout at this time was a small single-seat machine designed for special high-speed reconnaissance missions, being lighter and more manœuvrable than the standard two-seaters then in service. As such it was the obvious choice as an aircraft for attacking the larger, more cumbersome two-seaters.

The snag with this early adaptation, however, was that the gun had to fire through the area in which the propeller revolved, and therefore would probably shoot this off when fired. The important invention incorporated in Garros's aircraft was tough metal wedges screwed to the propeller blades to deflect any bullets which might hit them. In fact this was a really crude improvisation, and in use propellers were frequently thrown off balance by the impact of the bullets, resulting in immediate forced-landings.

Garros first put the invention to practical use on 1 April 1915, shooting down an unsuspecting German Aviatik. Two more victories followed in swift succession, together with two or three less decisive combats, but on 19 April engine trouble forced Garros to land behind the German lines, and he was taken prisoner. He had already been publicized as an 'Ace' by this time, though in fact he was never to be an ace in the sense that the term was later to be understood – a pilot who had shot down five or more opposing aircraft.

The Germans inspected Garros's Morane with interest, and then turned it over to the Dutch aircraft manufacturer Anthony Fokker with a request that he swiftly prepare a copy. Fokker was advised by his engineers that a more satisfactory interrupter gear, which caused the gun to stop firing when the propeller blade passed in front of the muzzle, had already been designed by a German named Franz Schneider. Fokker's own *Eindekker* monoplane scout was already in service in small numbers and, taking one of these, he incorporated Schneider's system to enable a Spandau-made Maxim machine-gun to fire over the nose. This was probably the first truly viable single-seat fighting scout, and production of the aircraft in its armed version was swiftly got underway. The aircraft were then issued to German units in small numbers for the protection of the two-seaters.

At first the *Eindekkers* were rather slow to make their presence felt, but by the autumn and winter of 1915 they were appearing in greater numbers and exacting a heavy toll of British and French reconnaissance aircraft. This period marked the start of what came to be known as the 'Fokker Scourge', during which the first great German aces appeared.

In an effort to combat the Fokkers, the Allies introduced special fighting units, the British using the two-seat 'pusher' Vickers Gunbus, followed by early examples of the similar FE 2. However, an effective answer soon followed when each nation put into service their own single-seater fighting scouts. The French Nieuport 11 *Bébé* was a classic little tractor biplane (i.e. with the propeller in front), while the

The man who began it all. Roland Garros, the first pilot to shoot down an opposing aircraft while flying a single-seat machine with a fixed, forward-firing machine-gun. He is seen here with a Morane Type 'L' parasol, one of the scouting types he flew during 1915. The Hotchkiss gun and the metal plate attached to the propeller blade to deflect its bullets can be clearly seen.

British introduced the DH 2 pusher early in 1916, followed by the similar FE 8 and the tractor BE 12, a single-seater conversion of the reconnaissance BE 2, which was destined to be a failure as a fighter. The Nieuport and the DH 2 both had the measure of the *Eindekker*, and during the spring and summer the Allies were able to achieve a measure of air superiority. The Germans were by now also grouping their fighters into special units, and in the summer of 1916 introduced a new organization of *Jagdstaffeln*, or *Jastas*. These were small units of fighters which were based all along the front. At the same time new aircraft became available, Halberstadt and Albatros biplane scouts reaching these new units early in the autumn.

These new fighters outclassed the early British and French scouts, but the latter were able to counter this threat with the introduction of improved Nieuports and the new Spad S.7. The British were still lagging behind in fighter development and production, having to acquire Nieuports from the French during 1916. The first Sopwith Pups were becoming available late in the year, but only in small numbers. On the French front at the end of 1916 and the beginning of 1917, the Spads were able to maintain the balance, but over the British lines in Flanders the Germans soon regained a good measure of superiority.

As the armies on the ground engaged in the massive and costly battles at Verdun and Arras and on the Somme, ever-larger formations of opposing aircraft locked in battle overhead. The German and French authorities were not slow to seize upon the morale and propaganda value of the new aces, giving wide publicity to the exploits of the more successful pilots, and keeping a careful count of the victory tallies of all their pilots. The British were much less enthusiastic, and never officially espoused the idea of the ace, which conflicted with the British policy of playing down the importance of the individual in favour of the team. However, with losses heavy in the air as well as on the ground, some element of publicity was given to certain individuals, such as Albert Ball, mainly by way of decoration citations which made clear the extent of their achievements. Soon the British public was avidly interested in who were the 'top-scorers' of the day.

At this stage it should be made clear that from the very start each of the three major combatants in the air had a different method of compiling their pilots' totals. With the Germans and French, only those aircraft which crashed on or behind the victor's lines, or those confirmed to have crashed by independent eyewitnesses, were included. In the German system, where more than one pilot took part in the shooting down of an aircraft, its destruction was credited only to the pilot considered to have played the major part in the combat. In similar cases the French adopted a system whereby each pilot taking part in the combat had one victory added to his score, but only one was added to the score of the unit as a whole.

The British adopted a modified form of the French system, giving it a more liberal interpretation. This stemmed not only from the fact that the British philosophy of taking the war to the enemy meant that most combats took place well over the German lines but also from a desire to show that British pilots had scores as high as their French and German counterparts at a time when British losses were high and morale was threatened. Aircraft seen falling apparently out of control were taken as being

The Sopwith Camel, one of the outstanding fighters of the war. Descended from the Pup and the Triplane, some 5,490 were produced from July 1917 until the Armistice.

The Belgian-designed Hanriot HD1 was used by the pilots of both that country and of Italy. A line of these machines in service with an Italian *squadriglia* are seen here on an airfield near the front.

victories and, although classed as a separate category, were included in a pilot's score right up to the end of the war. Thus a decoration citation might credit a pilot with 'Ten victories, six destroyed and four driven down out of control.'

Had the French used the same basis, it must be said that many of their aces would have had higher scores—substantially so in some cases—and the list of aces would have been much longer. It would not have made so great a difference in the case of the Germans, as most combats took place in areas where it was easy for their claims to be confirmed. Had the Allies adopted the German system of crediting shared victories to only one pilot, many Allied pilots would have had substantially lower scores. Even had they applied the system used by the

Americans and British during the Second World War, that of allotting fractions, totals would in many cases have been lower.

Among the other nations, the Austro-Hungarians accepted the German method, while the Belgians, Italians and Russians employed the French system. The Americans employed a dual system, which will be explained in more detail later. All nations included tethered observation kite-balloons among their victory totals. It should also be mentioned that during the war Germany and the Austro-Hungarian Empire—the Central Powers—considered ten, rather than five victories to be the mark of the ace, or *Aberkanone* as he was known to them.

During the spring of 1917 new British fighters began to appear over the front in growing numbers. In April the magnificent Sopwith Triplanes of the Royal Naval Air Service arrived to aid the Royal Flying Corps, and soon Spads built under licence in England and other new types, such as the DH 5, SE 5 and early Bristol F2A Fighters, followed them.

Despite the arrival of this new equipment, April 1917–'Bloody April'–was a month of terrible losses among the reconnaissance and 'Corps' units. With the advent of summer, the balance began to swing. Improved SE 5As and Bristol F2B Fighters arrived, joined in July by the first Sopwith Camels. The French introduced the much-improved Spad S.13, and before long the Germans' Albatroses were in

trouble. During the autumn many of the great German aces fell, though the leading French and British pilots, Guynemer and Ball, had also been lost by now. Late in the year the Germans introduced the Fokker Dr.I triplane to service, developed as a result of their admiration for the Sopwith scout of this configuration. The Pfalz D.III biplane also began to appear with the *Jastas*.

By now the Germans were becoming increasingly outnumbered in the air, and although Russia was out of the war, the United States had come in. Early in 1918 the Germans had one last chance to defeat the Allies before the mighty reserves of American manpower could reach the front. France was virtually exhausted, and if the British armies could be beaten, a favourable armistice might be forthcoming. In spring 1918 a massive offensive was launched which pushed back the British and took comparatively large areas of territory. The British threw in everything they had, aircraft in large numbers giving direct support to the troops on the ground, and the offensive was held. For the Germans it was the beginning of the end.

During 1918 re-engined SE 5As, Camels and Spad S.13s reached the front, as did the first American squadrons, but now it was the Germans' turn to introduce new equipment. In May the first examples of the excellent Fokker D.VII biplane reached service, and soon this became the predominant type. Other types appeared in smaller numbers, such as the

Siemens-Schuckert D.III and IV, the Pfalz D.XII and, at the end of the war, the new Fokker D.VIII monoplane. The British introduced the Sopwith Dolphin in small numbers during the early summer, while during the last weeks of the war the excellent Sopwith Snipe also reached the front. While fighter development continued in France, no major new type was introduced before the war ended.

During the final months of the war many pilots became aces, particularly those serving with the German Air Service, the Royal Air Force, which had been born on 1 April 1918 from the marriage of the old RFC and RNAS and was now a new independent third service, and the fledgling United States Air Service. Although outnumbered, the German fighter pilots achieved some considerable victories, the British losing twice as many aircraft as did their opponents during the summer and autumn. When the war ended in November 1918, the German Air Service was far from being a defeated force.

While air fighting on the Eastern Front, in Palestine and in the Balkans had been little more than desultory, in Italy it had steadily increased in tempo during 1917 and 1918. The battles which the Austro-Hungarians fought with the Italians and their British allies during 1918 frequently reached intensities approaching those witnessed over the Western Front. All three nations produced considerable numbers of aces on this important front.

Albatros D.III and V biplanes and Fokker Dr.I Triplanes on a German airfield.

ACES OF THE NATIONS 1915-1919

The French

It was the French who were the pioneers of air fighting. During 1915, while individual experiments by RFC pilots such as Lanoe Hawker were taking place, the French were developing the art of air fighting at a faster pace than anyone else. There had been a great deal of national interest in flying before the war, and France had a nucleus of experienced pilots on which to call in 1914, a number of these, including Roland Garros, Eugene Gilbert and Jean Navarre, serving together in *Escadrille MS 23* at the beginning of the war. The unit was equipped with both the two-seater Morane Type 'L' parasol monoplane and the single-seater Type 'N' mid-wing monoplane.

The Type 'L' could carry up to two movable Lewis guns, and it was with these aircraft that the French Air Service's first three victories were claimed. The first fell to Gilbert and his observer on 10 January 1915, and the third to

One of the earliest of the French aces was Jean Navarre. He is seen here early in 1916 in front of a Nieuport 11 of *Escadrille N 67*. Soon after this photograph was taken he was badly wounded after gaining his twelfth victory. He was to return to active duty two years later, but had achieved no further success when hostilities ceased.

Navarre on 1 April. When Garros began flying his armed Type 'N' that same month, he was not the only pilot to do so, Gilbert, Navarre, and Adolph Pégoud of *MS 49* also flying the Type 'N'.

During April Garros made six claims, three destroyed, one out of control and two forced to land, but only the first three were confirmed. He then came down in German territory and was taken prisoner. Escaping later in the war, he served in *Escadrille SPA 26* in 1918, flying Spad S.13s, and here he claimed one further victory before he was shot down and killed on 5 October, a month before the end of the war. With only four confirmed victories, he thus never became an ace in the accepted sense so far as the French system was concerned, though he would have been considered one had he served in the RFC.

It was left to Gilbert to become the first pilot to reach five confirmed victories, but he was then killed. Pégoud then moved into the lead on 11 July with his sixth victory, but on 31 August he too was killed, leaving only Navarre of the original band of fighters still at the front. By the latter part of 1915 the Fokker *Eindekkers* were beginning to appear over the front, and soon the 'Fokker Scourge' began.

The French soon had their answer to the *Eindekker*, the Nieuport 11, in production, the first examples reaching the front during the late summer of 1915. Promoted to *Sergent*, Navarre continued to fly the Type 'N' until the Nieuport became available, then joining *Escadrille N67* to fly this type over the Verdun area. His fifth victory was gained in February 1916, and his tenth on 19 May. With his score standing at twelve he was shot down on 17 June and badly wounded, not returning to operational flying.

However, he never reached the No. 1 position, for before he had exceeded Pégoud's score he had already been overtaken by a new generation of young pilots who had learned to fly since the outbreak of war. The outstanding character among the new arrivals was Georges Guynemer. A frail young man, he had been rejected as physically unfit for Army service. However, he finally persuaded the authorities to accept him as a trainee mechanic for the air service in November 1914. After much further persuasion, he talked them into allowing him to take pilot training in March 1915, joining *Escadrille MS 3* as a *Caporal* in June. His first victory came on 19 July when he and his observer accounted for a two-seater while flying a Morane Type 'L'. In September he was shot down for the first of seven times, but survived unhurt.

He later flew Nieuports and Type 'N's, and by June 1916 was among the leaders with nine victories to his credit. In September he received one of the first Spad S.7s, and on the 23rd of the month claimed three victories in one day. His score now rose fast, and by January 1917 he had claimed his thirtieth victory, the only Allied ace with a higher score at this time being the RFC's Albert Ball. After Ball's death Guynemer soon moved into the lead, and in July reached fifty. Now a *Capitaine*, he claimed his fifty-fourth victory on 6 September 1917, but on the 11th disappeared in a new Spad S.13. It was a cloudy day and at first no claim was forthcoming from the Germans, though they later announced that he had been shot down by *Leutnant* Wissemann (five victories). His body and aircraft were never found, apparently destroyed in no-man's-land in an artillery barrage.

Many other leading French aces served in *Escadrille SPA 3*, which was led by Alfred Heurtaux, an ex-hussar who had earlier flown in Moranes and Nieuport 11s. His 'crack' *escadrille*, known as the *Cigognes* (Storks), flew Nieuports until September 1916 as *N 3*, then receiving Spads and becoming *SPA 3*. With these aircraft its pilots claimed 200 victories in six months. Heurtaux's eighth victory was over the German ace Kurt Wintgens (eighteen victories), and his twenty-first fell on 4 May 1917. He was then wounded, not returning to the unit until September. On his return he was wounded again almost immediately, and

The greatest hero of the French Air Service was *Capitaine* Georges Guynemer. A frail young man, rejected for service in any other branch of the army on medical grounds, Guynemer became the greatest Allied ace of 1917, running up a score of fifty-four. He failed to return from a patrol on 11 September 1917, his ultimate fate remaining something of a mystery.

did not fly any further operations thereafter.

Two other great aces of 1916 in this unit were René Dorme and Albert Deullin. The former had flown Caudron two-seaters and Nieuports elsewhere before joining the *Cicognes*, while the latter, an ex-cavalryman, had flown Maurice Farmans. Dorme had sixteen victories by the end of the year, to add to one gained earlier, but was then wounded. In spring 1917, on his recovery, he raised his total to twenty-three, but was then shot down and killed by the German ace Ritter von Schleich. Deullin had eleven by February 1917, when the *Cigognes* unit was expanded into a *Groupe* of several *escadrilles*. He took command of one of these, *SPA 73*, leading this unit until spring 1918, by which time his score stood at twenty. He then commanded a full *Groupe de Chasse*, becoming an

Georges Guynemer's most famous mount was this Spad S.7, *Vieux Charles*. The *cigogne* (stork) of *Escadrille SPA 3* can be clearly seen painted on the fuselage side. In the left background is a Sopwith Triplane, which with the Spad was one of the most successful fighters at the front in spring 1917. It equipped several squadrons of the Royal Naval Air Service.

France's Ace of Aces was René Fonck. Flying in the *Cigognes Groupe* with Guynemer, he was rather a late starter. A prolific scorer, however, he overtook Nungesser in April 1918, and finally passed Guynemer's long-standing total during July. He twice claimed six victories in a single day, and at the Armistice his score stood at seventy-five, making him top-scoring Allied pilot of the war, and second only to the great von Richthofen.

Charles Nungesser's Nieuport 23, seen here late in 1917, carrying his personal 'coat of arms' – a black heart, surmounted by a skull and crossbones, a coffin and a pair of candlesticks.

Officer of the Légion d'Honneur, as had Guynemer, Heurtaux and Dorme.

Not all the great French aces served with the *Cigognes*, the most notable among the 'others' being Charles Nungesser. A young adventurer in South America before the war, he returned to France in 1914. After service in the cavalry, he joined the air service in January 1915, initially flying Voisin 'pushers'. Involved in several combats, he claimed one victory before joining *N 65* in November to fly Nieuports. After one victory with this unit, he was badly hurt in a crash in January 1916. He returned to the front in March, and at once began to build up his score. His tenth victory was over Otto Parshau (eight victories), and by late September, with seventeen victories, he was only one behind Guynemer.

Further spells in hospital later in the year,

having fractures re-set, kept him out of action from December until May 1917, but by August of that year he had raised his score to thirty, shooting down a Gotha bomber. However, his injuries had caused his health to deteriorate, and he was forced to cease flying and undertake a period as an instructor. During this time he was involved in a car accident, receiving further injuries.

He returned to action early in 1918, at which time he was top-scorer still at the front. However, he was now closely followed by a new star, René Fonck. For a while their scores kept pace, but in July Fonck's score shot ahead. With forty victories to his credit, Nungesser again went into hospital for a short spell. On his return he claimed four balloons in one day during two flights on 14 August, next day claiming his forty-fifth and last victory.

Heavily decorated by all the Allied nations, he was unable to settle after the war, becoming a barnstorming and stunt pilot. In 1927 he and *Capitaine* Coli, flying in a specially built Levasseur aircraft, the *Oiseau Blanc*, attempted an East–West crossing of the Atlantic. They took off on 8 May 1927, but were never seen again.

Other leading pilots of this period included Armand Pinsard, another cavalryman, who flew with Garros in *MS 23* early in the war. Forced down by engine failure, he became a prisoner, but escaped in early 1916 to fight again. Flying Nieuports and Spads with *Escadrille 26*, he claimed sixteen victories between August 1916 and June 1917, but was then badly wounded. A year later he claimed seven balloons in a short period, going on to finish the war with his score at twenty-seven. He later became a *Général* in the *Armée de l'Air*.

Georges Madon had been a qualified pilot since 1911, but early in 1915 he was interned in Switzerland following a forced-landing. Escaping, he became a fighter pilot in early 1917, flying with *Escadrille SPA 38* until the end

of the war, by which time his score stood at forty. He was killed in a crash on 11 November 1924. International rugby star Maurice Boyau became a pilot after early service as a driver. Flying with other athletes in the *Escadrille des Sportifs*, *N 77*, he shot down six balloons and five aircraft in six months. More victories followed, and by 15 September 1918 his score stood at thirty-four. Next day he shot down his last balloon—nineteen were included in his total—but at the same time his wingman was attacked by several German scouts. Boyau dived under the blazing 'gasbag' to his aid, but was struck by ground fire, went into a spin, and crashed to his death.

The great days for the French aces had been during 1916 and 1917; by 1918 most action was taking place over the British sector. Consequently many French pilots had to spend their time hunting balloons, and only a few were able to build up big scores against enemy aircraft. There were exceptions, however, the leading among these being René Fonck.

Initially trained as an engineer before he was allowed to take flying training, he was posted to fly Caudrons during 1915. He forced down his first enemy aircraft by rifle-fire on 1 March 1916, but this was not confirmed. In July machine-guns were fitted to the Caudrons, Fonck and his observer shooting down an Aviatik, which again was not confirmed. On 17 March 1917 two Caudrons, one of which was flown by Fonck, tangled with five Albatros scouts. Although the Caudron accompanying him was shot down, Fonck managed to account for one of the scouts.

Fonck was now given fighter training and posted to *Groupe de Chasse 12*, the *Cigognes* (*SPA 3, 26, 73* and *103*), joining *SPA 103*. His first claim here was also unconfirmed, but by 13 May he had gained his fifth official victory. This was only a start, for by January 1918 Fonck's score had risen to twenty-one, and by February he was level with Deullin and Madon, only Nungesser being ahead of him. Several double claims followed, and by the end of April he had thirty-five victories. Then came his greatest day to date, when in two flights on 9 May he shot down six aircraft, three on each mission. More doubles and trebles followed, and he soon passed Guynemer's score, reaching fifty-seven on 1 August. On 14 August he again claimed a triple, and on 26 September once more claimed six in two flights. Thereafter his score continued to climb in ones and twos, his last claim being made on 1 November 1918, to bring his total to seventy-five – the top-scoring Allied ace of the war.

After the war he became a stunt flyer and also attempted some record flights. He later rejoined the service, and in 1937 became *Inspecteur de l'Aviation de Chasse* (Inspector of Fighter Aviation), retiring in 1939. He died in 1953. By his own reckoning his total confirmed and unconfirmed victories amounted to 127.

The frequent injuries suffered by *Lieutenant* Charles Nungesser in crashes and air battles often kept him away from the front for weeks at a time. Despite this, he was able to claim forty-five victories, often flying when he was barely able to walk. The scarring to his jaw following one of his accidents can be clearly seen in this portrait, which epitomises the character of this tough and determined pilot.

The most successful French 'balloon-buster' was Michel Coiffard of *SPA 154*. Coiffard saw action with the army in North Africa before the war, transferring to the air service in 1917. During 1918 his score rose fast, and by July he had seventeen victories. Three months later he had doubled his score and had become unit commander, but he was then badly wounded during an escort mission, dying in the ambulance on the way to hospital. His score included no less than twenty-eight balloons, though like many of the other Allied aces a considerable number of his victories were shared with others.

In excess of 158 French pilots became aces during the war, fourteen of them claiming twenty or more, and thirty-nine more getting between ten and nineteen. One or two were to add to their scores in the early stages of the Second World War, as will be related later, while one pilot, Jean Darré (six victories), was to fly for the Spanish Republicans early in the Civil War, claiming at least three victories flying various French fighter types.

The leading French aces

Capitaine René P. Fonck	75
Capitaine Georges M. L. J. Guynemer	54
Lieutnant Charles E. J. M. Nungesser	45
Capitaine Georges F. Madon	41
Lieutenant Maurice Boyau	35
Lieutenant Jean-Pierre L. Bourjade	28
Capitaine Armand Pinsard	27
Sous-Lieutenant René Dorme	23
Lieutenant Gabriel Guérin	23
Sous-Lieutenant Claude M. Haegelen	23
Sous-Lieutenant Pierre Marinovitch	22
Capitaine Alfred Heurtaux	21
Capitaine Albert Deullin	20

The Germans

Initially the Germans lagged behind the British and French in the offensive use of aircraft, relying on them purely for reconnaissance and occasional bombing operations. However, once persuaded of the desirability of fighting scouts, they espoused the idea with characteristic energy, producing a large number of aces of high calibre. Many of the advantages lay with the Germans: most combats took place over their own territory, a factor aided by the prevailing wind which tended to push aircraft steadily eastwards during a fight.

Apart from the odd victory by two-seater crews, the first German scout victory was not achieved until July 1915, when the first few armed Fokker *Eindekkers* became available. The first pilot to claim was Kurt Wintgens, who had already been flying unarmed *Eindekkers* in Bavarian *Fliegerabtailung (FlgAbt.) 6b*. On 15 July he shot down one of the armed French Morane monoplanes that had been harassing the German reconnaissance aircraft, but it fell in French territory and could not be confirmed. He was later transferred to various *FlgAbt.* to escort reconnaissance machines, his score rising only slowly. By May 1916, when he was in a *Kampfeinsitzerkommando*–a special fighter unit, a few of which had recently been formed to group the available *Eindekkers* together–his score still stood at five. He was awarded the coveted Pour le Mérite (The Blue Max, as it was colloquially known) in July 1916, bringing his score up to eighteen before he was killed in action on 25 September 1916 when going to the aid of an observation aircraft.

The next pilot to score, and Germany's first ace, was Max Immelmann, a Saxon vegetarian and abstainer. He transferred to the air service in November 1914, serving as a pilot in *FlgAbt.10* from February until April, and then moving to *FlgAbt.62*. He engaged in some early battles in an LVG two-seater without success, but when two *Eindekkers* were delivered to the unit for the use of an experienced fellow-pilot, Boelcke, he flew one of these on 1 August 1915 to intercept a raid by French bombers, shooting one of them down for the first confirmed scout victory of the war. Flying regularly with Boelcke thereafter, he had gained three victories by September, at which point Boelcke was detached for bomber escort duties. Immelmann was now the sole defender of the Lille area, and during October he gained two more victories to become an ace. Late in 1915 the first special units of single-seaters were formed and he joined one of these, being awarded the highest Prussian award, the Pour le Mérite, in January 1916. By the end of March he had fourteen victories, many decorations and awards, and was the idol of the nation. However, he had twice shot off his own propeller when the Schneider synchronization gear malfunctioned, and on each occasion had to carry out a forced-landing.

On 18 June he claimed his fifteenth confirmed victory, but that evening, in a battle with seven FE 2Bs of 25 Squadron, RFC, his aircraft broke up in the air and he was killed. The Germans believed he had shot off his own propeller again, but the British credited Lieutenant McCubbin and Corporal Waller with shooting him down.

At the time of his death Immelmann had already lost his place as German top-scorer to his fellow-pilot, the true father of German air fighting, Oswald Boelcke, another Saxon. Boelcke had joined the army in 1911 and underwent flight training in June 1914, becoming a qualified pilot the day after the war broke out. Flying initially with *FlgAbt.13*, he first flew unarmed *Eindekkers* late in that year. In April 1915 he joined *FlgAbt.62*, and on 4 July, with his observer, was able to shoot down a Morane two-seater while flying an LVG. The arrival that month of the first armed *Eindekkers* for his use

At first German units were allocated one or two armed fighting scouts each, to protect their other aircraft when carrying out their normal duties. Typical equipment in summer 1915 is seen here serving with a *Marine-Feld Fliegerabteilung* on the Belgian coast. In the centre are two Fokker E-1 monoplanes.

promised more successes, but it was 19 August before he was able to claim again. Detached to Metz for bomber escort, he added four more victories by early December; he then rejoined *FlgAbt.62* at Douai. Like Immelmann, he achieved his eighth victory early in January 1916, receiving his Pour le Mérite on the same day as his comrade and rival.

Posted to *FlgAbt.203* for more escort duty, he made known his strongly held views that the dilution of scouts among reconnaissance units was not the best way to use them, and on 16 June he was ordered to form his own *Kampfeinsitzer Sivry*, for action over the Verdun area. In the meantime he had overtaken Immelmann, raising his score to eighteen with two victories on 20 May, and had become the youngest *Hauptmann* (Captain) in the Army next day. After Immelmann's death he was taken out of action, having scored nineteen victories, and sent on a tour of inspection in the Balkans and East.

On his return he helped set up the new *Jagdstaffeln* (*Jasta*–literally hunter, or fighter unit), and prepared his *Dicta Boelcke*, a set of basic rules for air fighting which was to become the bible of all German fighter pilots. He then took command of *Jasta 2*, which was filled with pilots hand-picked by himself. New aircraft arrived–Fokker D.III and Albatros D.I biplanes–and in one of the former Boelcke claimed his twentieth victory on 2 September. While training his men and awaiting more aircraft, he continued to fly, adding six more victories by the time Albatros D.IIs arrived on 16 September.

Deciding that the unit was now ready to operate, he took it into action. In its first combat eight Albatros scouts took on twenty-eight British aircraft and shot down four without loss. Among his young pilots where several who would soon become aces, including Manfred von Richthofen and Max Müller. By 17 October Boelcke's score had risen to thirty-five, and by 25 October to forty. Then disaster struck. On 28 October he engaged a force of British DH 2s, but collided with the Albatros flown by his closest friend, Erwin Boehme, and crashed to his death. Boehme survived, but was hysterical with grief. However, he was later able to take over the *Jasta* and lead it successfully. Boehme gained twenty-four victories before he was shot down in flames on 29 November 1917.

Another early ace was Rudolf Berthold, who transferred to the air service in 1913. Becoming a pilot in 1915, he flew *Eindekkers* the following year, receiving a Pour le Mérite the following October for ten victories. Despite receiving severe and painful wounds, he became leader of *Jagdgeschwader (JG) II* after the death of von Tutschek, bringing his score to forty-four by August 1918. Shot down six times, he ended the war in hospital at the Kaiser's personal order. His determination to continue flying while suffering from crippling unhealed wounds gained him the nickname of the 'Iron Knight'. During the political upheavals following the war, he led a *Freikorps* unit against Communists in Bavaria, and then against the Russian Bolsheviks. In March 1921 he was attacked and killed by a Communist mob in Harburg, who strangled him

Germany's first ace, *Leutnant* Max Immelmann. He invented the 'Immelmann turn', a half-loop and a roll off the top, which gained height and put him quickly on the tail of his enemy. He is seen here, with an *Eindekker* scout, on a German propaganda postcard.

The father of German fighter tactics was *Hauptmann* Oswald Boelcke. A contemporary of Immelmann, he outlived him by several months. During this time he formed and led one of the first pure fighter units, *Jagdstaffel 2*, and ran his own score up to forty. He remained top-scorer until surpassed by von Richthofen–one of his own protégés–during April 1917. Among Boelcke's awards, the cross of the Pour le Mérite (popularly known as the 'Blue Max') can be clearly seen at his collar in this portrait.

with his Pour le Mérite ribbon and then shot him six times in the back.

One of Boelcke's promising young pilots in *Jasta 2* was Manfred von Richthofen. This Prussian officer joined the air service after seeing action with the cavalry, being spotted by Boelcke after serving for some months as a pilot of observation and bomber aircraft. He had already claimed two victories during this period, but neither had been confirmed. However, on 17 September 1916, during *Jasta 2*'s first combat, he shot down an FE 2B, and by late November his score stood at eleven. A stealthy hunter rather than an aggressive dogfighter, his results were none the less impressive, and on 23 November he shot down the leading British ace, Major Lanoe Hawker, VC, in his hardest combat of the war.

In January 1917 he took command of *Jasta 11*, leading it to great success. By the end of March his score had risen to thirty-one, but then came 'Bloody April', the month of the Battle of Arras. During this fateful month the British suffered losses against the Germans in the air at the rate of five to one. By far the most successful unit was *Jasta 11*, with nearly four times as many victories as its nearest rival–eighty-nine victories coming in one month. Twenty-one of these were credited to von Richthofen, raising his score to fifty-two, well clear of Boelcke's record of forty, twenty-one to Kurt Wolff, eighteen to Lothar von Richthofen, the commanding officer's younger brother, and fifteen to Karl Schaeffer. On 26 April Schaeffer was posted to command *Jasta 38*; he was killed on 5 June with his score at twenty-four.

During April experiments were made with several *Jastas* flying together, and on 26 June the first *Jagdgeschwader*, *JG I*, was formed under von Richthofen's command. It incorporated *Jasta 4, 6, 10* and *11*. The 'Red Baron', as he was now known to the Allies, because of his red-painted Albatros fighter, was able to hand-pick his unit commanders, including his nearest rival, an old friend from *Jasta 2*, Werner Voss.

On 6 July, with fifty-seven victories to his credit, von Richthofen was wounded in the head in combat with FE 2Ds of 20 Squadron, and for the rest of the year his victories came more slowly. In September he flew one of the early Fokker Dr.I Triplanes for the first time, but was unimpressed, handing it over to Wolff and returning to his faithful Albatros. Later in the year he began flying the production Dr.I regularly. By the end of 1917 his score stood at sixty-three, but during the German spring offensive of 1918 he was once more to the fore, claiming his last seventeen victories between 12 March and 20 April to become the top ace of the war, with eighty victories. On 21 April he engaged Camels of 209 Squadron, getting on the tail of one. Before he could bring it down, he was shot down and killed. He was attacked by another Camel flown by Roy Brown, a Canadian ace (eleven victories), and was also fired on by Australian machine-gunners on the ground, both claiming to be responsible for his death.

Though officially credited to Brown, doubt remains to this day as to the responsibility for the death of the great ace. He was buried with full military honours by the British, but after the war his body was removed to a permanent resting-place in German soil. During his lifetime he received every decoration his nation had to award him, including one normally retained only for princes of the royal blood. It has been maintained that he preyed mainly on two-seater reconnaissance aircraft, which were easy victims. A study of his claims shows this not to be so. While seventeen BE 2s and eight RE 8s were included in his score, so too were thirteen of the tougher FE 2s, together with some forty fighting scouts of various types.

Among his pilots several shone, the three most successful being Karl Allmenröder, Kurt Wolff, and his brother Lothar. Allmenröder claimed thirty victories in five months, but was killed in action on 26 June 1917 by a chance shot fired from a Sopwith Triplane by the great Canadian ace Raymond Collishaw. Collishaw fired from long range, and although his aim was true, did not see the result and never claimed the Albatros as shot down. Wolff lived a little longer, his score reaching thirty-three before he was shot down in flames by a Camel on 15 September when flying one of the pre-production Fokker Triplanes.

Like his brother, Lothar von Richthofen was an ex-cavalry officer. Impetuous and agressive, he threw himself into air fighting, claiming twenty victories in his first four weeks at the front. He was credited with shooting down the great British ace, Albert Ball, but it seems that though he was himself wounded, he actually brought down a Triplane which was lost during

5 unserer erfolgreichsten
Kampfflieger.

Vizefeldwebel Festner† Leutnant Schäfer†
Leutnant Frhr. von Richthofen
Rittmeister Frhr. von Richthofen †   Leutnant Wolff †

Top-scoring ace of the First World War was *Rittmeister Freiherr* Manfred von Richthofen. He is seen here flanked by some of his most successful pilots in *Jasta 11* in spring, 1917. From left to right: Sebastian Festner (twelve victories); Karl Schaeffer (thirty victories); Manfred von Richthofen (eighty victories); Lothar von Richthofen (forty victories) and Kurt Wolff (thirty-three victories).

the same engagement. In September he replaced Wolff as commander of *Jasta 11*, but due to a combination of wounds and leave, he was to spend only seventy-seven days actually at the front, during which he claimed forty victories. He was badly wounded in August 1918, subsequently recovering to die in an air crash in 1922.

Manfred von Richthofen's nearest competitor during his lifetime was Werner Voss, a young hussar who transferred to the air service in 1915, becoming a very fine aerobatic pilot. After a period on two-seaters, he joined *Jasta 2 (Boelcke)* in November 1916, befriending von Richthofen. His first claim was made on 17 March 1917. On one occasion he shot down a BE in no-man's-land, landing alongside and taking the Lewis gun from the aircraft as evidence of his victory. Having gained twenty-eight victories by early April, he received the Pour le Mérite, and in May took command of *Jasta 5*. A brief move to *Jasta 39* followed, and then in July, at Richthofen's request, he took over *Jasta 10* in *JG I*.

He undoubtedly found the responsibilities of command worrying, and his rate of scoring dropped. In August he was given one of the two pre-production Fokker Triplanes and found this a delightful mount. With this aircraft he added ten more victories by 23 September to raise his score to forty-eight – only thirteen behind the 'Red Baron' and ahead of all others at that time. That afternoon, however, he was out alone over Ypres when he was engaged by 'B' Flight of 56 Squadron in probably *the* epic dogfight of the war. He fought brilliantly against British aces McCudden, Lewis, Mayberry, Bowman, Rhys-David and Hoidge, hitting several of the SEs and consistently escaping a critical shot from any of his opponents. After a long and inconclusive dogfight, eleven Albatros scouts approached. Voss made off in their direction, but Spads and Camels appeared and drove

all but one away. At last Rhys-David found himself below the Triplane, and pulling back his wing-mounted Lewis gun, sent several bursts into its underside. Pulling up behind, he then opened fire with both guns; the Fokker slowed, stalled, and fell into the Allies lines. Voss was buried by his enemies with full honours.

No other pilot seriously challenged von Richthofen's lead during his lifetime, though one was to approach his score before the war was over. This was Ernst Udet, a keen glider pilot. He became a fighter pilot early in 1916, flying for some time on the French front, where his unit frequently fought the French *Cigognes Groupe* – often with heavy losses. He later transferred to the Flanders front, but by mid-1917 his score still stood at only six. He then began to score more rapidly, and by early 1918 he had reached twenty.

Noticed by von Richthofen, he joined *Jasta 11* in *JG I* in March 1918, flying triplanes for the first time. In April he received the Pour le Mérite, and in May took command of *Jasta 4*. His busiest period was during the summer of 1918, and by late September, when he was shot down and wounded, his score had reached sixty-two. He became a well-known stunt flier after the war, also designing and building the successful Flamingo sports plane.

In 1936 he was persuaded by Goering to join the new Luftwaffe, becoming Inspector of Day Fighters and Dive Bombers and later Director of Technical Services. This job proved beyond his capabilities, and on 17 November 1941 he shot himself. He was reported killed in an accident and was given a State funeral which was attended by many leading aces of the Second World War.

Two aces whose lives were closely linked were Bruno Loerzer and Hermann Goering. Close friends, they transferred from the infantry to the

Albatros D.IIIs of von Richthofen's *Jagsgeschwader*. A fine aircraft, the D.III was nevertheless outclassed by the Sopwith Camel and the Spad.

air service, both later becoming pilots. Loerzer transferred to fighters first, gaining two victories early in 1916, but he was then badly wounded. Subsequently both pilots served in *Jasta 17*, which Loerzer commanded, throughout most of 1917.

At last in 1918 their careers diverged.

Second-ranking German ace, and later head of the Luftwaffe's Technical Services at the start of the Second World War, was *Oberleutnant* Ernst Udet.

Loerzer was given command of the new *JG III*, and a month later he was awarded a Pour le Mérite for twenty victories. His score rose quickly during the summer, many French Spads falling before his guns, and when the war ended his score stood at forty-five. Goering meanwhile commanded *Jasta 27* for a short time, and in July was chosen to lead the élite *JG I*. His score now stood at twenty, most of which were gained during late 1917, but with his new unit he claimed only two more victories. Thereafter he devoted most of his time to paperwork, flying only occasionally. A strict disciplinarian, he was not unduly popular with his pilots.

At the end of the war Goering encouraged his pilots to crash their Fokker D.VIIs while handing them over to the Allies, and soon afterwards, embittered by the peace, joined the infant Nazi Party in Munich. Badly wounded during the putsch of November 1923, he escaped abroad to avoid arrest. Treated with morphia for the pain caused by the wound, he eventually became addicted to the drug. He later returned to Germany and was elected to the Reichstag in 1928, becoming President of that assembly. His later career as Reichmarshal of the new Luftwaffe, his trial and suicide after the war, are well known to all, and do not need repeating in detail here.

After his rise to power, Goering recruited many of the old aces, including Udet and Loerzer, into the new Luftwaffe. Loerzer received swift promotion. He led Fliegerkorps II in Poland, France and the Battle of Britain, and was awarded the Knight's Cross in May 1940. He later commanded the Luftwaffe in Sicily for the attack on Malta, subsequently being appointed Chief of Staff. He died in August 1960.

The state of Bavaria provided many of its own units and many outstanding pilots during the war. Eduard Schleich rose to command a Prussian unit, *Jasta 21*, by March 1917, leading it to great success. His first victory was over the great French ace René Dorme. Within six months the unit had forty-one victories, seventeen credited to Schleich, who was by then flying an all-black Albatros.

Taken ill with dysentery after his twenty-fifth victory, he flew no more with the unit following an edict that Prussian units should in future be led only by Prussians. Taking over *Jasta 32*, he was awarded a Pour le Mérite at the end of 1917, but then fell ill again. During 1918 he commanded a unit of three *Jastas* known as *Jagdgruppe 8*, which was expanded into *JG IV* late in the war – the last *Jagdgeschwader* formed. Knighted with the Bavarian Order of Max Joseph, he became Ritter von Schleich, and was nicknamed the 'Black Knight'. He ended the war with thirty-five victories, later serving in Lufthansa and joining the SS. In 1938 he joined the new Luftwaffe, leading a dive-bomber *Staffel*, then *JG 131 Schlageter*, which later became the famous *JG 26*. Having filled a staff post, he became a general in 1941, commanding all Luftwaffe units in Denmark. He died in 1947.

Adolf Ritter von Tutschek received the Order of Max Joseph as an infantryman. Transferring to the air service after being badly gassed at Verdun, he later joined *Jasta 2* in 1917. His powers of leadership soon brought him the command of *Jasta 12*, and by July 1917 he had eleven victories. Having gained several more victories and a Pour le Mérite, he was then wounded in August, not returning to action until early 1918. Leading the new *JG II*, he raised his score to twenty-seven by mid-March, but was then shot down and killed.

Like the Allies, the Germans had pilots who specialized in destroying balloons, and the most successful of these was Heinrich Gontermann. Initially in the cavalry, he became a fighter pilot in 1916, flying in *Jasta 5*, and he soon became the unit's leading pilot. His sixth victory fell in March 1917, soon followed by his first balloon. During 'Bloody April' he made twelve claims, becoming commanding officer. With twenty-one victories by mid-May, he received both the Pour le Mérite and the Bavarian Order of Max Joseph.

During the summer he continued to hunt balloons, and by 6 August had shot down eleven of them. In the middle of that month he shot down four balloons in one day, three of them in three minutes. Attacked by a French Spad, he shot this down as well. His final victory came on 3 October 1917, raising his score to thirty-nine, eighteen of which were balloons. On the 30th of that month he tested one of the new production Fokker Triplanes, but it broke up in the air and crashed. He died of his injuries next day. Close behind him as a 'balloon-buster' came Friedrich Ritter von Roth, a Bavarian in *Jasta 23b*, who was credited with seventeen balloons among his twenty-eight victories.

One of the high-scoring aces of the latter part of the war was Fritz Rumey, who joined *Jasta 5* as an NCO in June 1917, shooting down a balloon the following month. By mid-May 1918 his score had risen to twenty, and the next month he was commissioned and awarded the Pour le Mérite. Scoring very swiftly in doubles and trebles, he had raised his total to forty-five by September, but on the 27th of that month, when in combat with SE 5As of 32 Squadron, RAF, the wheels of a British fighter hit his top wing and he crashed to his death.

Few German aces served as fighter pilots for long on fronts other than the Western Front, but one such was Rudolf von Eschwege, who was posted to Macedonia in late 1916, where a small German detachment was flying in support of the Bulgarians in the Aegean area. Only one Halberstadt scout was available at first, and in this von Eschwege quickly became the scourge of the Allied air units. Conditions were difficult and he frequently had to fly alone, so that many of his victories could not be confirmed. Nevertheless, he managed to obtain confirmation of nineteen by November 1917, two of these being balloons. On 21 November he again shot down a balloon, but it was a trap, a charge of dynamite being fired from the ground as he attacked, the resultant explosion sending his aircraft crashing to destruction.

The Bavarian ace, Eduard Schleich. Awarded the Pour le Mérite, he also received the Bavarian Order of Max Joseph, which made him a knight, Ritter von Schleich. He is seen here with his all-black Albatros scout in which he led *Jasta 32*.

following page, bottom
Every man a hero! All these pilots are holders of the 'Blue Max'. From left to right: Walter Blume, Josef Veltjens, Josef Jacobs, Oscar von Bönigk, Eduard von Schleich, Ernst Udet, Bruno Loerzer, Paul Bäumer, Hermann Goering and Heinrich Bongartz. No less than eight of Germany's twenty-two top-scorers are included in this group.

Germany's greatest 'balloon buster' was *Leutnant* Heinrich Gontermann, eighteen of his thirty-nine victims being tethered observation balloons. He is seen here (on the right with goggles) inspecting a British FE 2D which he had forced down in German territory.

Like most other nations, the Germans also boasted a naval air arm and, like the Royal Naval Air Service, this was eventually to provide fighting units for the Western Front, producing some notable aces. The first great navy ace had no such advantages, Friedrich Christiansen being credited with twenty-one victories while flying two-seater seaplanes, mainly of the Hansa-Brandenburg type. His score included a British

dirigible airship, shot down on 11 December 1917, and he was also credited with sinking the British submarine C-25, though in fact he succeeded only in damaging her.

Two pilots who gained great success with the *Marine-Feld Jagdgeschwader* during 1918 were Götthard Sachsenberg and Theodore Osterkamp. Sachsenberg, the senior of the two, rose to command the unit. He claimed thirty-one victories before being badly wounded. Osterkamp fought many hard combats, including one fight with Guynemer during 1917. In April 1918 he headed *Marine Jasta 2*, and on 12 August led twenty-two Fokker D.VIIs against twenty-two DH 9 bombers, his formation shooting down nineteen DH 9s for no loss. He later flew one of the new Fokker D.VIII monoplanes, gaining his thirty-second victory in September to become the navy's top-scorer. He missed the last weeks of the war with a bout of influenza.

After the war the two Pour le Mérite holders flew in support of the *Freikorps* Iron Division against the Bolsheviks in Lithuania, Estonia and Finland. In the Second World War, Sachsenberg served in the navy, but Osterkamp had joined the new Luftwaffe in the 'thirties, commanding the 'Horst Wessel' *Jagdgeschwader*. In 1940 he commanded *JG 51*, leading it as *Kommodore* until July 1940. Flying a Messerschmitt Bf 109E over France and the English Channel, he

Fokker Dr.I Triplanes of von Richthofen's *Jagsgeschwader*, which was formed in June 1917. Von Richthofen was shot down and killed while piloting one of these aircraft.

page 25
Leutnant Max Immelmann, Germany's first great fighter pilot of the First World War, circles over one of his victims, a BE 2C reconnaissance biplane of the RFC. Immelmann is flying his Fokker *Eindekker* scout.
By Michael Turner.

pages 26–27
Werner Voss's final combat. In his gaily decorated Fokker Dr. I Triplane, *Leutnant* Werner Voss of *Jasta 10* fights for his life against a patrol of SE 5As from 56 Squadron, RFC. At this time, 23 September 1917, Voss was Germany's second ace, with forty-eight victories. But in this combat all his opponents were aces, and he was to fall victim to one of them, Lieutenant A. P. F. Rhys-David. The nearest SE 5A in this scene is that flown by the leader of the British flight, Captain J. T. B. McCudden.
By Michael Turner.

opposite page
High above the Madrid Sierra during the summer of 1937, the leading ace of the Spanish Nationalist forces, Joaquin Garcia Morato, and his wingman surprise a Republican patrol of Polikarpov I–15s. Morato is flying his faithful Fiat CR 32, 3–51, in which he gained most of his victories between 1936 and 1939, and in which he subsequently lost his life.
By Michael Turner.

claimed six further victories thus becoming an ace in the new war, the most successful of several German pilots who gained victories in both conflicts. Promoted to *Generalmajor*, he was Fighter Commander (*Jafü*) English Channel, receiving the Knight's Cross in August 1940. He was later Fighter Commander in Italy, rising in rank to *Generalleutnant* before the end of the war. At the time of writing he is still living in Western Germany, the 'grand old man' of the German fighter pilots.

Some 363 German pilots were credited with five or more confirmed victories. A dozen had more than forty, twenty-one had between thirty and thirty-nine, and thirty-eight had between twenty and twenty-nine.

The leading German aces

Rittmeister Manfred von Richthofen	80	
Oberleutnant Ernst Udet	62	
Oberleutnant Erich Loewenhardt	53	
Leutnant Werner Voss	48	
Hauptmann Bruno Loerzer	45	
Leutnant Fritz Rumey	45	
Hauptmann Rudolph Berthold	44	
Leutnant Paul Bäumer	43	
Leutnant Josef Jacobs	41	
Hauptmann Oswald Boelcke	40	
Leutnant Franz Büchner	40	
Oberleutnant Lothar von Richthofen	40	
Leutnant Karl Menckhoff	39	
Leutnant Heinrich Gontermann	39	
Leutnant Theodore Osterkamp	38	(including 6 in the Second World War)
Leutnant Max Müller	36	
Leutnant Julius Buckler	35	
Leutnant Gustav Dörr	35	
Hauptmann Eduard Ritter von Schleich	35	

The British Empire

The first British ace of the war was Lanoe Hawker, who had flown with 6 Squadron since the outbreak of the fighting. A keen inventor and innovator, he was interested from the start in fitting armament to his aircraft for air combat. He had already been awarded a DSO for a daring lone bombing raid on German Zeppelin sheds, when his first combat successes were recorded. Flying an armed Bristol Scout biplane, he engaged in three flights on 25 July 1915, bringing down two German biplanes, one of them in flames. For this he received the Victoria Cross. Subsequently he flew two-seater FE 2 aircraft, claiming a further four victories during August and September.

He then returned to England where he helped form 24 Squadron, the RFC's first single-seat fighter unit, which was equipped with DH 2 'pushers'. He led the unit back to France in February 1916, and at first it achieved considerable success. However, the arrival of German Albatros fighters made life much more difficult, and on 23 November Hawker was shot down, after a long dogfight, by Manfred von Richthofen; he was the Red Baron's eleventh victim. At the time of his death he was credited with nine victories in the air.

The first really high-scoring ace of the RFC was Albert Ball, the archetypal 'lone wolf' pilot. He first flew over the front in February 1916 on reconnaissance duties, but showed an aggressive streak in attacking opposing aircraft. Posted to 11 Squadron, he began flying the new Nieuport *Bébé* scout, and at once achieved considerable success.

In late August 1916 he was posted to 60 Squadron, with his score standing at eleven, three of these having been destroyed in one day on 21 August. With 60 he claimed at an even greater rate, getting four on 28 August and three on three other occasions before the beginning of October. With his score standing at thirty-two, he returned to England on leave and was fêted as a national hero, collecting a DSO and Bar. He returned to France in the spring of 1917 with the 'crack' new 56 Squadron, which was equipped with the first SE 5s. Flying both these aircraft and a favourite personal Nieuport, he claimed a further fifteen victories between 23 April and 6 May. On 7 May he became engaged in a dogfight with some red Albatros Scouts, a Sopwith Triplane and a Spad. He was last seen disappearing into cloud and did not return, Lothar von Richthofen, brother of the Red Baron, being credited with shooting him down. His score of forty-seven was made up of twenty-one destroyed (one of them shared), five out of control, twenty forced to land, and one kite-balloon. Following his death, the announcement of the posthumous award of the Victoria Cross was made.

Alan Wilkinson and John Andrews both flew in Hawker's 24 Squadron early in 1916, Wilkinson claiming nine victories and Andrews fourteen (nine of which were not decisive). Wilkinson later led a flight in 48 Squadron, the first Bristol Fighter unit, and was one of the first to achieve any degree of success on the early F2As, raising his score to nineteen by the late spring of 1917. Andrews led a flight of new Sopwith Pups in 66 Squadron, raising his own score to twenty-four by summer 1917, at least six of his total being destroyed. He later served in the Mediterranean, and then in southern Russia in 1919, while Wilkinson ended the war as a squadron commander.

Among the first British high-scorers were a number of naval pilots, most of whom remained little known to the public at large. A large proportion of them came from the Empire, and this was certainly the case with two Australians, Roderick Dallas and Robert Little. Dallas flew Nieuport Scouts with 1 Naval Wing at Dunkirk in 1916, and in the following spring flew Sopwith Triplanes on the Western Front with 1 Naval Squadron. When the squadron withdrew to re-equip with Camels, he had well over thirty victories, at least twenty-five on Triplanes, fourteen of them gained during April alone. Returning to the front in February 1918, he gained two more victories, but in April, when the RAF was formed, he was posted to lead 40 Squadron, an old RFC unit equipped with SE 5As. A dozen more victories followed, but on 19 June he was involved in a fight with three Fokker Triplanes near Lieven, and was shot down and killed by *Leutnant* Hans Werner (seven victories), commander of *Jasta 14*. His final score totalled fifty-one, of which more than twenty-six were confirmed destroyed.

Little flew in the same unit at Dunkirk in 1916, but gained his first nine victories in Sopwith Pups. He then flew at the front, first with 8 Naval Squadron on Triplanes, and then with 3 Naval Squadron on Camels. On 27 May 1918 he attempted to attack a Gotha bomber at night, but was apparently blinded by a searchlight. He was then hit by return fire and shot through the thigh, whereupon his aircraft crashed near Noeux, killing him. His score of forty-seven included fifteen and three shared destroyed, eighteen and four shared out of control.

One of the greatest of all Allied aces was the Canadian Ray Collishaw. After early service with 3 Naval Wing and 3 Naval Squadron, which brought four victories, he joined 10 Naval Squadron to fly Triplanes over the Western Front. By the end of May 1917 he had brought his score to ten, and during June and July twenty-eight more victories followed. At this time he led a famous flight, known as the 'Black Flight', each aircraft carrying a name beginning with the word 'Black'. This all-Canadian flight claimed eighty-seven victories between mid-May and the end of July.

Later in 1917 Collishaw commanded 13 Naval Squadron on Camels, and early in 1918 took over 3 Naval Squadron, later 203 Squadron, RAF. By October of that year he had brought his score to sixty, but despite this high total he did not receive a VC—no naval pilot did—although he did receive the DSO and Bar, DSC and DFC. In 1919 he commanded a unit in southern Russia (47 Squadron), shooting down at least two Bolshevik aircraft to bring his score to sixty-two. This total included forty-two and one shared destroyed and nineteen out of control. He also had at least 100 indecisive fights during which fifteen aircraft were driven down but not claimed, including that of the German ace Allmenröder, who was in fact killed.

An ace of similar standing but much greater fame was 'Jimmy' McCudden. Joining the RFC before the war as a mechanic, he subsequently flew as an observer before becoming an NCO pilot with 29 Squadron in early 1916. Here he claimed his first five victories while flying DH 2s. Commissioned, he returned to England as an instructor until July 1917, when he joined 66 Squadron in France on Pups. Two months later he transferred to the 'crack' 56 Squadron to fly the new SE 5, and here he really shone. By the end of 1917 he had claimed thirty-two more victories, and during the first two months of 1918 another sixteen followed. His best days were 23 December 1917 and 16 February 1918, on each of which he claimed four victories, while on two occasions he claimed three in a day.

McCudden was a great hunter of German reconnaissance two-seaters, forty-five of his fifty-seven victories being claimed against these aircraft, including one LVG that he forced to land in Allied territory and which was captured intact. His younger brother John Anthony also became an ace, being credited with nine victories flying with 25 and 84 Squadrons. On 19 July 1918, after a leave in England, 'Jimmy' McCudden, who had by then received the Victoria Cross, was posted to command 60 Squadron. While on his way to join this unit, he crashed during a take-off and was killed.

Canadian Billy Bishop achieved great fame during the war, partly as a result of an excellent book, *Winged Warfare*, which he wrote while on leave and which was published in 1918. Originally a cavalry officer, he became first an observer and then a pilot, joining 60 Squadron in March 1917. Flying Nieuport Scouts, he showed an early flair for the 'lone wolf' type of fighting of Albert Ball, and within three months had built up a score of twenty-two. On 2 June came his most famous combat. Going out alone

Captain Lanoe Hawker, the first ace of the RFC. On 23 November 1916 he was shot down and killed by Manfred von Richthofen.

Captain Albert Ball gained a reputation in England approaching that accorded to Guynemer in France. Flying during the same period as the great French ace, Ball was well ahead of him in spring 1917, but on 7 May he was killed with his score at forty-four. He was awarded a posthumous VC.

A career serviceman in the RFC at the outbreak of war, Major James McCudden, VC, first flew as an NCO pilot. He later rose to command a flight in the élite 56 Squadron, and was then given command of his own unit. He was killed in a crash while on the way to take up his new command. His fifty-seven victories placed him fourth on the list of British top-scorers. He is seen here in the cockpit of a 56 Squadron SE 5.

at dawn, he attacked a German airfield where he claimed the destruction of three scouts which took off to intercept him. For this he was awarded the Victoria Cross to add to his DSO and MC. Eleven more victories followed by 20 July, raising his total on Nieuports to thirty-six. Converting to the new SE 5, he claimed eleven more by mid-August.

Having equalled Ball's score, he was rested, going to Canada for a recruiting drive. He returned to the front in May 1918 to lead 85 Squadron, but was ordered to do little operational flying. Ignoring this stricture, he flew often, and frequently alone, claiming no less than twenty-five victories in less than a month, including twelve in four days, 16–19 June. On the latter date he claimed five, bringing his score to seventy-two. He was at once ordered back to England, and in August returned to Canada to aid in the setting up of the new Canadian Air Force. After the war he ran a commercial aviation firm with another great Canadian ace, Barker, VC. During the Second World War he served as an Air Marshal; he died in September 1956. Until a counter-claim for Mannock of seventy-three victories was made after the war, Bishop remained British top-scorer. Indeed, in one list prepared by the Air Ministry just after the war, his score was given as seventy-five. Only one of his claims was shared.

Another great exponent of the Nieuport Scout was Philip Fullard of 1 Squadron. Between May 1917 and mid-November of that year he claimed fifty-two victories, making him RFC top-scorer at that time. However, he then broke his leg while playing football and was invalided home. He remained in the service after the war, rising to air rank during the Second World War. His

evacuation from France coincided with the arrival in 19 Squadron of 'Nick' Carter, a Canadian pilot. An ex-army major who had been badly wounded, Carter quickly became a most successful flight commander, and in under two months he claimed eighteen victories flying the Spad S.7 Scout with which the unit was equipped. Early in 1918 re-equipment with Sopwith Dolphins took place, and with these Carter made another thirteen claims to raise his total to thirty-one: twelve and two shared destroyed, fourteen and three shared out of control. On 19 May he was shot down behind German lines, wounded and taken prisoner. He was subsequently killed in an air crash early in 1919 when testing a German Fokker D.VII fighter.

Other great names at the front during late 1917 included Arthur Rhys-David of 56 Squadron, an old-Etonian who shot down the great German ace Werner Voss for his eighteenth victory on 23 September, a day which brought him three successes. The following month, with his score at twenty-three, he failed to return from a fierce dogfight. Tom Hazell flew with Fullard in 1 Squadron on Nieuports, bringing his score to nineteen by the end of the summer. After a spell as an instructor he returned to lead 24 Squadron on SE 5As, claiming another twenty-two victories, including ten observation balloons, by early October. Posted to command 203 Squadron late in the war when Collishaw was rested, he obtained his last victory on Bentley-engined Camels, raising his total to forty-three.

Besides their reconnaissance and spotting duties, two-seaters always played a big part in the RFC's and RAF's fighting activities during the war, producing many aces. Indeed, one of the first aircraft to take the measure of the Fokkers in 1916 was the FE 2 'pusher'. The greatest name among the pilots flying these cumbersome but successful machines was undoubtedly F. J. H. Thayre, all of whose victories were, of course, actually shot down by his gunners. After an early victory on a BE, he joined 20 Squadron in 1917, teaming up with Captain R. F. Cubbon. Their first two victories fell on 29 April, while on 3 May, having forced an Albatros two-seater to land, they were attacked by twenty-six Albatros scouts. They fought these single-handed, claiming two shot down. When their ammunition was gone, they fought on with their automatic pistols until the attackers gave up and flew off. By early June they had claimed seventeen victories: twelve destroyed, three out of control, and two forced to land. A few days later they were reported missing when their aircraft was hit by an anti-aircraft shell and destroyed. At this time Thayre's personal score was twenty-one, Cubbon's twenty; the latter was the RFC's top-scoring gunner.

The most successful two-seater fighter was the Bristol F2B Fighter, once pilots learned to

use it as a fighter and not as a well-armed reconnaissance machine. The first man to master the aircraft was another Canadian, Andrew McKeever, Joining 11 Squadron in May 1917, he achieved regular successes throughout the summer, culminating on 30 November when he claimed four victories to raise his total to thirty aircraft and one balloon. Of these at least nineteen were shot down by McKeever himself with his front gun, and at least ten by the gunner in the rear seat, seven of these being credited to Sergeant L. F. Powell, his most frequent companion. McKeever was posted to England in early 1918 to become an instructor. He was killed in a motor accident the following year.

Learning from McKeever, many Bristol Fighter pilots later became aces, several of them with scores in excess of twenty, but none of them exceeded his total while flying this aircraft. McKeever was not, however, to retain his position as top-scoring two-seater pilot, this honour being wrested from him by another Canadian, A. C. Atkey, in the summer of 1918. Atkey proved an aggressive bomber with 18 Squadron, claiming four hostile scouts shot down while flying DH 4s. Posted to 22 Squadron, the one Bristol unit which was a pure fighter, rather than a fighter-reconnaissance, unit, he joined C. G. Gass to form the squadron's most successful team. During their first combat on 7 May they claimed five Fokker D.VIIs shot down, and two days later they claimed three more of D.VIIs and two Pfalz scouts. More multiple claims followed, and by the end of May their score stood at twenty-seven. Their final combat on 2 June brought their joint total to twenty-nine, fifteen credited to the front gun and fourteen to

Gass's rear gun, thus bringing Atkey's personal score to thirty-three.

Air Chief Marshal Sir Keith Park, famous commander of Fighter Command's 11 Group during the Battle of Britain, was also a Bristol Fighter ace of some note. Flying with 48 Squadron, this dashing New Zealander claimed some twenty victories, his best day being 17 August 1917, when he shot down four Albatros scouts.

The naval pilots of the RNAS also continued to do well, not least of these being another Canadian, Joe Fall. Flying Sopwith Pups on the Western Front with 3 Naval Squadron, he claimed eight victories during spring 1917. Subsequently he flew Camels with this unit. He then transferred to 9 Naval Squadron, raising his score to thirty-four by the end of the year, of which eleven were shared with other pilots. Eleven of his individual victories and seven of those shared were classed as destroyed. R. J. O. Compston, a vicar's son, flew Nieuports, Triplanes and Camels with 8 Naval Squadron, claiming twenty-five victories between late 1916 and early 1918. His total included nine shared victories.

The year 1918 brought a considerable escalation of aerial fighting, both sides pushing new units of all kinds to the front. In the RFC and RNAS, which jointly became the Royal Air Force on 1 April 1918, many new aces appeared, a good number of whom had received their early baptism of fire during the previous year. The main fighting scouts throughout the year remained the SE 5A and the Camel, reinforced by the Dolphin in growing numbers, and right at the end of the war, in October 1918, by the first of the new Sopwith Snipes.

Canadian Major 'Billy' Bishop, VC, was one of the best-known RFC aces of the war, and was widely held to be the top-scorer until long after 1918. Seen here with his Nieuport 17 in August 1917 while serving with 60 Squadron, he had just passed Ball's score and become Britain's top-scorer at that time. He later returned to France to lead 85 Squadron during 1918, when he claimed an incredible twenty-five victories in under a month to raise his total to seventy-two.

Henry Woollett was one of the minor aces of 1917, claiming six victories with 24 Squadron, the first two while flying DH 2s and the remainder on DH 5s. Early in 1918 he joined 43 Squadron as a flight commander to fly Camels, returning to France in the spring. In the first two months at the front he claimed twenty-one victories, including six scouts in one day on 12 April. He was only the second single-seater pilot in the RAF to claim such a total in one day. His final claim on 9 August raised his total to thirty-six, none of which were shared. At least twenty-three were confirmed as destroyed, nine of these being balloons.

Widely listed as British top-scorer, Edward 'Mick' Mannock, a man of humble parentage, was reported to have been almost blind in one eye. On the outbreak of war he was interned in Turkey, where he was working for a telegraph company. However, he was later repatriated owing to this poor physical condition. Joining the Medical Corps, he transferred to the RFC, and was posted to 40 Squadron in France in 1917 to fly Nieuports. His first claim, on 7 May, was against a balloon, his next not following until a month later. Success during the summer raised his total to seventeen, following which the unit converted to SE 5As during the winter. He made at least one more claim at the start of 1918, some sources quoting his score at this stage as being between twenty and twenty-three.

Returning to England, he was posted as a flight commander to the newly formed 74 Squadron, and when this unit moved to France in April was soon in the thick of the fighting again, making about thirty to thirty-five more claims by mid-June. Posted to command 85 Squadron after Bishop's return to England, he made a further eight claims by 22 July. On 26 July, accompanied by Lieutenant Inglis, he attacked a DFW CV ground attack aircraft and shot it down. He was then hit by machine-gun fire from the ground and crashed to his death in flames.

As will be seen, the basis of his score remains obscure. The citation for his posthumous VC states fifty victories, but admirers who served with him subsequently insisted that he had seventy-three—one more than Bishop. Rigorous study of the records—and these were generally quite well kept in 1918—indicates a maximum number of between sixty and seventy claims, many of which were decidedly questionable and some of which are known to have been disallowed. His total is probably in excess of fifty, but may well not actually be as high as the seventy-three with which he is listed. He was, however, undoubtedly a great leader, and was worshipped by his men.

South Africa's top-scorer was Anthony Beauchamp-Proctor, who joined the RFC in 1917 after service in South-West Africa with the South African Army. He was posted to 84

Squadron on its formation and, flying SE 5As, made his first claim on 3 January 1918. Thereafter he scored regularly and consistently throughout the rest of the war. By mid-June, when he went on leave, his score stood at twenty-eight: fifteen destroyed and thirteen out of control. After his return to the front he was able to improve the ratio of those destroyed, claiming twenty-six more by early October, all but four of them destroyed. Twelve of these latter were balloons, and he was in fact probably the RAF's top 'balloon-buster', with sixteen 'gasbags' brought down in flames among his fifty-four victories. He was awarded the Victoria Cross in November 1918. He was killed in a crash while flying a Snipe in 1921.

Two virtually unknown aces of this period were A. A. N. D. 'Jerry' Pentland, an Australian, and W. E. 'Moley' Molesworth. Pentland flew as a corps pilot first, subsequently flying Spads with 19 Squadron in 1917 and Dolphins in 87 Squadron in 1918, his total score reaching twenty-two by the end of the war. Molesworth saw service with 60 and 29 Squadrons, being one of the last pilots in the RFC to fly Nieuport scouts in action. His score by spring 1918 stood at nineteen, of which twelve, including one balloon, were credited as destroyed.

Ireland's top ace was George McElroy, another ex-soldier who had been gassed. Flying SE 5As with 40 Squadron, he first claimed in December 1917, and had twelve by mid-February 1918. Posted as a flight commander to 24 Squadron, he made seventeen more claims by 7 April. Having made three claims on 7 April, he crashed into a tree and was injured. On recovery he returned to 40 Squadron in June. In July alone he claimed sixteen aircraft and a balloon, his total reaching forty-nine, including eight of the tough Hannoveranner two-seaters. On 31 July 1918 he failed to return from a patrol, shot down by an obscure young pilot of *Jasta 56* for his first victory. Only two of McElroy's victories were shared, and at least thirty-one—including three balloons—were classified as destroyed.

Three more high-scoring Canadians were Don MacLaren, Fred McCall and A. T. Whealy. MacLaren was retained as an instructor until late 1917, when he finally arrived in France to fly Camels in 46 Squadron. He first scored in March 1918, continuing to claim regularly until the end of the war, his last victory on 9 October bringing his score to fifty-four. 46 Squadron was a very 'ace-conscious' unit, and made sure that its pilots' names were to the fore for decorations, MacLaren being the unit's greatest star. His score was made up of twenty-three destroyed, ten of them shared, six balloons, and twenty-five out of control, five of them shared. Late in 1918 he helped in the formation of the new Canadian Air Force, but resigned his commission in 1920 and went into commercial aviation.

McCall flew RE 8s on observation duties with

13 Squadron early in 1918, fighting off attacking enemy aircraft with such determination that he was able to claim six victories. Transferred to 41 Squadron as a scout pilot, he claimed thirty-seven victories between May and August while flying SE 5As, including fourteen and three shared destroyed, eleven and one shared out of control, one Fokker D.VII forced down in Allied territory and captured, and three driven down damaged. He was taken ill late in August and spent the rest of the war in hospital.

Whealy, a naval pilot, flew Pups with 3 Naval, Triplanes in 9 Naval, and then Camels with 3 Naval Squadron (later 203 Squadron). He claimed seven victories during 1917 and twenty the following year. Sixteen of his total were classed as destroyed, two of them shared.

During 1918 two scout squadrons of the Australian Flying Corps served in France, one with Camels and the other with SE 5As. Each produced several aces, the most successful of whom was Arthur Cobby, a Camel pilot in 4 AFC Squadron. From February to August 1918 he made thirty-two claims, including nineteen and two shared destroyed, three and one shared out of control, five balloons, one aircraft forced to land and crash, and one destroyed on the ground. New Zealander R. B. Bannerman served with 79 Squadron during 1918, where he was one of the most successful Dolphin pilots, claiming fifteen aircraft destroyed and one out of control in a period of three months ending on 4 November.

An unusual case was that of Sam Kinkead, a South African in the RNAS. He first saw service in the Dardanelles during 1916 with 2 Naval Wing, claiming three victories. Serving in France during 1917 with 1 Naval Squadron, he claimed some of the last Sopwith Triplane victories. He then flew Camels, raising his score to fifteen by the end of the year. He doubled this score during 1918, and then in 1919 led the Camel Flight of 47 Squadron in southern Russia. Here he was reported to have been the most successful pilot, at least five and possibly ten victories being credited to him here.

During a combat in May 1919 he had shot down two Bolshevik aircraft when he was hit by a Fokker D.VII and had to force-land on the steppe. Setting light to his aircraft, he climbed under the centre section of the top wing of Lieutenant Daley's Camel, which had landed alongside, and was flown back to base. Subsequently he was assigned to fly the Supermarine S.5 seaplane racer in the Schneider Trophy Race in 1928, but was killed in a crash during practice.

During the war the British flying services maintained fighting units elsewhere than in France. In Macedonia, where British, French, Serbian, Italian, and later Greek forces were fighting the Germans, Turks and Bulgarians, 17 and 47 Squadrons bore the brunt of the action, though aerial combat was generally

South Africa's top-scorer, Captain Anthony Beauchamp-Proctor, VC, gained all his fifty-four victories during 1918 while flying SE 5As with 84 Squadron. Sixteen of his successes were against balloons, making him the RAF's top 'balloon-buster' of the war.

Widely believed to be the British Empire top-scorer, Major Edward 'Mick' Mannock's reported score of seventy-three remains highly contentious. Undoubtedly a great leader and pilot, he was in action throughout much of 1917 and 1918. He was shot down and killed by ground fire on 26 July 1918 when at the head of 85 Squadron—a unit previously commanded by Bishop; like Ball, he received a posthumous VC.

limited. The most successful pilot in the early days was Gilbert Murlis-Green, who reached 17 Squadron during 1916. Flying the very poor, makeshift BE 12 Scouts, he was able to put these to good use against the two-seaters and Friedrichshaven twin-engined bombers which opposed him. He shot down two in December 1916 and six more in early 1917, including two Friedrichshaven aircraft in one day. In July he borrowed a lone French Spad, shooting down one more two-seater, before returning to England late in 1917. Here he took command of 44 Home Defence Squadron, equipped with Camels modified for night fighting, and on 18 December he made the first successful night interception of a Gotha bomber, which he shot down. This brought his score to ten; his total has been quoted as high as thirty-one, but this is manifestly incorrect.

Meanwhile the units in Macedonia gradually received more and newer scouts, and by 1918 had a number of Bristol M-1C monoplanes, some SE 5As and a few Camels. In May the fighter flights of 17 and 47 Squadrons were detached to form 150 Squadron, several pilots in the unit becoming aces around this time. During April Canadian A. E. deM. Jarvis claimed his first three victories in an M-1C, two of them shared. Late in May he claimed another in a Camel, followed by four more during July, all shared, while he was flying an SE 5A.

A few units served in Palestine against the Turks, but the other main front was in Italy. In November 1917, following the disastrous defeat of the Italians at Caporetto, three Camel squadrons were sent to bolster the Italian air strength. These units, 28, 45 and 66 Squadrons,

produced many aces in Italy. A Bristol Fighter unit, 139 Squadron, was later formed in Italy during 1918.

The most famous RAF ace on the Italian front was a Canadian, W. G. Barker. After service with observation units, with which he claimed two victories, he became a scout pilot late in 1917, going to France in October with the newly formed 28 Squadron. After five more victories over this front, he went with the unit to Italy, where by the end of March 1918 he had claimed a further nineteen, including nine balloons. Five of these were destroyed with another pilot during one sortie on 12 February.

During April he was posted to 66 Squadron, and in the next three months made a further sixteen claims. Posted again, this time to command the new 139 Squadron, he took his Camel with him and in short order gained six more victories. Sent back to England as an instructor during September, he went to France in October to 'get up to date' on the latest combat conditions, taking one of the new Snipes with him. Attached to 201 Squadron, but with a roving commission, he fought his last battle on 27 October, just as he was preparing to return to England. After shooting down a two-seater, he was attacked by a large formation of Fokker D.VIIs. In an epic battle, he managed to shoot down three of his attackers, but was wounded three times and crashed into the British lines. He survived to collect the Victoria Cross to add to his DSO, MC and two Bars; he was killed in a flying accident in March 1930 in Canada.

On the British scoring system nearly 800 fighter pilots of the British Empire became aces, including twenty-seven with thirty or more victories, fifty-seven with scores of twenty to twenty-nine, and 226 with scores of ten to nineteen. Additionally some sixty-five pilots of bombers and Corps observation aircraft were credited with five or more victories, as were about fifty gunners.

The leading British aces

Major E. C. Mannock	British	73 (approximately, but possibly less)
Major W. A. Bishop	Canadian	72
Major R. Collishaw	Canadian	62 (including 2 in southern Russia)
Major J. T. B. McCudden	English	57
Captain A. W. Beauchamp-Proctor	South African	54
Captain D. M. MacLaren	Canadian	54
Major W. G. Barker	Canadian	52
Captain P. F. Fullard	English	52
Major R. S. Dallas	Australian	51
Captain G. E. H. McElroy	Irish	49
Captain A. Ball	English	47
Captain R. A. Little	Australian	47
Major T. F. Hazell	Irish	43
Major J. Gilmour	Scots	40
Captain J. I. T. Jones	Welsh	40
Captain F. R. McCall	Canadian	37
Captain W. G. Claxton	Canadian	36
Captain J. S. T. Fall	Canadian	36
Captain H. W. Woollett	English	36
Captain A. C. Atkey	Canadian	35
Captain S. M. Kinkead	South African	35–40 (including 5–10 in southern Russia)

The Russians

The revolution in Russia in 1917 brought an end to the war with the Central Powers at a time when aerial combat was just coming of age. Air activity on the Eastern Front was always limited, and none of the leading German or Austro-Hungarian aces gained any of their victories there. However, it was claimed that at least eighteen Russian pilots became aces, although not all of them achieved all their victories in this area.

Following the revolution, civil war broke out, together with conflicts with several neighbouring states in both the Baltic and the Balkans. There was a certain amount of aerial activity which mainly took place during 1919, but few details are available and the only pilots known to have scored victories are those who served with RAF units supporting the White Russians.

Even by 1917 the strength of the Russian air arm was no more than four groups, each containing three or four small squadrons equipped with a variety of aircraft types. Fighters used included Morane Type 'N's, Nieuport Scouts, Sopwith 1½ Strutters, and a few Spad S.7s. Russian top-scorer was Alexander Kazakov, who, like so many other pilots in the nations at war, began his military service in the cavalry. Training as a pilot late in 1914, he gained his first victory on 18 March 1915 when the first French claims were being made on the Western Front. Flying a Morane, he trailed a long steel cable beneath it with a small anchor on the end,

hoping to grapple an enemy Albatros with this contraption. In fact he finally brought the Albatros down by ramming its top wing with the undercarriage of his aircraft, thus causing it to crash-land.

Given command of the XIX Corps Squadron in August 1915, he fought with the first Fokker *Eindekkers* to appear in the area that winter. He shot down two of these during spring 1916, and another two in the following autumn. On 16 July 1916 he engaged in one of the few big air battles on this front, a dozen Russian aircraft meeting an equal force of Germans. One Albatros was shot down by Kazakov during this battle. Several of his later victories were against Brandenburg two-seaters of the Austro-Hungarian air force, his last victory during the war being over one of these on 29 August 1917. By this time he was in command of the new 1st Fighter Group, leading four squadrons of fighters.

With his score standing at seventeen at least, he was posted to the RAF Mission in northern Russia during the civil war. Promoted to the rank of major, he led a Slavo-British squadron for a year from August 1918. He was believed to have shot down several 'Bolo' (Boleshevik) aircraft during this period, but on 3 August 1919, while in an extremely depressed mood, he crashed while taking off and was killed.

Ivan Smirnoff joined Kazakov's XIX Corps Squadron as a sergeant in 1915, having previously been wounded while serving in the infantry. His first victory was brought down while flying a Morane Type 'L', but he later flew the Type 'N', and then the Nieuport. In two years he claimed a total of twelve victories, his last falling as late as 10 November 1917. He had been commissioned in the meantime, but as a popular member of the squadron was warned that the Bolsheviks intended to shoot all officers, enabling him to make good his escape. He subsequently reached England and became a major in the RAF. He was on his way to southern Russia when the fighting ended, and he remained in the West. In 1922 he joined KLM, the Dutch airline, beginning a long and distinguished career in civil aviation. In early 1942 his Douglas DC 3 was shot down by Japanese fighters while evacuating Java, but he survived a crash-landing with his crew and passengers and was rescued. He retired in 1949 and died in 1956.

Alexander P. de Seversky is best known as an aircraft designer, his Seversky Aero Corporation in the United States later becoming the famous Republic Aviation, responsible for the Thunderbolt fighter in which many Americans became aces during the Second World War. He was, however, an ace in his own right. A naval officer, he had attended the School of Aeronautics in Russia before transferring to the Imperial Naval Air Service in 1915. Posted to the 2nd Bombing Squadron in the Baltic, he was shot down during a night raid on 2 July 1915; his bombs detonated when the aircraft crashed, the force of the explosion blowing off his right leg.

On recovery, he was given command of a bombing squadron, and later became Chief of Fighter Aviation in the area, shooting down thirteen German aircraft in fifty-seven sorties. One of his epic combats occurred on 31 July 1916; he engaged in a two-hour fight between his seaplane and seven hostile aircraft, two of which he shot down. In September 1917 he was sent to the United States by the Kerensky Government with a Naval Air Mission, but while he was there the Bolsheviks took over. Deciding to remain, he became an American citizen, forming his own aircraft manufacturing company, which was later to supply the Air Corps with its P-35, P-43 and P-47 fighters.

Several Russian aces served as members of the French Flying Service, having been resident in that country on the outbreak of war. The most successful of these was Paul d'Argeyev (French spelling d'Argueef). Wounded with the infantry, he transferred to the air service and was posted to *Escadrille SPA 124* in 1917. By chance this unit was detached to the Eastern Front to aid the Russians, and it was here that d'Argeyev claimed his first six victories. Returning to the Western Front later in the year, he claimed nine victories in five months, ending the war well up in the French and Russian lists of aces. He remained in France after the war, dying in 1922.

The leading Russian aces

Major A. A. Kazakov	17 (at least, but could be as high as 32)
Capitaine P. V. d'Argeyev	15 (all with French units, 9 on Western Front)
Lieutenant Commander A. P. de Seversky	13
Lieutenant I. W. Smirnoff	12
Lieutenant M. Safonov	11
Captain Boris Sergievsky	11
Ensign Eduard M. Thomson	11

The Belgians

Involved in the war from the very outset, the Belgians played a significant part in all aspects of the fighting on the Northern Sector of the Western Front. In 1916 the small air arm's *1ère Escadrille* became a fighter unit, equipped with Nieuport 11s, and before the year was out the *5ème Escadrille* was also converted to this role, both units receiving Nieuport 17s as the year wore on.

The first Belgian ace was Fernand Jacquet, who had engaged in aerial combats from the very beginning of the war while flying Farman two-seaters. He shot down his first aircraft on 17 April in a Farman armed with a Lewis gun. Further victories followed, his fifth falling on 1 February 1917. Now commanding the *1ère Escadrille*, he flew Spad S.11 two-seaters later in the year, and then in 1918 he led the first and only Belgian fighter *groupe*, claiming two further victories during the last month of the war.

Jan Olieslagers flew in Blériots as an observation pilot early in the war, but in 1915 was posted to the *1ère Escadrille* and began flying one of the small number of Nieuport 11s then on hand. He served right to the end of the war with the unit, being officially credited with six victories, though it was believed he had shot down a substantial number of others over German territory; as he never put in claims, it was impossible to confirm these.

The first big ace was a young solicitor, Edmond Thieffry. In 1914 when war threatened, he had just finished two years' conscription, and he was called back into the infantry in July 1914. A year later he transferred to the air service. After several crashes early in his flying career, he was retrained on fighters, and early in December 1916 joined the *5ème Escadrille* to fly the Nieuport. His first victory was claimed on 15 March 1917, and another victory followed a week later. He was shot down the following day, but escaped unhurt. In spring 1917 the unit received Spads, and in one of these he made his third claim on 12 May. His fifth went down in June, but again he was shot down himself. On 3 July he shot down two Albatros scouts, and by the end of August had brought his score to nine.

In February 1918 *1ère* and *5ème Escadrilles* were renumbered *9ème* and *10ème*, and a third unit, the *11ème Escadrille*, was formed with Sopwith Camels, the three units forming the new Belgian *Groupe de Chasse*. At this stage Thieffry, with ten victories, was the leading ace. However, on the 23rd he was shot down and crashed in German territory. Injured in the crash, he became a prisoner, and although he later managed to escape on four occasions, he was recaptured each time. In April 1929 he was killed in an air crash during a tropical storm over the Belgian Congo.

The next ace to appear was André de Meulemeester, who joined the air arm in 1916 and was posted to the *1ère Escadrille* at the end of the year. Flying Nieuports, he shot down his first enemy aircraft on 30 April 1917, claiming others during the year to bring his score to six by the end of December. During the autumn he had been offered one of the first Hanriot HD 1s, but had rejected it, handing over the little Belgian-built scout to his wingman, Willy Coppens. At the end of October he finally agreed to fly the HD1, painting it yellow overall. He later formed a special flight of three yellow Hanriots. In February 1918 he became the leading Belgian ace at the front when Thieffry went down, and

during May he shot down two aircraft to equal the latter's score of ten. He did not claim again until 5 October; on that date he shot down a balloon, but on that same day his old wingman, who had long since passed his score, claimed his own thirty-fourth victory.

Willy Coppens was indeed the Belgian 'Ace of Aces' – and by a huge margin. Called up into the infantry, he transferred to the air arm in September 1915, learning to fly in England. Going to the front, he joined the *6ème Escadrille* in July 1916, flying Sopwith 1½ Strutters, in one of which he fought his first combat in May 1917. In July he was posted to the *1ère Escadrille*, on Nieuports, but soon converted to the new Hanriot, which was passed to him by André de Meulemeester, on whose wing he initially flew. Flying many sorties, success still eluded him. He tried attacking balloons, but had no initial success against these. On 25 April 1918 he at last managed to shoot down a German fighter, and was then given some incendiary ammunition. Using this, he at once shot down two balloons, and more soon followed. On 14 October he shot down his thirty-sixth balloon to bring his total score to thirty-seven, but was hit and wounded. He crashed and was taken to hospital, where one leg was amputated. He was the highest-scoring 'balloon-buster' of the war of all nations.

Highly decorated and made a Baron by the King of the Belgians, Coppens remained in the air force after the war, but in May 1940, following the Belgian surrender to the Germans, he took up residence in Switzerland.

The leading Belgian aces

2/Lieutenant Willy Coppens de Houthulst	37
Adjudant Andre de Meulemeester	11
2/Lieutenant Edmond Thieffry	10
Capitaine Fernand Jacquet	7
Lieutenant Jan Olieslagers	6

The Austro-Hungarian Empire

The forces of the Austro-Hungarian Empire were initially concentrated on the Eastern Front, a theatre of war in which there was little air fighting. The entry of Italy into the war on the Allied side brought a new front into being, and it was here that the first Austro-Hungarian fighter units served. The air force of this power was never large, and for most of the war the main emphasis was given to the two-seater reconnaissance units. By 1917 seven small *Jagdfliegerkampagnien* were in existence, but the presence of British squadrons in Italy, and improved Italian fighter equipment reaching the front late in the year, forced an increase in strength during 1918 to thirteen units,

though these could only be kept operational at a level substantially below established strength.

About thirty Austro-Hungarian pilots became aces, but more than half of these had scores of ten or above, and the leaders did very well indeed. Main equipment in 1915–16 was the home-produced Brandenburg D-I 'Star-Strutter', though in 1917–18 these were supplemented and then replaced by the Berg D-1 and Phoenix D-I, and by licence-built Albatros D.II and D.III aircraft.

The most successful pilot was Godwin Brumowski, who was born in Poland. Transferring from army to air service as an observer in August 1915, he taught himself to fly, and was later given command of *Fliegerkampagnie 12*. When the Germans began forming *Jastas* in 1916, he was sent to study the organization and results and on his return was given command of *Fliegerkampagnie 41 Jagd (Flik 41J)* the first Austro-Hungarian *Jasta*, equipped with 'Star-Strutters'. Flying on the Italian front, he was soon scoring regularly, and in summer 1917 his unit was re-equipped with Austrian-built Albatros D.IIIs.

When the Germans began forming *Jagdgeschwadern*, Brumowski visited the Western Front again, and was greatly impressed by Manfred von Richthofen, attempting to model himself and his unit on the German's example. Continually pressing for the strength of his unit to be increased, he met sustained opposition from above. The greatest size his *Flik* was ever to reach was a strength of eighteen aircraft. By the end of the war Brumowski's personal score stood at forty.

During summer 1917 his position as top-scorer was frequently challenged by one of his pilots, another Polish-born officer, Frank Linke-Crawford. Called up into the cavalry in 1914, Linke-Crawford was remustered to the infantry in February 1916. In April he transferred to the air service. In the autumn he joined *Flik 12*, and a few months later was posted to Brumowski's *Flik 41J*. Here he scored rapidly, particularly when flying the Albatros D.III. Late in the year he was given command of the new *Flik 60J* on the Piave front, and here he met the English Camels for the first time. He finally fell in action on 31 July 1918, by which time his score had reached thirty. He met his death in a Phoenix D-I scout on a sortie on which he was leading a formation of novice pilots in Albatros D.IIIs. It is believed that he was shot down by Captain Jack Cottle of 45 Squadron, RAF (eleven victories).

Julius Arigi was born in the area of the Empire now known as Czechoslovakia. He transferred to the air service early in the war, and had become a pilot by November 1914, subsequently flying on the Russian front and then in the Balkans. Here on 4 September 1916 he and his observer shot down an Italian Farman. In early 1917 he converted to fighters and was posted to the Italian front. Later in the year he joined Linke-Crawford's *Flik 60J*, with which he swiftly became top-scorer. The most decorated NCO in the Empire, he was frequently recommended for a commission, but the rigid hierarchy of the system made this impossible. He ended the war second only to Brumowski, with a score of thirty-two. During

the Second World War he served in the Luftwaffe as an instructor, his pupils including two great future aces, Walter Nowotny and Hans-Joachim Marseille.

Viennese-born Benno Fiala, Ritter von Fernbrugg, described as a true Austrian gentleman, was a qualified engineer at the outbreak of war, and went straight into the air service. At first he was retained as an engineer officer, but eventually he became an observer, serving on the Eastern Front. On his return he again undertook engineering duties before joining *Flik 10* on the Italian front. On 2 May 1916 the Italian dirigible airship M-4 raided Lubiana at night, but suffered an engine failure and was unable to leave the area. Next morning a Brandenburg CI gave chase with Fiala in the gunner's cockpit, and he was able to shoot down the drifting M-4 for his first victory. In summer 1916 he undertook pilot training, and between the autumn of 1916 and the spring of 1917 claimed five more victories while flying two-seaters. He was then allocated a 'Star-Strutter'. In autumn 1917 he was posted to command *Flik 51J*, now flying against the British.

On 3 March 1918 he took part in a combat with Camels of 66 Squadron, RFC, during which he shot down Lieutenant Alan Jerrard (eight victories). Jerrard was subsequently awarded the Victoria Cross for his part in this action, the details of which were reported by other members of his squadron on their return; Jerrard himself became a prisoner of war. When the war ended, Fiala had twenty-nine victories. In the Second World War he served in the Luftwaffe, commanding an airfield.

A small naval air force was also active over the Adriatic during the war, the most successful pilot in this service being Gottfried Banfield, a naval officer since 1912. Banfield flew the Hansa-Brandenburg CC fighter flying boat, making bombing raids and intercepting Italian attacks. He also attacked observation balloons, his first four victories being against these. During summer 1916 he shot down three Italian flying boats and a Caproni trimotor, while in January 1917 he fought an indecisive combat with the leading Italian ace, Baracca. His final score was nine.

The leading Austro-Hungarian aces

Hauptmann Godwin Brumowski	40
Offizierstellvertreter Julius Arigi	32
Oberleutnant Franke Linke-Crawford	30
Oberleutnant Benno Fiala,	
Ritter von Fernbrugg	29

The Italians

Italy entered the war in May 1915, having been one of the first powers to exploit air power—

against the Turks in Libya in 1911. By the latter part of 1915 a fighting squadron had been formed, *8ª Squadriglia*, equipped with French Nieuport 11 Scouts which were built under licence in Italy. Early in 1916 this unit was renumbered *70ª Squadriglia*; gradually others were added until there were twelve Nieuport *squadriglie* available by the spring of 1917. These were later re-equipped with Spads or Belgian Hanriot HD-1s.

Piero Ruggiero Piccio had served originally in the infantry, but became one of the first military aviators in Italy. In 1914 he commanded *5ª Squadriglia*, and on the outbreak of war the following year led *8ª Squadriglia*, making a name for himself as a fighter pilot when the first Nieuports arrived. In his unit were two other promising young pilots, Francesco Baracca and Fulco Ruffo di Calabria.

Baracca had transferred from the cavalry as early as 1912, first flying with Piccio in *5ª Squadriglia*. Summer 1915 found him flying Nieuport two-seaters in *8ª Squadriglia*, until the arrival of the first single-seaters late in the year. His first victory, with what had now become *70ª Squadriglia*, was claimed against an Aviatik on 7 April 1916. On 25 November of that year he claimed his fifth victory to become Italy's first ace. By 1 May 1917 his score had risen to nine, and at that stage one flight of the unit was used to form a new 'crack' *squadriglia, 91ª*, which was equipped with new Spad S.7s. Initially Baracca commanded one flight of this unit, scoring his first Spad victory on 13 May. In June he took command of the whole unit, and by late September his score stood at nineteen. The next three highest scorers at this time, Ruffo di Calabria with thirteen and Piccio and Luigi Olivari with twelve each, were all flying with the same unit.

On 21 October Baracca claimed his first double – two Albatros D.IIIs – during the Battle of Caporetto, five days later claiming two Aviatiks to raise his total to twenty-four. The unit was then re-equipped with Spad S.13s, but now found itself frequently engaged by Brumowski's 'crack' *Flik 41J*. During November, Baracca claimed five more victories, and his score soon reached thirty. After a month away from the front advising on the new Ansaldo Ballila fighter, he returned early in 1918, claiming two further victories during May, and two on 15 June. He disappeared while strafing on 19 June. Austrian troops found his burnt-out Spad a few days later; Baracca's body lay nearby, untouched by the flames but with a bullet hole in the forehead. He had apparently been thrown clear by the impact of the crash.

While outshone by Baracca, Piccio continued to fly with *91ª Squadriglia* on every possible occasion, although he had been promoted to the rank of *Tenente-Colonello* during 1917. He claimed two victories on 25 October 1917, but was badly shot up on 23 November while flying a Spad S.13 on the Piave front. He survived the war with twenty-four victories, receiving Italy's

Italy's handsome and dashing Ace of Aces, Francesco Baracca. Like so many of the leading aces who lost their lives, Baracca's death on 19 June 1917 has never been adequately explained. It is likely that he was a victim of ground fire. Italy's premier fighter unit was named in his honour during the Second World War. His personal score was thirty-four.

highest award, the *Medaglio d'Oro*, which was awarded to only seven pilots.

Fulco Ruffo di Calabria's career closely followed that of Baracca. His first victory was claimed on 7 June 1917, his thirteenth before the end of September. Like Piccio, he claimed two victories on 25 October, but thereafter his rate of scoring dropped and he ended the war with twenty victories and the *Medaglio d'Oro*. His score was just beaten by Torello Baracchini,

Most of Italy's aces of the first war gained their victories during 1917 flying Spads with the 'crack' *91ª Squadriglia*. A most notable exception was Silvio Scaroni, who operated during 1918, flying a Hanriot HD1 fighter with *76ª Squadriglia*. He finished the war with twenty-six victories, second only to Baracca.

who though serving with *76ª Squadriglia* during 1917, frequently flew with Baracca. He was killed in action during 1918.

The year 1917 had been *91ª Squadriglia*'s year of glory, for during 1918 the Camels of the RAF squadrons bore the brunt of the air fighting. However, one bright new star was to appear in the Italian sky in the person of Silvio Scaroni. After early service as a reconnaissance pilot in *4ª Squadriglia*, flying Caudron G IVs, Scaroni was trained as a fighter pilot in mid-1917, joining *76ª Squadriglia* in November 1917 as it was beginning to augment its Nïeuports with Hanriots. His first victory came on 15 November, five more following by 19 December. On 26 December his base at Istroma was raided by twenty-four Austrian aircraft, and he broke all Italian records, shooting down two Knoller two-seaters and a twin-engined Gotha.

Four more victories followed in January 1918 and two in February. However, his sixteenth – a balloon – was not claimed until 3 April. On 25 June he shot down an Albatros which disintegrated in the air, the engine falling on another Albatros and bringing that down too. With *Sergente* Romolo Ticconi (eight victories), he engaged Phoenix and Berg scouts over Ariago on 7 July, shooting down two Bergs and a Phoenix and bringing his score to twenty-four, making him second only to Baracca. He had also made six more claims, which were not con-firmed. Five days later in a big dogfight in which Hanriots and Camels fought many Austrian fighters, he shot down an Albatros and a Phoenix, but was hit and lost consciousness. Recovering just before his aircraft reached the ground, he was able to crash-land, but was taken to hospital with serious wounds, remaining there for the rest of the war. He received the *Medaglio d'Oro*. He later commanded a fighter *gruppo* in 1927, subsequently serving as Air Attaché in the United States. In the Second World War he was recalled to Italy, serving as a *Generale*.

The Italian navy also operated an air arm, flying mainly over the Adriatic. Several pilots gained victories flying various types, but only one became an ace. This was Orazio Pierozzi, who served in the *Squadriglia San Marco*, where he achieved seven victories. Altogether, forty-three Italian pilots became aces during the war, ten of them having scores of over ten.

The leading Italian aces	
Maggiore Francesco Baracca	34
Tenente Silvio Scaroni	26
Tenente-Colonello Pier Ruggiero Piccio	24
Tenente Flavio Torello Baracchini	21
Capitano Fulco Ruffo di Calabria	20
Sergente Marziale Cerutti	17
Tenente Ferruccio Ranza	17
Tenente Luigi Olivari	12

The Americans

The story of the American aces of the First World War is a complex one. Although the United States did not enter the world conflict until April 1917, idealism or the desire for adventure had caused many young Americans to join the forces of France and Britain long before that date. Soon they were finding their way into the air services of these nations as pilots and observers, and early in 1916 the French authorities decided to form an all-American unit, to be equipped with Nieuport fighting scouts. Officially christened *Escadrille N 124*, it was popularly referred to as the *Ecadrille Americaine*, until objections from the German Government through diplomatic circles led to its being renamed *Escadrille Lafayette*.

In the British forces no such special units were formed, and because of the French flair for publicity, the Americans in French service typically received far more acclaim than did their compatriots serving with the RFC or RNAS. Nevertheless, several of the latter did extremely well – better probably than most of those serving with the French.

When US units began arriving in France late in 1917, *Escadrille N 124* was transferred to the US Air Service, becoming the 103rd Aero Squadron. It would later form part of the 3rd Pursuit Group. However, until sufficient units could be formed, a large number of USAS pilots were attached to the RFC to gain operational experience. At least twenty of these pilots became aces with British units during 1918. In the summer many of these pilots were transferred to two new USAS squadrons equipped with Sopwith Camels, which flew under RAF control until October 1918.

As a result of this duality of service, those Americans serving with the RFC, RAF and in the USAS Camel units – the 17th and 148th Aero Squadrons – had their scores assessed under the British system, while those in the French Air Service, and in the rest of the USAS units, which to some extent were trained and equipped by the French, had their scores assessed by the French method. As a result, the scores of all American pilots are not strictly comparable with each other in all cases.

The claim of being the first American ace of the war has been made for Frederick Libby, an ex-cowboy from Colorado who joined the Canadian army in 1914, transferring to the RFC as an observer in 1916. Flying in 22

Squadron during the summer of 1916, it is claimed that he shot down an aircraft during his first flight over the front on 15 July, claiming his fifth on 27 August. However, the incomplete records of this squadron list none of these victories, Libby's name first appearing with 11 Squadron on 14 September 1916, and again twice more in October, enemy aircraft being driven down out of control by Libby and his pilot on each occasion. On 14 November the award of a Military Cross was gazetted, the citation crediting him with five shot down at that time, rather than the ten claimed for him. Retrained as a pilot, he joined 43 Squadron in March 1917 to fly Sopwith 1½ Strutters, two further victories being credited to him and his gunners with this unit. He later flew DH 4 bombers in 25 Squadron before transferring to the USAS at the end of 1917. It has been claimed that he gained fourteen victories as a pilot, but this seems highly unlikely; it is more probable that he claimed a further two with 25 Squadron to raise his apparent total claims to fourteen, though no record has been found of these claims.

Almost certainly the first American pilot ace was one of the members of the *Escadrille Lafayette*—either Raoul Lufbery or Norman Prince. The latter, after service in two Voisin units, flew Nieuports with *N 124* from April 1916. He shot down his fifth aircraft on 12 October while escorting a bombing raid on the Mauser Works at Obendorf. On his return he hit a high-tension wire and crashed, dying of his injuries. Lufbery claimed his fifth victory during this same combat, going on to become one of the most famous American pilots of the war.

A French-born American, Lufbery was an adventurer before the war, having seen army service in the Philippines and subsequently working as a mechanic for the French aviator Marc Pourpe. In 1914 he followed Pourpe into the French forces via the Foreign Legion, and on Pourpe's death in action requested pilot training. He became a scout pilot in May 1916, joining the new *N 124*. By June 1917 he had increased his score to ten, following which he was commissioned. Later in the year, with his total at seventeen, he transferred with the unit to the USAS, becoming a major. Early in 1918 he commanded the 95th, and then the 94th Aero Squadrons, but was frequently in hospital with rheumatism. He led the first flight over the front by USAS fighters during March 1918, but on 19 May his Nieuport 28 was seen to fall in flames after attacking a German two-seater. Lufbery apparently preferred a quick, clean death, for he leapt from the cockpit of the blazing machine far above the ground.

Meanwhile, other aces had appeared with the British. Listed as a Canadian but in fact a US citizen, John J. Malone joined the RNAS. Flying in 3 Naval Wing and then 3 Naval Squadron on Sopwith Pups during early 1917, he claimed eight victories in two months before he was shot down and killed on 30 April. Clive Warman, a Philadelphian, had an equally meteoric career. He joined 23 Squadron, RFC, in summer 1917 to fly the Spad S.7. In July he made five claims, and in August eleven more, including a balloon, a two-seater and two scouts

Raoul Lufbery, the first well-known American ace. In 1914 he joined the French forces, later serving in the all-American *Escadrille Lafayette* and the USAS. He was shot down and killed in May 1918, leaping to his death from his blazing aircraft.

in one day on the 16th. All but three of these victories were classed as destroyed, and only one was shared. He was wounded before the end of August, however, and saw no further action.

Not all Americans in the French service flew in the *Escadrille Lafayette*, and two of those previously listed as doing so in fact served elsewhere. David Putnam became a pilot in October 1917 and was posted to *MS 156*, the only unit to fly the Morane AI monoplane fighter operationally. With this unit he gained three victories in early 1918 and four more during June. Posted to *SPA 38* to fly Spads, he made two more claims before transferring to the 139th Aero Squadron of the USAS. Five more victories followed, the thirteenth and last falling on 12 September. However, during this combat he was shot down and killed.

Frank Baylies never lived to transfer to the USAS. Joining the air service in May 1917, he first saw combat with *SPA 3* in the *Cicognes Groupe*. His fifth victory was claimed on 12 April 1918, and by June his score stood at twelve. On the 17th of that month, however, he was killed in a fight with four German scouts.

In the spring of 1918 the first pilots attached to the RAF by arrangement with the British Government began seeing action, many of them serving in SE 5A units. Those gaining most fame were the pilots who later served in the USAS Camel squadrons, but once again they were not necessarily the most successful. Reed Landis and Louis Bennett Jr joined 40 Squadron, with which Landis claimed twelve victories, eight of them during August. He later commanded the 4th Pursuit Group, comprising the USAS Camel squadrons. Bennett was also very active during August. Between the 15th and 22nd of that month he claimed three aircraft and seven balloons. Then on the 24th he was seen to shoot down two more balloons and head for a third. Ground fire struck his aircraft and it burst into flames. He leapt from it at low level and was carried to hospital by the gunners who had shot him down, but died as his wounds were being dressed. His death came before he could be recommended for a decoration, his brief but brilliant career remaining unrecognized by an award.

Several Americans served in 1 Squadron, the most successful being Howard Kuhlberg. His first eight victories were all shared, but seven of the next eight were individual claims. His total of sixteen included two balloons and one aircraft forced down in the Allied lines; the remainder were classed as destroyed.

Among those serving in both air forces was George Vaughan, who flew in 84 Squadron, claiming six aircraft and a balloon. Transferred to the 17th Aero Squadron as a flight commander, he added six more victories flying Camels. Elliot White Springs flew under 'Mick' Mannock in 85 Squadron, claiming four vic-

tories, but was shot down and wounded. Later serving with the 148th Squadron, he claimed eight more, becoming squadron commander late in the war. Field Kindley, a fellow flight commander in the 148th, had first flown Camels with the RAF, claiming one victory with 65 Squadron. Eleven more followed between July and October 1918 to equal Springs's twelve.

Frederick Gillet and Frederick Lord both served with 79 Squadron, flying Sopwith Dolphins. Gillet was very successful, claiming fourteen aircraft and three balloons destroyed between 3 August and 3 November; none were shared. Lord claimed ten between June and September, seven of them destroyed. He subsequently served briefly as a pilot with the Republicans during the early days of the Spanish Civil War, flying on the Basque front in the north.

Oren Rose flew SE 5As in 92 Squadron, claiming fourteen destroyed and two out of control between 30 July and 4 November. He was the unit's top-scoring pilot. In 20 Squadron, a Bristol Fighter unit, the Iaccaci brothers, August and Paul, both did well. August claimed eighteen victories between May and September, while Paul got eleven in the same period. Both claimed their first victories on 19 May, and of August's total twelve were classed as destroyed, seven by the rear-seat gunner. Nine of Paul's victories were destroyed, six by the gunner.

Most successful of all was William Lambert, an SE 5A pilot in 24 Squadron, whose final score totalled twenty-two, although this included three aircraft forced to land. Amongst the total were at least ten aircraft destroyed, including one shared. One of these was a rare Siemens-Schukkert D.III fighter. He also claimed one balloon destroyed, and at least six aircraft out of control.

Kenneth Unger was not a member of the USAS, having been rejected for service in 1917. He joined the RFC in Canada, already possessing a pilot's licence, and in April 1918 joined 210 Squadron. Flying Camels, he claimed fourteen victories between June and November, including five aircraft—two of them shared— and a balloon destroyed, and eight aircraft— three shared—out of control.

An unusual case was that of David S. Ingalls, the only US navy ace of the war. One of the early American naval aviators, he flew coastal patrols in France in 1918. In his spare time he flew Camels with the RAF's 213 Squadron, based nearby on the Belgian coast. He shared in destroying two Albatros two-seaters on 11 August, and after this success was formally attached to the squadron to gain air fighting experience. During September he made three more shared claims and then three individual ones, raising his score to eight.

Meanwhile early in 1918, the first USAS units had arrived on the French sector of the front, the first fighter unit to enter action being

the 94th Aero Squadron, which was initially equipped with Nieuport 28s. The first sorties were flown in March, and on 14 April Douglas Campbell became the first pilot with all-American training to gain a victory. A few weeks later, he also became the unit's and the USAS's first ace, but on 6 June, soon after his sixth victory, he was wounded in action and was invalided home.

Another of the unit's pilots was Edward Rickenbacker, who was to emerge as America's top ace of the war. A racing driver and engineer before the war, his valuable engineering knowledge prevented him from joining an active unit for some time. Joining the 94th, he took part in the first patrol with Lufbery and Campbell on 19 March 1918, claiming his first victory the following month. By the end of May he had five, but was then hospitalized with a severe ear infection. On his return in September, he found the unit now flying Spad S.13s.

During the last two weeks of that month he claimed six victories, becoming unit commander and receiving the Congressional Medal of Honor, America's highest award. In October, the last full month of the war, he made fourteen more claims, and when the war ended in November his total stood at twenty-two aircraft – three of them shared – and four balloons. He subsequently played a major part in commercial aviation between the wars, returning to the US Army Air Force during the Second World War for special duties.

Frank Luke was the true American 'maverick', his period of action at the front reading like a highly romanticised Hollywood movie. After a period as an instructor, he obtained a posting to the 27th Aero Squadron

in the 1st Pursuit Group, flying Spads. He proved to be a good pilot and marksman with considerable fighting spirit, but was not particularly popular as he was something of a braggart and also had a tendency to be a 'loner'.

His first claim, in August, was disallowed because he had broken formation without permission. Thereafter he flew alone whenever possible. During September he and another pilot, Joseph Wehner, frequently went hunting balloons. Between the 12th and the 18th Luke shot down ten balloons and four aircraft; Wehner also claimed eight victories, but was shot down and killed on the 18th. By now Luke had overtaken Louis Bennett's record 'bag' of the previous month. After a short leave he shot down another balloon, but again the pilot with him was killed. Depressed, he twice went absent overnight, and was grounded as a punishment. Ignoring this ban, he took off on 27 September and shot down three more balloons, although he was hit by ground fire and badly wounded. Despite this, he strafed some German troops nearby, and then force-landed. Surrounded and called on to surrender, he drew his .45 and opened fire. He was shot dead at once.

A posthumous award of the Congressional Medal of Honor was announced only four days after the award to Rickenbacker. The citation spoke of seventeen victories in as many days, but it appears that at least one of Luke's was not included. His score has been quoted as eighteen, nineteen or twenty-one, but the official figure is eighteen – four aircraft and fourteen balloons. The irony of the situation is that had Luke returned alive he would have faced a court martial, which his commanding officer had

Captain 'Eddie' Rickenbacker became top-scoring American ace of the war during 1918 while flying with the 94th Aero Squadron. In his relatively short time at the front, he scored at a far higher rate than any other USAS pilot other than the 'balloon buster', Frank Luke. Awarded the coveted Congressional Medal of Honor, he is seen here with his Spad S.13, which is clearly marked with the 94th's 'Hat in the Ring' marking.

Awarded a Medal of Honor posthumously when he failed to return from his last flight on 27 September 1918, Lieutenant Frank Luke would have faced a court martial for disobeying orders in taking off, had he returned alive. A 'loner' in the best Hollywood tradition, Luke enjoyed a brief but meteoric combat career, claiming all his eighteen victories in under two months, fourteen of them against observation balloons.

ordered on finding that he had taken off in defiance of the ban on his flying.

The last American ace of the period was another member of the RAF, Marion Aten. Joining 203 Squadron to fly Camels late in the war, he was injured in an accident before seeing any action, not recovering until after the fighting had ended. Subsequently he was recruited by his old commanding officer, Raymond Collishaw, to volunteer for the Camel Flight of 47 Squadron for service with the White Russian forces of General Denikin in southern Russia in 1919. Here during the spring he was to prove one of the most successful pilots, claiming the destruction of five Bolshevik aircraft – three Nieuport Scouts, a Fokker D.VII and a Fokker Triplane. His last victory, the D.VII, was painted black overall and was believed to have

been flown by the top Bolshevik ace at the time, who had previously shot down Sam Kinkead's Camel, and was reputed to have about a dozen victories. Like many of the other American pilots, Aten was decorated by the British for his exploits in their service.

Altogether, about twenty-two Americans became aces flying with the British forces only, six with the French services only, and eighty-two while serving in the USAS for at least a part of their combat careers. The one naval pilot brings the overall total to about one hundred and ten. Two more high-scoring pilots with the British forces, S. W. Rosevear and A. M. Wilkinson, have been listed as Americans, but in fact Wilkinson was an Englishman, and Rosevear a Canadian from Port Arthur, Ontario.

The leading American aces

Captain Edward V. Rickenbacker	26 (all with USAS)
Captain William C. Lambert	22 (all with RAF)
Captain August T. Iaccaci	18 (all with RAF)
Second Lieutenant Frank Luke Jr	18 (all with USAS)
Captain Frederick W. Gillet	17 (all with RAF)
Major Raoul Lufbery	17 (all with French flying service)

Captain Howard A. Kuhlberg	16 (all with RAF)
Captain Oren J. Rose	16 (all with RAF)
Captain Clive W. Warman	15 (all with RAF)
First Lieutenant David E. Putnam	13 (French/USAS)
First Lieutenant George A. Vaughan Jr	13 (RAF/USAS)
Second Lieutenant Frank L. Baylies	12 (all with French flying service)
Lieutenant Louis Bennett Jr	12 (all with RAF)
Captain Field E. Kindley	12 (RAF/USAS)
Major Reed G. Landis	12 (all with RAF)
Captain Elliot W. Springs	12 (RAF/USAS)
Lieutenant Paul T. Iaccaci	11 (all with RAF)
Lieutenant Kenneth R. Unger	11 (all with RAF)

The Greeks

The Greeks were supplied with small numbers of Nieuport Scouts, Spads and Camels during the war. At least one Greek pilot became an ace, Commander A. Moraitinius, who served in the Naval Air Service. He took part in a large number of bombing raids, anti-submarine patrols, fighter escorts and defensive patrols. In twenty air fights he was credited with shooting down nine enemy aircraft. Tragically, he was killed in an air accident on 12 December 1918 while undertaking a flight from Salonika to Athens.

The fate of thousands of aircraft on the Western Front—the tangled remains of a shot-down Albatros.

AIR COMBAT
THE WORLD OVER
1932-1945

Air Combat The World Over
THE BACKGROUND

The lessons of the First World War had been learned, at least in part, by many countries, and before long air components were being added to the military forces of most nations. While aircraft were frequently used throughout the world to subdue dissidents in colonial territories, or to aid in suppressing internal unrest, battles of one aircraft against another were not to be seen again for something over ten years.

Late in 1931, Japanese forces which had occupied Manchuria became involved in combat with the Chinese. During these hostilities the Japanese made good use of their modern and efficient air arm, against which the defenders had no effective riposte. Consequently, an American Mission was invited to the country to advise on the formation of a Chinese Air Force. When Japanese troops were landed at Shanghai early in 1932, ostensibly to protect national interests in that region, the Chinese resisted and carrier-borne aircraft from the aircraft carrier *Kaga* attacked the Chinese quarter. One raid was intercepted by a single Boeing 218 export demonstration biplane fighter, flown by one of the American instructors, this being shot down by three Japanese Nakajima A1N1 fighters for the first Japanese aerial victory. Chinese authorities claimed that three of the attackers had been shot down first, but this claim was motivated by a desire for propaganda rather than fact, the Japanese actually suffering no loss.

Far away during that same year of 1932, aerial combat on a larger scale erupted in a somewhat unlikely setting – South America. A series of incidents over a territorial dispute between Paraguay and Bolivia broke out into full-scale war during 1932, fighting continuing until 1935, by which time both nations were economically exhausted. A number of air battles took place between the very small Paraguayan air force, equipped only with Potez 25 reconnaissance-bombers and Fiat CR20 fighters, and the somewhat larger Bolivian air force, which fielded Curtiss Hawk fighters, Curtiss Osprey and Falcon, and Junkers W.34 reconnaissance and bomber aircraft. Aircraft on both sides were shot down, but not in sufficient numbers for any one pilot to become an ace in the accepted sense. One Bolivian pilot, Major Rafael Pavon, did better than most, claiming about three victories, and was then referred to as the Bolivian 'Ace of Aces'.

The development in Europe and the United States of fast monoplane fighters with multiple gun armament and high-speed monoplane bombers led during the 'thirties to a growing official belief that the lessons of the First World War were to a great degree no longer valid. It was thought that the speed of modern aircraft would give no opportunity for dogfighting in the old style, and that new aces were unlikely to appear. It was believed that co-ordinated formation attacks would be the order of the day, with individual victory credits generally proving to be impossible to allot.

This fallacious view, which would again be put forward when jet fighters were introduced into general service, has consistently been proved mistaken in the light of experience. It was later replaced by the equally mistaken views that missiles had made the day of the manual interceptor fighter a thing of the past, or that guided missile armament made the carriage of machine-guns, or cannon, by fighters unnecessary. Yet every conflict has only strengthened the basic ground rules of aerial conflict: the man with the gun, who enjoys surprise, or superior speed, or greater manœuvrability, or greater experience – or an amalgam of any or all of these factors – is most likely to achieve the best results.

The first indications that the new doctrines were not as infallible as they perhaps seemed began to emerge in the midsummer of 1936 on the outbreak of the Spanish Civil War. In a politically conscious and strife-torn Europe, this conflict polarized the struggle between Left and Right, and soon both sides were receiving substantial aid in both men and modern military equipment. While many individual volunteers were motivated by deeply held beliefs, for the dictatorships of Europe, Spain proved an excellent testing ground for their military theories and their new equipment.

While the government forces of the Republic were aided by Soviet Russia, the Nationalist insurgents received their support from Mussolini's Italy and Hitler's Germany. During the course of the war, increasing numbers of Spanish pilots, trained after the outbreak of hostilities, took their places at the front, but initially the main burden of combat was borne by foreign personnel. The eventual top-scorer was a Spaniard, but German, Italian and Russian pilots all did well with their respective legions. When the war finally ended early in 1939, many of the aircraft which were to play an important part in the Second World War had

received their initial baptisms of fire over Spain.

Meanwhile, outbreaks of armed conflict were occurring elsewhere with increasing frequency. During July 1937 a large-scale, but undeclared war between China and Japan broke out, the Japanese playing down its scope by referring to it only as an 'incident'. The poorly trained Chinese quickly suffered heavy losses at the hands of the highly efficient Japanese naval air force by which they were principally opposed, and would have been virtually wiped out by the autumn had not Russian aid arrived. Not only aircraft of modern design but also full volunteer squadrons from the Red Air Force fought in China, allowing aerial opposition to be maintained against the invaders during much of 1938.

In Europe the occupation of the Sudetenland, followed by the full occupation of Czechoslovakia and the setting up of a separate Slovakian State by the Germans, occurred during this period, setting the scene for more fighting in the air. On this occasion the fighting was between Hungarian and Slovakian forces, Hungary laying claim to territory within the Slovakian borders. The fighting was not widespread and was brought to a speedy conclusion.

The next outbreak was almost totally overlooked by the Western world, and only recently has its full scope become apparent. During May 1939 Russo-Mongolian and Japanese forces went to war on the Mongolian-Manchurian frontier in another undeclared 'incident'. Until mid-September a fierce campaign was prosecuted, during which large formations of aircraft, sometimes in strengths running into hundreds, battled in the skies. While the Japanese army was soundly defeated on the ground, in the air the Army Air Force appears to have got very much the better of the conflict. Large numbers of Japanese and some Russian pilots became aces, some of the former claiming scores, both in total and in individual combats, which were certainly not equalled in Spain, nor until well into the Second World War.

Western attention had, of course, been occupied by the increasing tension in Europe which finally led at the start of September 1939 to the invasion of Poland by Germany, and to the outbreak of war between that country and France and the United Kingdom. After the initial fighting during the conquest of Poland, the war settled down into the 'Phoney War' period, when little took place except patrol activity, reconnaissance and occasional clashes over the border.

The main action occurred further north, over the eastern territory of Finland, which Russian forces invaded during November 1939. However, they found themselves with a severe fight on their hands. Both in the air and on the ground the small Finnish forces put up a terrific fight, not accepting an armistice until March 1940, when they were finally overwhelmed by the vast numerical superiority of the Soviet forces.

During April 1940 the Germans invaded Denmark and Norway in an attempt to forestall an Allied landing in Norway and protect iron ore supplies from Sweden. This brought a brief outbreak of aerial combat, but ranges were too great for this to be of any great intensity over a protracted period, and before long the British and French forces which had gone to the

The Fiat CR 32, mainstay of the Nationalist air force in the Spanish Civil War, had a 600-hp A30 engine and was fitted with either two or four machine-guns.

Queen of the skies over South China in 1937–38 was the Mitsubishi A5M carrier fighter of the Imperial Japanese Navy, later code-named 'Claude' by the Allies. This particular aircraft is seen aboard the carrier *Soryu* during late 1939. The pilot of this aircraft was Lieutenant Tamotsu Yokoyama (five victories) who is standing, left. Next to him, with moustache, is NAP1/C Matsuo Hagiri (thirteen victories).

opposite, top
One of the truly great fighters of the war, and built in larger numbers than any other fighter before or since, was the Messerschmitt Bf 109. More victories were claimed by the pilots of these aircraft, and more of their pilots became aces, than on any other type employed by the air force of any nation. This is an example of the E sub-type, used throughout 1939–40 and during much of 1941 and 1942. This particular aircraft is seen in flight over the White Sea area of northern Russia in 1942. The pilot is *Hauptmann* Günther Scholz, *Kommodore* of *III Grüppe, Jagdgeschwader 5*. He personally claimed thirty-two victories; note the three lines of victory 'bars' on the rudder.

aid of the Norwegians were forced to withdraw.

The real battles began on 10 May 1940, when the great German *Blitzkrieg* offensive was launched against France, Belgium and Holland. Fierce aerial fighting commenced at once, both sides losing large numbers of aircraft. Increasing numbers of British aircraft were thrown into the fray, particularly during the Dunkirk evacuation, when for the first time Fighter Command aircraft, operating from bases in southern England, were able to wrest local air superiority from the Luftwaffe. On 10 June 1940 Italy declared war on France and the United Kingdom, fighting then breaking out in southern France and in the Mediterranean. In the latter area the small British forces in Egypt clashed with the Italians across the Libyan border, while aircraft from Sicily attacked the British naval base at Malta.

When France capitulated before the end of June, the scores of many of the combatant pilots had begun to rise well into double figures, the victorious Luftwaffe fighter pilots in particular having enjoyed many opportunities to make claims. Two German pilots had by now claimed in excess of twenty victories, while several more, as well as a number of RAF pilots, were fast approaching this score.

Throughout July 1940 the British awaited a German invasion which never came. Fierce fighter battles raged over convoys at sea during the month, and in August an all-out bombing campaign was launched against the south of England, designed to destroy the RAF as a preliminary to the invasion. This series of battles, which extended well into the autumn, has become famous as the Battle of Britain.

Despite the apparent German superiority in numbers, those fighter pilots who had taken part in the French campaign remained in action throughout the fighting of 1940; British pilots, on the other hand, were frequently rotated to rest areas, or to instruct new pilots. As a result, during the tremendous air battles of August and September 1940, German scores tended to reach higher levels than did those of their opponents. By the late autumn the three leading German aces had scores of over fifty, but many of these had been claimed over France, and the scores of the top-scoring pilots of the opposing air forces actually claimed between August and November 1940 were not markedly different.

In the winter of 1940 German bombers began a series of night raids of increasing intensity over England, but the first clumsy airborne radar sets allowed British night fighters to begin taking an increasingly heavy toll of these raiders. At the same time British bombers were regularly raiding German territory by night, and German pilots were also beginning to find ways and means of intercepting them with some degree of regularity.

In the spring of 1941, the RAF's Fighter Command went on to the offensive, flying sweeps and escort missions over western France, Belgium and Holland in an effort to bring the Luftwaffe to battle. These raids could not penetrate deeply into Europe, owing to the restricted range of the British fighters, but despite this the Luftwaffe met them regularly at first, and a long series of battles began in which, it must be admitted, the RAF generally came off worst.

Already, however, Luftwaffe units were withdrawing from France to move to the East. In the Mediterranean a British offensive in December 1940 had driven the Italians out of eastern Libya, while an Italian invasion of Greece during late 1940 had foundered badly. The Yugoslavs were also proving a problem to the Germans, having forced their King to abdicate and having repudiated the Axis Pact which he had signed earlier. Hitler was about to launch an ambitious invasion of Soviet Russia, and not wishing to face possible attacks from British forces on his southern flank, he sent support to bolster up the Italians in Sicily and Africa in March 1941, while in April he launched an invasion of Yugoslavia and Greece.

Resistance crumbled before the Axis forces,

and Yugoslavia and Greece were swiftly occupied, Libya was retaken, and Malta was neutralised, all to the accompaniment of fierce fighting in the air, mainly with the RAF. In May an airborne invasion of Crete was successfully carried out, albeit with large loss of life, but then the German forces withdrew for the attack on Russia, leaving only a relatively small contingent in Libya.

The British had undergone a series of disasters, and only in East Africa, where a war with the Italian garrisons in Eritrea, Ethiopia and Somaliland was being brought to a successful conclusion, was any success attained. The initial British aim was to consolidate the position in the eastern Mediterreanean. During May a revolt in Iraq was crushed, this involving some air fighting with the Iraqi Air Force, and then in

June the French colony of Syria was occupied. This led to some severe fighting with the Vichy French garrison, which had been reinforced, and some fierce air battles ensued. At the same time, the first of a series of offensives was launched against the Axis forces in Libya, though these failed totally. In Malta, however, the defenders enjoyed more success against the Italians, and efforts were at once instituted to reinstate this base's offensive capacity.

Meanwhile on 22 June 1941, the German invasion of Russia was launched, initiating air fighting on an unprecedented scale. The highly experienced German pilots enjoyed an enormous advantage over the Russians, and in no time the scores of many pilots began to increase at phenomenal speed. Before July was out the leading Luftwaffe ace of the time, *Obstlt.*

Obsolete PZL P11 interceptors were the mainstay of the Polish fighter force which faced the shattering impact of the German *Blitzkrieg* in September 1939.

Werner Mölders had passed von Richthofen's unbeaten First World War score and had reached the magic 100.

Other nations, among them Italy, Hungary and Rumania, had joined the Germans in their attack on Russia, while the Finns were soon also in the war, quickly retaking the territory which they had lost in 1940. It was the Germans, however, who bore the brunt of the combat, and by 1942 a hundred victories on the Russian Front was becoming as commonplace as had been twenty in the West.

A British offensive in North Africa in November 1941 again drove the Axis forces back across Libya, resulting in the withdrawal of units from Russia to restore the balance. This led, among other things, to a renewal of German air attacks on Malta, where a severe siege began. In Africa the British were finally held, and then driven back to the Gazala area, half the lost territory being regained.

At the same time came the final act which brought the war to virtually the whole of the world. On 7 December 1941 Japan launched an undeclared war in the Far East on America, Britain, Australia, New Zealand and the Dutch East Indies. An initial air strike on the great American naval base at Pearl Harbor, in the Hawaiian Islands, put the US Fleet out of action, while invasions of Thailand, Malaya and the Philippines were launched.

Against fragmented opposition, the experienced and highly trained fighter pilots of the Japanese Army and Navy Air Force cut a swathe through all opposition, and while American, British Commonwealth and Dutch pilots did what they could, it was only a matter of time before the initial objectives fell to the Japanese, followed by the Dutch East Indies, Singapore and Burma.

May 1942 found the Japanese in New Guinea, from which they were threatening the northern territories of Australia, and at the Indian frontier in north Burma. The British fleet base at Ceylon had been raided by carrier-based aircraft, and it seemed that nothing could stop the Japanese. At this juncture, the Axis attacked in North Africa, retaking the whole of Libya, including the port of Tobruk, and crossing the Egyptian frontier to press on towards the vital Suez Canal.

In the Soviet Union renewed German offensives in southern Russia had taken much territory and inflicted terrible losses. Mid-1942 was undoubtedly the lowest point in the war for the Allies. Gradually, however, things improved everywhere. In June 1942 the US Navy inflicted a crushing defeat on the Japanese Navy at Midway, great air battles being fought by the opposing carrier forces. In Russia the Germans were first held, then surrounded and defeated at Stalingrad during the autumn and winter. In Africa, too, success was on the way. In October the Alamein offensive was launched, finally throwing the Axis forces out of Egypt and Libya. During November Anglo-American landings in French North Africa took the Axis in the rear. Heavy fighting in Tunisia continued until early May 1943, but by then the German-Italian forces had been defeated.

North Africa had seen some very heavy aerial combat, and during 1942 the German had enjoyed considerable success in fighter battles, despite the fact that the British retained overall

Numerically, the most important British fighter during 1940 was the Hawker Hurricane. This aircraft, seen on a wintry airfield at the end of that year, is flown by the commanding officer of 257 Squadron, Robert Stanford-Tuck (twenty-nine victories).

superiority in the air. At this time *Hpt*. Hans-Joachim Marseille brought his score to 158, the most successful pilot of the war against the British. Other pilots also built up big scores over Tunisia, but Anglo-American strength gradually overwhelmed them, and it was to be virtually the last time the Luftwaffe enjoyed any real success against the fighter forces of the Western Allies.

Late in 1942 the Americans went on to the offensive in the South Pacific, Marines landing in the Solomons on the island of Guadalcanal, where the Japanese had been building an airfield. Marine fighters were flown in, and during October a series of heavy air raids was launched, the great 'blitzes' on this island and on Malta virtually coinciding. Fierce carrier battles were also fought around the Solomons, during which some of the most experienced pilots in the Japanese Naval Air Force were lost.

A Ju 52 crashes in flames during the air battles over Crete as the Germans launch an airborne invasion in May 1941. The RAF defenders were finally reduced to a mere handful of Hurricanes and Gladiators. This Ju 52 transport is one of the 220 Luftwaffe aircraft shot down during the invasion.

With Japan's entry into the war in December 1941, the presence in service of the superlative Mitsubishi A6M Zero-Sen with the naval fighter units came as an unpleasant shock to the Allies. However, this aircraft had made its debut in China over a year earlier, but reports of its presence from American observers were ignored. This early A6M1 of the *12th Fighter Kobutai*, a land-based unit, is seen over China during 1940.

The P-51 Mustang, one of the outstanding fighters of the war. Fitted with a licence-built Rolls-Royce Merlin engine, the Mustang was a superb escort fighter. These aircraft are part of the 1st Air Commando Group, operating in Burma.

The year 1943 marked the beginning of the end for the Axis powers. In Russia the Germans staked everything on a great offensive at Kursk, but they spent too long preparing and the Russians were ready for them. In one of the greatest battles the world has ever seen, millions of men and thousands of tanks locked in battle, while overhead vast armadas of aircraft clashed in the biggest series of combats of the whole war.

Even as the battle was at its height in early July, Anglo-American forces invaded Sicily, clearing the island in little more than five weeks. Landings in Italy followed in September, and the Italian Government capitulated, signing an armistice after deposing Mussolini. Precious German forces had to be made available to take over in Italy, forming a defence to stop Allied troops pressing on into southern Europe.

From England, Bomber Command was now launching telling night raids over Germany, anything up to 1,000 bombers making area attacks on industrial towns and other targets, sometimes with devastating effect. The first elements of a powerful American strategic bomber force were also starting to make deep penetration daylight attacks to bomb selected industrial targets with more accuracy. Hence defence became the first priority of the Luftwaffe, fighter units being pulled out from other fronts for this purpose, while more night-fighter units were also formed. At this stage the American bombers were only escorted by fighters as far as France, and some very heavy losses were inflicted on them; by night improved radar-directed interceptions were also taking a heavy toll of the British bombers. In Russia, too, the Germans continued to achieve great success. In October 1942 one pilot, Hermann Graf, had reached the incredible score of 200. It was nearly a year before any other pilot matched this achievement, but in the autumn of 1943 four more pilots topped this figure, and one, Walter Nowotny, reached 250.

Early in 1944 American escort fighters began to accompany the heavy bombers deeper and deeper into Germany, taking an increasingly heavy toll of the defending interceptors during the course of some very big battles. The spring brought a huge Russian offensive, which was steadily to roll the Axis back, the Soviet forces retaking their own territory before moving on into Rumania, Hungary, Poland and East Prussia. In Italy a further Allied offensive reached Rome in June 1944, while two days later a great invasion began in Normandy.

All remaining Luftwaffe units in Italy, and many from Russia, were rushed to the new Western Front, but here they were merely fed into the great grinding machine of Anglo-American air superiority, and were swiftly destroyed.

In the East the weakened German fighter force fought on with continued success, but it simply could not be everywhere. Over the Reich the battles against the bombers continued, but with ever-increasing losses and decreasing success. Even the introduction of jet fighters in the autumn had little real effect. At night the fighters still enjoyed a measure of success, but increasing numbers of escorting Mosquitos were now appearing, while radio and radar counter-measures continued to make the task of the fighter pilots difficult. Bombers were now appearing regularly from the south, flying from bases in Italy; the Reich was becoming impossible to defend.

Generally never taken off operations except for occasional leaves, the Luftwaffe pilots either died or built up big scores–particularly in the East. By the end of 1944 one pilot had passed 300, and when the war in Europe ended in May 1945, one more had done so too. Indeed, the score of the greatest ace of all time, Erich Hartmann, stood at 352. Those pilots who could, fought on to the very end on all fronts, as did a number of Italian and Hungarian pilots,

but there was nothing they could do to forestall the inevitable.

Meanwhile in the Far East, steady progress had been made during 1943 as US Marine and Army forces invaded key islands on which air bases and naval facilities were developed, other islands being by-passed and neutralised by air attack. Throughout this period Army and Marine fighters saw considerable combat over Japanese bases in New Guinea and New Britain, where regular Allied air raids were made. In Burma and China the war continued, British, American and Chinese forces struggling to regain the initiative, the air forces fighting a long, hard battle with the units of the Japanese Army Air Force.

As in the West, 1944 was to see a succession of Allied successes. From India the first big American B-29 Superfortress bombers began attacking the Japanese home islands, while island bases in the Pacific from which these bombers could operate were taken by the combined forces during the year. The invasion of the Marianas for this purpose in June 1944 brought out Japanese aircraft in great strength, only for them to be massacred in equally great numbers by the waiting fighters of the US Navy.

During September the Philippines were invaded, and a great naval battle in Leyte Gulf ensued, during which the remaining strength of the Japanese navy was destroyed. Every possible air unit was pushed out to the Philippines by the Japanese, and the first suicide missions were flown against US shipping. However, the Japanese were simply cut to pieces by the US Navy, Marine and Army fighters in the area.

In Burma the final Japanese attempt to press into India was held at Kohima and Imphal early in 1944, a counter-offensive then driving the Japanese back, clearing them steadily out of northern and central Burma, Rangoon being retaken in January 1945. The one area where no

great success had been gained was in China, and an offensive by the Japanese here in late 1944 looked threatening for a time, but in the event was held.

During 1945 B-29 raids and attacks by carrier aircraft played havoc on the mainland, most Japanese air units now being brought home for defensive purposes. However, the Japanese met with scant success as the technical superiority of American aircraft was by now generally substantial. The Americans, now joined by a British carrier force, steadily moved closer, first Okinawa and then Iwo Jima being captured. An invasion of the Japanese islands themselves appeared imminent, and a final great battle was in preparation, the Japanese planning many suicide attacks. However, with the intention of saving Allied lives, two atom bombs were dropped, at Hiroshima and Naga-saki, and a few days later, in August 1945, the Japanese surrendered unconditionally, bringing the Second World War to a close.

During the last few days of the war Russia also declared war on Japan, attacking Japanese forces in Manchuria and Korea. However, the surrender came before any substantial amount of combat could take place. Between 1936 and 1945 thousands upon thousands of aircraft of many nations were shot down and several thousand pilots became aces. Circumstance and chance governed which nationalities were to have the greatest opportunities to gain aerial victories, and this was the major factor in allow-ing the Axis nations to produce pilots with higher scores than those of the Allies. Germany, Japan and Finland produced the top scorers of all time. It is true that their pilots were well trained, highly experienced and generally equipped at the appropriate time with better aircraft, as well as being members of warrior races, but circumstance was the greatest factor in accounting for their success, and in this they were uniquely placed.

After initial service with the 8th Air Force as an escort fighter, the Republic P-47 Thunderbolt – or 'Jug' as it was affectionately known to its pilots – was employed as a fighter-bomber. In the latter role this P-47D of the 354th Fighter Group, 9th Air Force, is seen on a forward airstrip in France late in 1944. The pilot is the 9th's top-scorer, Captain Glenn Eagleston (twenty and a half victories). The man on the wing is directing him, as his vision is obscured by the cowling of the big engine.

ACES OF THE NATIONS 1936-1945

The Americans

The Americans retained a considerable interest in military aviation during the years between the wars, though successive reduced budgets during the years of depression steadily brought down the strength of Army, Navy and Marine Air Forces. The wars of the late 'thirties produced a number of American pilot 'soldiers of fortune', some of these serving in Spain and China. In the former country a collection of miscellaneous aircrews reached Republican territory during 1936, most of whom remained for only a short time. Several returned with lurid tales of their massive successes, but in reality many of these did not even operate over the front. Of those who actually reached units, two did achieve some success, both these men initially serving in squadrons equipped with Polikarpov I-15 biplanes.

Frank G. Tinker had served as a pilot in the Marine Corps and was to prove the more successful. During March and April 1937 he claimed two Fiat CR 32s and a He 51, while his compatriot, Albert J. 'Ajax' Baumler, claimed one of each, one shared and one probable. In May both pilots were moved to an I-16 unit, and flying the faster monoplane during June and July, Tinker claimed three more CR 32s and two of the first Messerschmitt Bf 109Bs to appear over Madrid, while Baumler claimed two more CR 32s and a probable. At this stage their contracts expired, and as adequate numbers of Spanish pilots were becoming available, they were released and returned to the United States.

In China an equally heterogenous collection of Americans put in an appearance, but few seem to have achieved any concrete success. One, George Weigel, is reputed to have claimed five victories, four of them in one engagement, while flying a Curtiss Hawk 75 fighter, but was killed in a landing accident.

The war in Europe offered further opportunities for Americans to participate, volunteers reaching both the United Kingdom and Finland during 1940. In the latter country the war ended before any of the volunteers could get into action, but in England a growing number arrived, many coming via Canada. At first they went to a variety of units, but in 1941 an all-American unit, 71 'Eagle' Squadron, was formed. Two more such units, 121 and 133 Squadrons, were later formed, all serving with Fighter Command and taking part in cross-Channel sweeps. Several of these Americans became aces, the first being William R. Dunn, who claimed five victories before being wounded in combat.

Gregory A. 'Gus' Daymond claimed his first victory in 71 Squadron on the same day as Dunn. In 1942 he became commander of the unit, later receiving a DFC and Bar for seven victories. Top-scoring 'Eagle' ace was Carroll W. 'Red' McColpin, who claimed six victories with 71 Squadron, twice getting two Bf 109s in a day. In 1942 he commanded 133 Squadron, claiming two more victories and a probable. He later flew with the US 9th Air Force, raising his score to twelve late in the war when he caused three Bf 109s to spin into the ground without firing a shot.

Other Americans served with the RAF in various squadrons in Malta, the Middle East and Far East, some remaining with this service long after their own nation had entered the war. Several did very well, including John J. Lynch, who claimed twelve victories over Malta with 249 Squadron during late 1942–early 1943, and David C. Fairbanks who commanded a squadron of Tempests (274) in Europe with 2nd TAF late in the war, being credited with twelve and a half victories. Claude Weaver III also flew in Malta, claiming eleven and a half in about six weeks during the summer of 1942. He later added two more over Western Europe with 403 (Canadian) Squadron, but both he and Fairbanks were posted missing before the war ended.

Lance C. Wade was turned down by the USAAF, but joined the RAF late in 1940. Posted to the Middle East, he flew Hurricanes with 33 Squadron, claiming fifteen victories between November 1941 and September 1942. After a rest, he led 145 Squadron, flying Spitfires during the Tunisian campaign and the invasions of Sicily and Italy. During 1943 he added ten more victories to bring his score to twenty-five, making him at the time Desert Air Force's top-scorer. He was killed in a crash during a routine non-operational flight on 12 January 1944.

Elsewhere during 1941 General Clair Chennault, American air adviser to the Chinese Nationalist forces, began, with the tacit agreement of the US authorities, to recruit a body of American volunteer pilots from the various US forces to operate over China. The American Volunteer Group (AVG), better known as the 'Flying Tigers', reached Burma during late 1941, where they were formed into three squadrons equipped with Lease-Lend P-40C Tomahawks. Training was completed and one unit moved into China at the beginning of December 1941, but no action had been seen when Japan attacked US, British and Dutch territory in the Far East to begin the Pacific War.

As a result it was regular US servicemen who saw action before the AVG. At Hawaii several pilots took off in defence of Pearl Harbor without orders, the most successful being George S. Welch, who flew three times, claiming four victories on 7 December. He later served in New Guinea, and exactly a year later shot down three more Japanese aircraft while flying a P-39 Airacobra. On 2 September 1943, while flying a P-38 Lightning, he claimed four more in a day, raising his total to sixteen. In October 1954 he was killed while test flying an F-100 Super Sabre.

In the Philippines, Boyd D. 'Buzz' Wagner became the first USAAF ace of the war, shooting down five Japanese fighters in two combats in his P-40 and claiming ten more destroyed on

Albert 'Ajax' Baumler, soldier of fortune and veteran of the Spanish Civil War. He is seen here in front of the 'shark's teeth' painted on the nose of one of 23rd Fighter Groups P-40 Warhawks.

Colonel David 'Tex' Hill of the 23rd Fighter Group climbs into his P-51 in China in October 1945.

One of the best American fighters at the start of the war in the Pacific was the Grumman F4F Wildcat. The Wildcat was flown by Naval and Marine Corps aces during 1942, bearing the brunt of the fighting at the Battles of Midway, Coral Sea and Santa Cruz, and during the defence of Guadalcanal.

the ground. As a staff officer in New Guinea during 1942, he flew occasionally, bringing his score to eight during June. He was later killed in an air crash in the United States.

The AVG went into action over both China and Burma late in December 1941, flying in the latter theatre alongside the RAF in defence of Rangoon. Employing tactics devised by Chennault to maximize the Tomahawk's best features, the group achieved some outstanding successes. During a long fighting retreat through Burma, it continued to operate as long as possible, despite the loss of many aircraft on the ground. In the air over 200 victories had been claimed by the early summer of 1942, for only light losses. During July the group was incorporated into the USAAF, becoming the 23rd Fighter Group. However, disgruntled by conditions and the terms of transfer, most of the original pilots then returned to the US.

Top-scorer was former naval dive-bomber pilot, Robert H. Neale, who claimed sixteen, fourteen of them between 20 January and 28 February 1942, in Burma. Decorated by the British, he was at this time top-scoring US pilot anywhere in the world since 1918. David L. 'Tex' Hill, with twelve and a quarter, and Charles H. Older, with ten and a half, both remained in China, both becoming Colonels. Hill added six more victories with the USAAF, and Older eight more. John Van Kuren Newkirk also claimed ten and a half, but was shot down by

ground fire on 24 March 1942. Altogether the AVG produced some thirty-eight aces.

'Ajax' Baumler, the Spanish Civil War pilot, arrived in China too late to join the AVG, but was inducted into the Air Force and joined the 23rd Fighter Group. Here he added six Japanese aircraft to his earlier score, including two bombers during the night of 30 July 1942.

The first US Navy ace of the war was Edward H. 'Butch' O'Hare, who was flying Grumman F4F Wildcats with Squadron VF-3 aboard the carrier *Lexington* during early 1942. On 20 February he intercepted a raid on his ship by eight Mitsubishi G4M bombers, and in quick succession shot down five of these and damaged a sixth for the expenditure of about 360 rounds of ammunition. In each case he concentrated his fire on one of the bomber's engines. For this outstanding exploit he was awarded America's highest decoration, the Congressional Medal of Honor. Flying Hellcats he later increased his score to twelve, but was shot down by mistake by the gunner of an American bomber at night on 26 November 1943. O'Hare International Airport, Illinois, is named in his honour.

During the Battle of the Coral Sea in May 1942, a young dive-bomber pilot, Stanley W. 'Swede' Vejtasa, claimed three Zero fighters while operating his Dauntless as a fighter in defence of his carrier, *Yorktown*. These victories were claimed during an epic twenty-five-minute fight against eight of these aircraft. Retrained as

a fighter pilot, he joined VF-10 on *Enterprise* and in October 1942 was involved in the Battle of Santa Cruz as the US Navy fought in the Solomons in support of the forces which had invaded Guadalcanal Island. During this battle Vejtasa claimed five torpedo-bombers and two dive-bombers in a single sortie in his Wildcat. A few days later he claimed his eleventh victory, making him the Navy's top-scorer of 1942.

At this stage of the war it was the US Marine Corps fighter pilots who were making the headlines. Apart from a brief defence of Wake and Midway Islands, the defence of Guadalcanal was their first major achievement of the war. VMF-223 arrived on the island in August, followed in September by VMF-121, both these squadrons being equipped with Wildcats. The fighting threw up several great aces, who soon became the top American scorers of the day. In VMF-223 Marion Carl, who had already claimed two victories over Midway in June, raised his score to sixteen and a half by October, while John Lucian Smith, the commanding officer, became US top-scorer with nineteen, for which he received the Congressional Medal of Honor.

In VMF-121 a flight led by Joseph J. Foss did particularly well, claiming seventy-two victories and producing six aces. Foss was the most successful, with twenty-three victories before the end of the year, including five in one day on 25 October. In January 1943 Foss raised his score to twenty-six, equalling Rickenbacker's First World War score and becoming top Marine Corps ace of the war. He received a Medal of Honor, both he and Carl returning for further tours later in the war. Carl gained two more victories, but Foss saw no more enemy aircraft.

More units arrived on Guadalcanal in 1943, and soon numbers of the excellent Vought F4U Corsair fighters began to replace the Wildcats. James E. 'Zeke' Swett of VMF-221 shot down seven dive-bombers during his first operational sortie of the war on 7 April 1943, being credited with an eighth as a probable. This was the last great Wildcat combat over the island, for which Swett, whose final score was to reach sixteen and a half, was awarded the Medal of Honor.

With the arrival of the Corsair, multiple claims against the lightly built Japanese aircraft became common, and soon other new aces were appearing. Kenneth A. Walsh of VMF-124 claimed twenty victories during the middle of 1943, while during the next six months Robert M. Hanson and Donald N. Aldrich of VMF-215 claimed twenty-five and twenty respectively, Hanson gaining twenty of his victories in just six combats during the latter part of January 1944. 'Pappy' Boyington, a hard-drinking hellraiser who had claimed six victories over Burma with the AVG, returned to the Marine Corps to lead VMF-214 – 'The Black Sheep' – over the Solomons. In two months he claimed a further

The early versions of the Vought F4U-1 Corsair began reaching the Solomons during 1943. The 'bent-wing bird' was to prove a great 'ace-maker' for the US Marine Corps, several of the leading aces, such as Boyington, Hanson, Walsh and Aldrich, flying them.

First USAAF ace against the Western members of the Axis – Germany and Italy – was Lieutenant Lyman Middleditch. Flying a Curtiss P-40F Warhawk with the 57th Fighter Group, he served in North Africa, operating in support of the British 8th Army. From just before the Battle of El Alamein in October 1942 until the fall of Tunis in May 1943, he claimed six victories, including three Messerschmitt Bf 109s in one fight on 27 October 1942.

fourteen victories, including five on 16 September 1943. After a brief leave he claimed a further five in two combats to raise his total to twenty-five. On 3 January 1944 he claimed three more, but was shot down into the sea, picked up by a Japanese submarine and became a prisoner. Not until after the war was it known that he had survived and that his final score of twenty-eight had exceeded Foss's total. However, only twenty-two of these were actually claimed while Boyington was flying with the Marines.

Boyington, Walsh and Hanson all received Medals of Honor, Walsh later flying from Okinawa in 1945 and claiming one further victory. Hanson was shot down by anti-aircraft fire and killed early in February 1944, and Aldrich was later killed in an aircraft accident in the United States.

During the mid-war months, the Navy, which was building up its carrier strength, enjoyed fewer opportunities to participate in aerial combat. However, a new ace, Ira C. 'Ike' Kepford, appeared early in 1944. In 1943 it had been decided that the Corsair was unsuitable for carrier operations – a decision subsequently reversed – but VF-17 was equipped with these aircraft, and late in the year was sent to operate from land bases in the Solomons alongside the Marines. Here the 'Jolly Rogers' claimed 154 victories in seventy-nine days, producing thirteen aces, of whom the most successful was Kepford, who was credited with seventeen.

On the other side of the world American aircraft began arriving in England during mid-1942, while at the same time units reinforced the British Desert Air Force in Egypt. The first USAAF ace to emerge in the struggle against the European Axis was Lyman D. Middleditch of the 57th Fighter Group, who claimed five fighters shot down during the Battle of El

Alamein in October 1942, including three Messerschmitt Bf 109s on 27 October. He later claimed one more over Tunisia in April 1943, all his successes being achieved while flying P-40F Warhawks.

Several American units took part in the invasion of French North Africa in November 1942, and in the ensuing Tunisian campaign; they flew P-40s, P-38s and Spitfires borrowed from the RAF. The most successful pilot here was Levi R. Chase of the 33rd Fighter Group, who claimed ten victories over Tunisia during the period December 1942 – April 1943, also while flying a P-40. Nine of these were German and Italian fighters. He subsequently commanded a Mustang unit in Burma late in the war, and during the early 'fifties led a jet fighter-bomber wing in Korea.

Sylvan Feld was the USAAF's most successful Spitfire ace, claiming nine victories with the 52nd Fighter Group by June 1943. Top ace in the US 12th Air Force in the Mediterranean was William J. Sloan, a P-38 pilot with the 82nd Fighter Group. He claimed twelve victories during the first seven months of 1945. Later in 1943 the P-38 units were transferred to the strategic 15th Air Force.

In England the 8th Air Force steadily increased in strength during early 1943, P-47 Thunderbolt units arriving to escort B-17 and B-24 heavy bombers over Europe. At first the P-47s lacked the range to penetrate very far

inland, and victories mounted slowly. However, gradually their range was increased by the provision of drop-tanks, and on 30 July 1943 Charles P. 'Joppo' London of the 78th Fighter Group claimed his fifth victory to become the 8th's first ace.

Other aces soon appeared, and late in the year scores began to mount swiftly. Walter C. Beckham of the 353rd Fighter Group pushed into first place, running his score up to eighteen, but was soon overtaken by Walker M. 'Bud' Mahurin of the 56th Group. Before he could regain his position, Beckham was shot down and taken prisoner.

The 56th was a proud and successful unit, which had been the first to receive the P-47, and was one of the first to arrive in England. The unit's first ace was Gerald W. Johnson, who claimed his fifth victory on 19 August 1943, running his total up to eighteen by early 1944. Close behind him came the Group's commander, Hubert Zemke, a brilliant leader who became an ace on 2 October, Mahurin getting his fifth two days later.

During the early months of 1944 the 8th launched a concerted assault on the German air defences, the P-47s and P-51s ranging ever further into Germany until they were able to accompany the bombers all the way to their targets and back. The battle reached a climax during March 1944, the Luftwaffe suffering grievous losses of aircraft and pilots during this

month. It was at this time that most of the great American aces of the 8th reached their peak, and the 56th Group was in the forefront of the fighting.

Mahurin was brought down during March with his score at twenty, though he evaded capture and later got back to Allied territory. However, he had already been overtaken by

Colonel Harrison Thyng led a squadron of Spitfires with one of the first USAAF units to fly from England in 1942, the 31st Fighter Group. After seeing his first action over Dieppe in August, he moved with the unit to Algeria during the Anglo-American landings there in November 1942. Here he claimed five victories, four of them German aircraft and one Vichy French. He later led a Thunderbolt group in the Pacific area, claiming one success against the Japanese. He was in action over Korea during the early 'fifties, flying an F-86 Sabre jet fighter in which he shot down five MiG-15s to raise his final total to eleven. He is seen here in his Spitfire with the 31st Fighter Group in 1942.

Colonel Jim Howard was the only fighter pilot to be awarded a Medal of Honor for operations over Western Europe. On 11 January 1944 he single-handedly drove off a force of German fighters which was attacking an unescorted bomber formation, claiming three of them shot down and three damaged. His 354th Fighter Group P-51B Mustang is decorated with his twelve and a half victories—six and a half gained against the Japanese while flying with the AVG in 1942.

First 8th Air Force pilot to pass Eddie Rickenbacker's First World War score of twenty-six victories was Lieutenant Robert Johnson of the 56th Fighter Group.

became the second in 8th Air Force to convert to P-51B Mustangs, and at once began to achieve considerable success. Several of the leading pilots had flown with the RAF, including the top-scorer Don S. Gentile, who claimed nineteen and a half air and six ground victories, and the group commander, Don Blakeslee, with fifteen and a half. Other leading pilots were John Godfrey, who claimed sixteen and a third, but was shot down and taken prisoner, and Ralph K. Hofer with sixteen and a half. Hofer was reported missing in his Mustang *Salem Representative*, during a shuttle mission to Italy on 2 July 1944. It is suspected that he was shot down over the Alps by the top German ace Erich Hartmann.

Another successful unit was the 352nd Fighter Group, which produced four aces with over fifteen victories. The top two were George E. 'Ratsy' Preddy and John C. Meyer. Preddy claimed twenty-five and five-sixths, including six Bf 109s in one combat on 6 August 1944, but was hit by American AA fire while chasing a German fighter at low level over Belgium on Christmas Day 1944 and was killed. Meyer gained his last victories on 1 January 1945 to raise his total to twenty-four, including eleven in nineteen missions during the autumn. He also claimed thirteen destroyed on the ground, and later flew in Korea, shooting down two MiGs.

The 8th Air Force produced far more aces than any other US air force, twenty-six of them having scores in excess of fifteen. Also operating from England until summer 1944, when it moved to France, was the tactical 9th Air Force, which also produced a number of aces. The most successful served in the 354th Fighter Group, the first unit to fly the P-51. On arrival in England this group was at first attached to the 8th Air Force, flying many bomber escort missions during early 1944. Its first important ace was James H. Howard, the group commander. Howard had flown with the AVG, claiming six and a half Japanese aircraft. Over Europe on 11 January 1944 he made a single-handed attack on a large force of German fighters which were savaging a bomber formation, claiming three of them shot down to raise his score for the mission to four. For this action he received the only Medal of Honor awarded to a fighter pilot operating over Western Europe during the war. His total score was twelve and a half.

Top-scorer in the 9th Air Force was Glenn T. Eagleston, also a member of the 354th, who claimed eighteen and a half in two tours. He later claimed two MiGs over Korea. An unusual 9th Air Force ace was Clyde B. East, a tactical reconnaissance pilot in the 67th T R Group, who shot down thirteen German aircraft while flying low-altitude armed reconnaissance missions.

Flying missions similar to those undertaken by 8th Air Force fighter groups were the escort

Robert S. Johnson, a member of the same unit, who had twenty-eight by early May. It was thought that he was the first American pilot to exceed Rickenbacker's score, but when he arrived back in the United States, it was to discover that Dick Bong had reached twenty-eight in the Far East shortly before him.

Several more pilots took up Johnson's mantle, but only Francis S. 'Gabby' Gabreski was to equal his score. He was hit while ground strafing during July and was taken a prisoner. He later flew in Korea, adding six and a half MiGs to his score. Zemke also became a prisoner later in the year, with his total standing at seventeen and three-quarters, while David Schilling claimed twenty-one and a half in the air and ten on the ground during two tours, his score including five in one day on 23 December 1944. At the end of the war the 56th was well in the lead in terms of air victories, and of the nine 8th Air Force aces with scores in excess of twenty, five were members of this unit.

During 1944 the Group was hotly pursued by the 4th Fighter Group. This unit had been formed late in 1942 from the three RAF 'Eagle' squadrons, but had been slow to achieve much success early on. At the start of 1944 the unit units of the 15th Air Force based in Italy. Ranging far into southern Europe and the Balkans, this air force produced several aces, the most successful of whom was John J. Voll, a Mustang pilot with the 31st Fighter Group. During his last combat on 16 November 1944 he shot down a Ju 88 and three fighters to raise his score to twenty-one.

In the East, too, the USAAF was again coming to the fore in the closing stages of the war, as improved aircraft became available. In China the 23rd Fighter Group remained the most successful, gradually supplementing its P-40s with P-51s. Top ace here was an 'elderly' pilot of thirty-five, John C. 'Pappy' Herbst. After one victory in Europe, he claimed eighteen more over China during late 1944–early 1945. He was killed during 1946 in a crash in a new P-80 jet fighter.

In the Solomons the 13th Air Force did not enjoy as much success as the Marine units, but one pilot did particularly well, emerging as USAAF top-scorer in that theatre. Robert B. Westbrook flew with the 18th Fighter Group, claiming seven victories while flying a P-40, and eight more in a P-38, all these being claimed during 1943. A further five during a second tour in late 1944 raised his total to twenty.

It was the 5th Air Force in New Guinea which enjoyed the greatest success, and while it was never as large as the 8th Air Force, consequently producing less aces overall, it was to produce the two top-scorers of the USAAF, together with five other pilots with twenty or more victories. Most of these pilots flew P-38s, which were the supreme fighters with the 5th, and by 1943 a race for the top-scoring position was underway. Early contenders were Richard I. Bong and Thomas Lynch of the 49th Fighter Group. Late in the year the 348th Fighter Group arrived with P-47s, and the Group Commander, Neel E. Kearby, quickly caught up with the leaders. On 11 October 1943 he claimed seven fighters shot down, his gun camera confirming six before the film ran out. By March he had overtaken Lynch, but on the 9th of that month he was shot down and killed after raising his score to twenty-two. A few days later Lynch fell to anti-aircraft fire from a ship.

Bong reached a score of twenty-eight in April to become American top-scorer and the first known to have passed Rickenbacker's score; he was then sent home on leave. Thomas B. McGuire of the 475th Group, with sixteen, and Jay T. Robbins of the 8th, with thirteen, remained, both scoring regularly in multiples to raise their scores to twenty-one apiece. While Robbins ended his tour after his twenty-second, McGuire remained with twenty-eight to challenge Bong, who now returned for a second tour. Awarded a Medal of Honor later in the year, Bong became the all-time American Ace of Aces on 17 December, when his total reached forty. He then returned to the States

again. McGuire ran his score up to thirty-eight, but on 7 January 1945, in the Philippines area, he stalled during a combat between four P-38s and a single Japanese fighter and crashed to his death in the sea. He received a posthumous award of the Medal of Honor. Bong was killed in a crash in a P-80 the following August.

Two more 5th Air Force pilots subsequently became high-scorers, both flying P-38s. Gerald R. Johnson (not to be confused with the 8th Air Force's Gerald W. Johnson) was credited with twenty-two confirmed and twenty-one probable victories in three tours, while Charles H. MacDonald, commander of the 475th Fighter Group, raised his total to twenty-seven by the end of the war to become the third-ranking USAAF ace in the Pacific area.

On the vast reaches of the Pacific Ocean, the revitalized US Navy carrier task forces, boasting powerful new *Essex*-class carriers and F6F Hellcat fighters, began a series of strikes on Japan's island garrisons during 1944. Now at last the Navy was in a position to produce aces with scores similar to those of the Air Force and Marine Corps, and soon multiple claims became the order of the day.

The top-scoring Navy pilot was David

Colonel John C. Meyer, photographed in January 1945. He gained his twenty-four victories flying Mustangs with 352nd Fighter Group.

McCampbell, a pilot who had joined the service in 1934. In May 1944, as commander of Air Group 15 aboard the *Essex*, he led his fighters in strikes on Marcus Island. The following month he took part in the Saipan invasion and also participated in the Battles of the Philippine Sea and Leyte Gulf later in the year. During the Saipan operations Japanese aircraft, flown by inexperienced young crews, were thrown in in droves only to be massacred by the confident Hellcat pilots in a slaughter that became known to the Americans as the 'Marianas Turkey Shoot'. During this battle of 19 June 1944, McCampbell personally shot down seven of the attackers. Over the Philippines in September, he claimed four on the 12th and three next day. His greatest day was yet to come, for on 24 October, over Leyte Gulf, he and wingman Roy Rushing engaged forty Zeros which made no real attempt to evade their attacks, or to fight back. Following the formation for ten minutes, McCampbell shot down no less than nine aircraft—an American record—while Rushing, who would end the war with thirteen victories, claimed six more. By the end of the year when Air Group 15 returned to the US, McCampbell's score stood at thirty-four, plus twenty destroyed on the ground. Awarded the Medal of Honor, he was not only the top Navy ace but also the top-scoring American to survive the war.

Eugene A. Valencia served on *Essex* with VF-9 during 1943, claiming seven victories in three sorties over Rabaul, Tarawa and Truk. Returning to the States, he trained his four-plane flight in his own 'mowing-machine' tactics, whereby a continual attack could be kept up on an enemy formation. Returning to the Pacific early in 1945, the tactic was first tried in action on 16 February over Tokyo, six victories being claimed. More successes followed, and when the tour ended Valencia had claimed sixteen more victories, the other three members of his section having all become aces as well.

Other leading Navy aces included Cecil Harris of VF-18 on *Intrepid*, who claimed twenty-four in two tours, claiming four in a day on at least three occasions. Alexander Vraciu also undertook two tours, his second with VF-16 on *Lexington*, when he raised his score to nineteen in the air and twenty-one on the ground. Over the Marianas he shot down six dive-bombers in a single eight-minute combat. Shot down over the Philippines in December, he survived the war as a member of the local guerrilla forces.

Cornelius N. Nooy flew two tours with VF-31 during 1944 and 1945, claiming a total of eighteen victories. On 21 September 1944 he claimed five fighters shot down while still carrying a 500-lb bomb under his Hellcat. Patrick D. Fleming of VF-80 also shot down five fighters, in one combat, this time on 16 February 1945, while flying from *Hancock*. He survived the war with nineteen victories, but died in a crash in

1956. Top-scoring Navy pilot to be lost in action was Douglas Baker of VF-20, who also made a number of multiple claims, but was lost late in 1944 after his sixteenth victory.

During 1945 groups of P-51 Mustangs of the 20th Air Force were operating from Iwo Jima and Okinawa Islands, escorting B-29 heavy bombers over Japan. Pilots from these units became the last US aces of the war. On 13 August 1945 Oscar Perdomo of the 507th Fighter Group shot down four fighters and a trainer to become the final ace of the Second World War.

Few American pilots became aces as night fighters, most night fighting in the European and Mediterranean theatres being left to the RAF.

However, several pilots were attached to RAF squadrons for night-fighting experience, A. A. Harrington claiming seven victories, John Luma and Clarence M. Jasper getting five each in such circumstances. In the Pacific Carroll C. Smith was successful, claiming two victories in a modified P-38, and five more in the specialized P-61 Black Widow night fighter, four of them in one night.

The Navy and Marines fitted some of their fighters with radar for night defence, John W. Dear and Frederick L. Duncan claiming seven each in Navy units, while Robert Baird claimed six in a radar-equipped Corsair with Marine Squadron VMF-533(N). Altogether, America produced about 1,280 aces during the war.

opposite, top
Lieutenant Colonel Robert Westbrook (twenty victories) in the cockpit of his Lockheed P-38 Lightning.

opposite, bottom
The USAAF's two top aces, Bong (left) and McGuire, confer after arrival at Leyte in the Philippines late in 1944.

following page
Lieutenant Commander David McCampbell led Air Group 15 on the first of the new American fast fleet carriers, USS *Essex*, during 1944. Over the Philippines and Marianas he achieved many successes, including seven in one day on 19 June. On 24 October over the Philippines, he and his wingman, Roy Rushing (thirteen victories), shot down between them fifteen Zeros from a formation of forty. Nine of these were credited to McCampbell, an American record. With a final total of thirty-four, he was top scoring Navy pilot by a wide margin; he also destroyed twenty-one more aircraft on the ground. In this photo he is in his Grumman F6F Hellcat, *Minsi III*.

The leading American aces

United States Army Air Force

Major Richard I. Bong	40 (5th Air Force, South West Pacific)
Major Thomas B. McGuire	38 (5th Air Force, South West Pacific)
Colonel Francis S. Gabreski	28 (8th Air Force, Western Europe, plus 6½ more in Korea)
Major Robert S. Johnson	28 (8th Air Force, Western Europe)
Colonel Charles H. MacDonald	27 (5th Air Force, South West Pacific)
Major George E. Preddy	25 5/6 (8th Air Force, Western Europe)
Colonel John C. Meyer	24 (8th Air Force, Western Europe, plus 2 more in Korea)
Major Raymond S. Wetmore	22.6 (8th Air Force, Western Europe)
Colonel David C. Schilling	22½ (8th Air Force, Western Europe)
Lieutenant Colonel Gerald R. Johnson	22 (5th Air Force, South West Pacific)
Colonel Neel E. Kearby	22 (5th Air Force, South West Pacific)
Major Jay T. Robbins	22 (5th Air Force, South West Pacific)
Captain Don S. Gentile	21.84 (8th Air Force, Western Europe; includes 2 with RAF)
Major Frederick J. Christensen Jr.	21½ (8th Air Force, Western Europe)
Major Walker M. Mahurin	21 (8th Air Force, Western Europe, includes one with 5th Air Force: 3½ more in Korea)
Captain John J. Voll	21 (15th Air Force, Southern Europe)
Major Thomas J. Lynch	21 (5th Air Force, South West Pacific)
Lieutnant Colonel Robert B. Westbrook	20 (13th Air Force, South Pacific)

United States Navy

Commander David S. McCampbell	34
Lieutenant Commander Cecil E. Harris	24
Lieutenant Commander Eugene A. Valencia	23
Lieutenant Commander Patrick D. Fleming	19
Lieutenant Commander Alexander Vraciu	19
Lieutenant Cornelius N. Nooy	18
Lieutenant Ira C. Kepford	17
Lieutenant Charles R. Stimpson	17
Lieutenant Douglas Baker	16

United States Marine Corps

Lieutenant Colonel Gregory Boyington	28 (6 with American Volunteer Group)
Major Joseph J. Foss	26
Lieutenant Robert M. Hanson	25
Captain Kenneth A. Walsh	21
Captain Donald M. Aldrich	20
Lieutenant Colonel John L. Smith	19
Major Marion E. Carl	18½
Captain Wilbur J. Thomas	18½
Major James E. Swett	16½

The Belgians

Unlike most of the small countries which became embroiled in the Second World War, Belgium already had a fighter pilot tradition dating from the First World War. Indeed one Belgian, Count Rodolphe de Hemricourt de Grunne, had joined the Nationalist forces in Spain during the Civil War, gaining considerable success flying Fiat CR 32 biplanes with Franco's premier fighter unit, the 3 *Escuadra Azul* (Blue Group).

Flying with such great Spanish aces as Garcia Morato and Salas Larrazabal, he was credited with ten victories over Republican fighter aircraft. Following the German invasion of Belgium in 1940, he escaped to England, joining the RAF. Initially he flew Hurricanes with 32 Squadron, claiming three German aircraft shot down and one probable during the Battle of Britain. He was then shot down and badly burned. On recovery, he joined 609 Squadron to fly Spitfires, but was shot down over France on 21 May 1941 and killed.

Four Belgian pilots, Jaques Phillipart, Daniel Leroy du Vivier, Jean Offenberg and Victor Ortmans, all fought briefly in defence of their country in May 1940, but all except Offenberg flew obsolete Fairey Fox biplanes, and were able to achieve little. Offenberg, in a more modern Italian Fiat CR 42 biplane, managed to shoot down one German bomber before hostilities ceased. All four pilots then escaped via France to England.

Here they all joined Hurricane squadrons of the RAF in time to participate in the Battle of Britain. Phillipart shone at once, claiming six victories in a fortnight in August 1940, flying from Exeter with 213 Squadron. His meteoric career ended on 25 August, the day of his final victory, when he was shot down into the sea and drowned. His score included three Messerschmitt Bf 110s shot down in one day on 15 August.

The mantle was then donned by Offenberg and Ortmans. Flying with 229 Squadron, the latter claimed two and one shared victories during September, while the former had claimed five and a probable with 145 Squadron by early 1941. Ortmans then joined du Vivier in a special

Belgian flight of 609 Squadron to fly Spitfires. During the summer he claimed three Bf 109s shot down and another shared, but was himself shot down into the Channel twice. On 21 October he went down for a third time, but on this occasion was taken prisoner.

Meanwhile Offenberg had also joined 609 Squadron late in the spring, rising to command the Belgian Flight. He enjoyed less success with the Spitfire, adding only one further confirmed victory, though his score also included four probables and three damaged at this time. Tragically, on 22 January 1942 he was killed in a collision with another aircraft.

Another member of this flight, Count Ivan Du Monceau de Bergandal, had been training as a pilot in 1940 in Belgium when war came. Known to his friends as 'The Duke', he had also flown Hurricanes in 1940, but without success, and not until the summer of 1941 was he to make his first claim. His slow start was followed by success, and in the spring of 1942 he was posted to the all-Belgian 350 Squadron, which had just been formed. By the end of the year his score had reached eight, making him top-scoring Belgian pilot of the Second World War. He later commanded the other Free Belgian squadron, 349, but gained no further victories.

Leroy du Vivier also served briefly in 609 Squadron, having been wounded during the Battle of Britain. His powers of leadership were considerable, and in the spring of 1941 he was posted as a flight commander to the RAF's 43 Squadron. Flying Hurricanes on intruder missions over France, he claimed three Ju 88 bombers shot down and shared in the destruction of two more. Early in 1942 he was promoted to command the squadron, but was then posted out to the Mediterranean area as a wing commander, and later led 324 Spitfire Wing in Italy.

Later in the war Remi van Lierde, Raymond Lallemant and Charles Detal all became aces while flying the Hawker Typhoon with 609 Squadron, van Lierde also becoming the RAF's second-highest-scoring pilot against the V-1 flying bombs during 1944, flying the later Tempest fighter.

The leading Belgian aces

Lieutenant Count Rodolphe de Hemricourt de Grunne	13 (10 in Spanish Civil War)
Major Count Ivan Du Monceau de Bergandal	8
Flight Lieutenant Jean H. M. Offenberg	7
Flying Officer Charles F. J. Detal	6½
Squadron Leader Remi van Lierde	6 + 40 V-1s
Flying Officer Victor M. M. Ortmans	6
Pilot Officer Jaques A. L. Phillipart	6
Squadron Leader Raymond A. Lallemant	5½
Wing Commander Daniel Leroy du Vivier	5

The British Commonwealth

In the Second World War, as in the First, the British authorities refused officially to acknowledge the concept of the ace, stressing the team and the unit in preference to the individual. Although they were prepared to allow the press to seek aces as heroes of the moment for propaganda purposes, they kept none of the careful score records maintained by certain other air forces—notably those of Germany, France and the United States. The RAF was also to be involved in a number of campaigns—particularly during the earlier stages of the war—in which retreats and evacuations resulted in records being destroyed. On other occasions, particularly at times of stress, incomplete records were kept, while a lack of standardisation in the keeping of records in the early years of the war ensured that the task of ascertaining the exact scores of many pilots serving in British units would always be a difficult one.

The outbreak of the Second World War in September 1939 found the RAF with a substantial fighter force in the United Kingdom, equipped to a large extent with modern Spitfire and Hurricane aircraft and deployed mainly for home defence. This force was supported by the world's first comprehensive radar defence screen, which would prove of very great assistance to the fighters during 1940.

On the outbreak of hostilities, an RAF element, including several squadrons of Hurricanes and Gloster Gladiator biplanes, accompanied the British Expeditionary Force to France. At first, contacts with the Luftwaffe were rare, but they increased in frequency during the spring of 1940. During March a young New Zealand Flying Officer, E. J. 'Cobber' Kain, became the first RAF ace of the war, receiving much attendant publicity.

Fighting in Norway in April and May 1940 provided opportunities for several other pilots to gain victories, while on 10 May the German attack on France and the Low Countries brought a sudden, violent upsurge in aerial activity. More Hurricanes were rushed over from England, and during the next month a number of pilots became aces, Kain, with his early start, emerging as the most successful pilot to date, with seventeen victories by the end of May. Early in June, leaving 73 Squadron to fly back to England, he attempted a farewell 'beat-up' of the airfield, but crashed and was killed.

Among other pilots becoming aces in France were Newell Orton of 73 Squadron, who claimed some sixteen victories and others like Aitken, Allard, Carey, David, Dutton, Gleed, Lacey, Lewis and Stephens, of whom more later. The Dunkirk evacuation, which took place late in May, involved more units of Fighter Command from their bases in England, Spitfires and two-seat Defiant turret fighters entering the fray for the first time. Many pilots who would later play an important part in the Battle of Britain were deeply involved in this fighting, and a considerable number of pilots claimed at least five victories during this desperate venture.

With the end of the fighting in France late in June, the defence of the British Isles became the major task. It was some time before the Luftwaffe had made good the attrition of the Battle of France, and while a number of fierce battles were fought over the English Channel during July, the numbers involved were generally not very large. In August the Battle of Britain began in earnest, large forces of heavily escorted German bombers attacking airfields, radar stations and other elements of the defences in southern England. Fighting for their lives, the RAF squadrons struggled to continue operating while their airfields were subjected to frequent bombing raids and the confident German fighters tried to bring them to battle.

Losses on both sides mounted swiftly, the RAF rotating the more experienced units out of the battle zone whenever possible to rest and make good their losses, sending in new units to take their place. This was not always a success, some of the more inexperienced squadrons being decimated, whereupon the tired, battle-hardened units had to be thrown back into the fight. In September the Luftwaffe diverted its main attack from airfields and aircraft factories to London, providing a welcome respite for Fighter Command. No longer under the same degree of attack themselves, the fighter pilots were able to intercept raids more effectively, so that by the end of the month the Luftwaffe bombers were ordered to stop attacking by day. Thereafter for the rest of the autumn, the battle became virtually an all-fighter affair, as the Spitfires and Hurricanes intercepted daily high-altitude sweeps by German Bf 109s and various hit-and-run fighter-bomber attacks.

During the battle a large number of pilots became aces, some of them future top-scorers, while others were to gain no further victories. Having already seen combat over France to a much greater degree than the Spitfires, it was the Hurricane units which produced the majority of the great aces early in the battle, 'Mike' Crossley of 32 Squadron claiming fourteen victories during July and August to raise his total to twenty-two, the first RAF pilot of the war to pass the twenty mark. Close behind him was Roy Dutton, whose total reached nineteen and a third during August, while early in September 'Sammy' Allard of 85 Squadron pushed his 'bag' up to over twenty-three. Others

were close behind them, and in October Allard's total was equalled by James 'Ginger' Lacey, an NCO pilot in 501 Squadron.

All these pilots had gained the first part of their scores over France earlier in the summer, but undoubtedly the top-scoring Hurricane pilot during the battle itself was Archie McKellar of 605 Squadron. A Scot, McKellar first went into action on 15 August, one of the busiest days, when he claimed three Heinkel He 111s shot down and a fourth probable. On 9 September he attacked three more Heinkels head-on, his fire causing the centre bomber to explode and take down those on either side of it. He then shot down a Bf 109. He again claimed three victories on 15 September, and on 7 October put in claims for five Bf 109s, four of them shot down in less than ten minutes. By the end of October his score stood at twenty, one of them at night, but on 1 November he was seen to dive, inverted, into the ground and was killed. An unclaimed Bf 109 was found nearby, and it seems that this was credited to him, bringing his total to twenty-one.

By September the Spitfires were coming into their own, one of the first great exponents of these aircraft being a little-known Australian, Paterson Hughes, who had claimed over fifteen victories when he was killed on 7 September after crashing into the wreckage of a bomber which he had just shot down. Later in the month an Auxiliary Air Force pilot, Eric Lock, who had only been called up during the previous May, passed Hughes's score. He had claimed eleven in two weeks, baling out three times himself, to bring his own total to seventeen. Six more victories by mid-November made him top-scorer of the Battle of Britain period, but he was then severely wounded. He returned to operations in 1941, claiming two further victories before being reported missing on 3 August.

Others doing well in 1940 included Hurricane pilots Dennis David with twenty, Albert Lewis, a South African in 249 Squadron, with eighteen –twelve of them in just two days–and 'Jim' Hallowes, whose score was also near to twenty. There were fewer high-scoring Spitfire pilots, but Harbourne Stephen of 74 Squadron had nineteen, and 'Sailor' Malan of the same unit had eighteen, while New Zealander 'Al' Deere of 54 Squadron was close behind with seventeen, having been shot down seven times himself. Other promising pilots included Desmond McMullen with thirteen (he would finish the war with a tantalizing nineteen and five-sixths), 'Bob' Tuck with over twenty on Spitfires and

One of the RAF's top-scorers, Squadron Leader 'Ginger' Lacey, is seen here in the cockpit of his Hurricane. After notable service throughout 1940, he later led a squadron in Burma, shooting down one Japanese fighter to raise his score to twenty-eight.

Flying Officer Albert Lewis is decorated with the DFC by King George VI. Flying a Hurricane, Lewis shot down five Messerschmitt Bf 109s in one day during the Battle of France and seven in one day during the Battle of Britain. His final score was eighteen.

Hurricanes, and the gallant, legless Douglas Bader, whose total stood at twelve and a half.

Among many others of note was John Dundas, top-scorer of 609 'South Yorkshire' Auxiliary Squadron, who shot down Helmut Wick, *Kommodore* of *Jagdgeschwader 2* and Luftwaffe top-scorer at the time. Wick, with fifty-six victories to his credit, fell to Dundas near the Isle of Wight on 28 November, bringing the latter's own total to thirteen and a half. The victor did not live to celebrate, falling victim at once to Wick's wingman.

During 1940 the Defiant had proved to be a disaster when operated by day, sustaining terrible losses at the hands of German fighters. Nevertheless, there was an exception to the rule, a successful NCO team, Flight Sergeants Edward Thorn (pilot) and Frederick Barker (gunner), claiming twelve victories during the period May–August, and later adding one more at night.

It will probably have been noticed by now that the names of most of the top-scorers during the Battle of Britain are not particularly familiar. While many of the aces who later won great public acclaim served in the battle, it was during 1941 that they were to come to the notice of the public. Early in that year the RAF began offensive action once more, despatching strong forces of fighters, with or without bombers, across the Channel to engage the German fighters in combat. To lead these large formations of aircraft, some of the more successful Battle of Britain pilots still with the squadrons were appointed to a new post of wing leader, with the rank of wing commander, each leading a force of three or four squadrons. Among the first to be appointed were 'Sailor' Malan, leading the Biggin Hill Wing, Douglas Bader, heading the Tangmere Wing, and Bob Stanford Tuck, leading that at Duxford.

Throughout the spring and early summer of

1941 the RAF fighters clashed with their German opposite numbers, and soon new top-scorers began to emerge. During June Malan claimed ten Bf 109s to bring his total to at least thirty-two, making him the clear-cut top-scorer at this time. Tuck's score had reached twenty-seven, while Bader had claimed twenty-three by the end of July. Bader was shot down and taken prisoner on 9 August, but it seems that he shot down two more German fighters on this date which were not credited to him. Among other pilots now up with the leaders, Michael Lister Robinson, commander of 609 Squadron, had claimed nineteen and a half by this period; 'Jamie' Rankin brought his score to fourteen after getting eight Bf 109s during June. A young Irish pilot, Brendan 'Paddy' Finucane, claimed his twenty-fifth, the last twenty having been claimed in three months. Later in the year 'Don' Kingaby, a young NCO pilot with 92 Squadron, brought his total to seventeen and a half, sixteen of them Bf 109s. At this stage, however, the great reduction of German fighter strength on the western coastline of Europe, occasioned by the invasion of Russia, led to a considerable reduction in the scale of air fighting in this area, and thereafter the scores of the RAF fighter pilots rose at a very much slower rate.

From the very beginning of the war, efforts had been made at night interception, but few successes were achieved, those that were made resulting more from luck than any other factor. However, development of airborne radar was underway, and during the summer of 1940 the first attempts to employ this system in Blenheim fighters were made; the Blenheim lacked both performance and fire-power and little success was achieved. The first truly effective night fighter to enter service was the powerful Bristol Beaufighter, the first examples of which reached units late in 1940, just at the time that the 'Blitz' was raging. The transfer of German bombers from day to night attack had made the need for successful interception that much more urgent, and the first Beaufighter victory was gained during the night of 19 November when John Cunningham of 604 Squadron shot down a Ju 88.

This first victory was to prove no accident, for during December Cunningham, with the aid of his regular radar operator, 'Jimmie' Rawnsley, shot down two more bombers, followed by another in February 1941. During April and May they enjoyed a terrific run of success as the spring weather brought the bombers out in force, ten Heinkel He 111 bombers being shot down in this period, three of them in one night. The last two were claimed on 31 May, when His Majesty King George VI was a guest in the squadron's control room and followed the combats on radar screen and radio.

The attack on Russia in June 1941 led to a reduction in the level of attack, and it was not until the following spring that Cunningham claimed his sixteenth victory. He later made a further tour in 1943 flying Mosquitos, raising his final total to twenty, all but one of them at night. Although not the RAF's top-scorer at night, he remains beyond doubt the most famous night fighter in that service. He later achieved more fame as de Havilland's chief test pilot, flying the prototype Comet jet airliner.

During 1941 several Hurricane squadrons became 'intruder' units, flying over the western coastal area of occupied Europe at night, attacking targets of opportunity, particularly around Luftwaffe airfields. While the pilots engaged on these activities did not have the advantage of radar, several enjoyed considerable success. The most successful of these was thirty-two-year-old Richard Stevens of 151 Squadron, whose score ran Cunningham's very close during 1941. An airline pilot before the war, he was already highly experienced in night flying. It was reported that his family had been killed early in the 'Blitz' and that as a result he flew with a total disregard for his own safety. Between January and October he shot down fourteen German bombers, several times claiming two in a night. His run of luck ended on 12 December when he failed to return from one of his nocturnal sorties.

Other night-fighter pilots who began their activities in 1940 and continued to operate throughout the war included the Honourable Max Aitken, son of the then-Minister of Aircraft Production, Lord Beaverbrook, who gained sixteen victories by 1944. Edward Crew, who served with Cunningham for some time, finally leading his own squadron, 96, in 1944; he ended the war with fifteen bombers and thirty-one and a half V-1s to his credit.

J. R. D. 'Bob' Braham was flying Blenheims in 1940 with 29 Squadron, gaining one of the rare night victories with these aircraft during

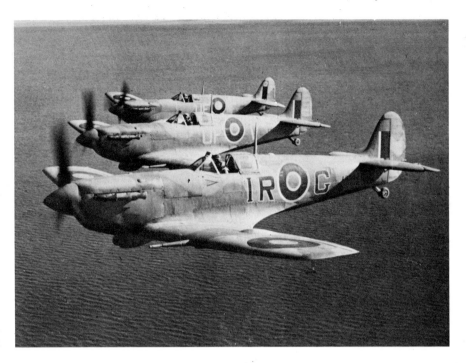

These Spitfire Vs feature 'clipped' wingtips for low-altitude operations. They are aircraft of 244 Wing, Desert Air Force, over southern Tunisia in early 1943. The nearest aircraft is that of the wing leader, Ian R. Gleed (fourteen victories), the others being from 601 Squadron.

August. Converting to Beaufighters, he raised his score to seven by the end of 1941. After a spell as an instructor, he raised his total to twelve during 1942, and was then given command of 141 Squadron. During the early summer of 1943, this unit's Beaufighters were fitted with a device code-named 'Serrate', which allowed them to home on to German night fighters, which were beginning to take a frightful toll of Allied night bombers. They were the first RAF night fighters to give support to the bombing offensive, and initially were able to catch the Luftwaffe at a disadvantage.

On 17 August, with his score standing at sixteen, Braham shot down two Messerschmitt Bf 110s of *Nachtjagdgeschwader 1*, which were flown by the German aces Heinz Vinke (fifty-four victories) and Georg Kraft (fourteen victories). On 29 September he despatched another of this unit's aces, August Geiger (fifty-three victories). His score now stood at twenty, and with nineteen of these at night he was at the time the RAF's top-scoring night fighter. Posted to a staff job, he managed to fly a number of intruder missions in Mosquitos of 2 Group during periods of bad weather, these sorties enabling him to claim nine further victories. Shot down near Denmark on 12 May 1944, he was rescued from the sea by an Allied craft, but on his very next flight on 25 June he was again shot down in the same area, spending the rest of the war as a prisoner.

In June 1940, war with Italy had broken out in the Middle East, where the RAF had a small contingent, the fighter element being equipped with Gladiators and a few Hurricanes. Hostilities between Italian forces in Libya and British units in Egypt were at first desultory, but a number of air combats were fought, and during the summer John Lapsley, a pilot with 80 and later 274 Squadrons, shot down six Savoia SM 79 trimotor bombers in three combats. At

The classic Supermarine Spitfire. This Mark Ia is being rearmed after a combat in October 1940. It is an aircraft of 19 Squadron, RAF, one of the most successful units, which produced a considerable number of aces.

the same time two other pilots became aces. Peter Wykeham-Barnes, who like Lapsley would later become an Air Marshal and who served in the same units, claimed two victories during June while flying a Hurricane, and four more in August while flying Gladiators. Canadian-born Vernon Woodward, serving with 33 Squadron, claimed the RAF's first victory of the war in North Africa on 14 June in his Gladiator, adding four more and one shared by the end of July.

On 9 December 1940 the British launched the brilliant First Libyan Campaign, which was to drive the Italians right across Libya with great losses of men and equipment. Air fighting was fierce during this period, Lapsley and Wykeham-Barnes both having increased their scores to eleven before the campaign ended, while Woodward brought his total up to ten and a half. However, they were all overtaken by E. M. 'Imshi' Mason, another 274 Squadron pilot, who had claimed fifteen and two shared in a five-week period by mid-January 1941.

'Pat' Pattle also served in North Africa with 80 Squadron during 1940, claiming his first two victories on 4 August, although he was shot down on that day and barely escaped with his life. He claimed two further victories a few days later, but in November moved with the squadron to Greece to provide air cover for the Greek army, which was locked in combat with an Italian force which had invaded north-western Greece the previous month. Before the year was out he had claimed ten more victories, plus shares in two others.

During January and February 1941 this exceptional South African pilot continued to achieve great success, claiming four victories on 28 February and three on 4 March, by which time his score stood at over twenty-four, the first RAF pilot in the Mediterranean area to exceed twenty. He was then posted to command 33 Squadron, having in the meantime begun flying Hurricanes. On 6 April 1941, with his score already over twenty-five, he faced the German attack on Greece and Yugoslavia, and was able on the first day to claim two Bf 109s. Thereafter the destruction of records during the Allied retreat has caused his further successes to remain little known to the public. In *Pattle: Supreme Fighter in the Air*, E. C. R. Baker has indicated that Pattle's score rose to at least forty or forty-one, but information available subsequently points to even greater success. Fighting almost every day, he had claimed six more German and two Italian aircraft by 12 April. Then on the 15th he appears to have claimed five in five sorties. Four more sorties on the 19th brought a further six victories, while next day he again flew three times, claiming three on the first two sorties. On the third occasion, over Eleusis Bay, Athens, he was seen to shoot down two twin-engined aircraft, but then dived to aid a Hurricane under attack and was himself shot down into the bay by a Bf 110 and killed. It would thus appear that he gained a final score of the order of fifty-one, plus four shared, eight probables and five destroyed on the ground. While his final total can never be confirmed, and as a result he has never been officially announced as RAF top-scorer, there can no longer by any doubt that he was in fact the holder of that position.

The fighting in Greece was among the fiercest

of the war for the RAF, and Pattle was not the only successful ace to appear. In 80 Squadron with him were several others who did well, including William 'Cherry' Vale, and Nigel 'Ape' Cullen. Vale claimed nine Italian aircraft between November 1940 and February 1941, and then in April claimed seven Ju 88s and two Ju 87s at least, his last three being claimed over Crete. In one day in May he shot down four Ju 52 transports over Maleme Bay, bringing his score to at least twenty-two. However, his squadron subsequently noted that while flying from Crete he had shot down thirteen aircraft, and as only seven are accounted for in his known score, this may indicate that his final total was as high as twenty-eight.

Cullen, an Australian, gained his first victory late in 1940. In the New Year his score began to rise fast, including four and one shared on 28 February. On 2 March he attacked a formation of six Cant Z.1007bis trimotor bombers with one other pilot, personally shooting down four of them to bring his score to sixteen and a half. Next day he failed to return from a sortie, the cause of his fate remaining unknown. By this time 33 Squadron had arrived in Greece from Egypt, and here Vernon Woodward added to his score. On 6 April he too attacked a formation of Z.1007bis bombers, shooting down three out of four. By the time he was evacuated from Crete, his total score had risen to over eighteen, and he was later to add two more over the Desert in summer 1941. He remained top-scoring Canadian until late in 1942.

In the Desert 3 RAAF Squadron had arrived from Australia, and was destined to become Desert Air Force's top-scoring unit, producing

many aces. The first was Peter Turnbull, who shot down four Bf 110s on 3 April while flying a Hurricane, adding five Vichy French aircraft over Syria two months later after the unit had converted to Tomahawks. He would later fly Kittyhawks in New Guinea with 75 Squadron, RAAF, claiming three Japanese aircraft shot down in early 1942 before he was killed by ground fire while dive-bombing Japanese troops invading Milne Bay on 26 August 1942.

Throughout 1941 and 1942 the Mediterranean area remained the main focus of attention for the British forces, campaigns in the Libyan Desert swaying first one way and then the other. For much of this period the main fighter types employed by the RAF were of American manufacture – the Curtiss Tomahawk and Kittyhawk, the first Spitfires not arriving

A pair of Hawker Hurricane Is of 501 Squadron, RAF, scramble during the Battle of Britain. The aircraft on the left is flown by Flying Officer K. N. T. Lee (six victories).

Squadron Leader John Gibson, a New Zealander, flew Hurricanes and Spitfires during the period 1940–42, claiming thirteen and a half victories against the Luftwaffe. He later flew Curtiss Kittyhawks over the Solomons with his native RNZAF; gaining his final victory against the Japanese.

During the summer of 1941, Wing Commander Adolf 'Sailor' Malan emerged as Fighter Command's leading ace. When taken off operations at the end of the year, his score stood at thirty-two at least. This total was not exceeded by an Allied pilot in the Western European theatre until 1944. A South African, Malan listed the basic rules of air fighting, which were subsequently adhered to throughout the RAF. He is seen here inspecting a wooden idol presented to his unit, 74 Squadron, late in 1940.

1941 was the year of the great wing leaders, and none of them was more colourful than the famous and indomitable Douglas Bader. This legless ace is seen here in typical style, aiding one of his artificial legs into the cockpit of his Spitfire, marked with his own initials. He was brought down by an aircraft of *JG 26* in July 1941, spending the rest of the war in a prison camp. This photograph was taken after his return to England in 1945, as he prepared to take part in the Victory Flypast over London.

until well into 1942. This period culminated in the great battle at El Alamein, immediately following which an Anglo-American invasion of French North Africa, further to the west, sealed the fate of Axis forces on the African continent.

During the Desert fighting several new aces made their names, most of them while flying the American fighter types. Alfred Marshall remains little known but was one of the most successful pilots in this area. After brief service in France in 1940, he reached Africa with 73 Squadron late in 1940, shooting down six SM 79 bombers in his first three combats there. Taking part in the defence of Tobruk during April 1941, he achieved more success, and by the end of the year his score stood at fifteen and a half, all but two of them gained in Africa. He later flew a second tour on Kittyhawks as a flight commander in 250 Squadron, adding a further three to his total. He was killed in an accident over England in 1944, with his final score at nineteen and a half plus one V-1.

250 Squadron produced several notable aces, being the first unit in the Desert to operate Tomahawks. Clive Caldwell claimed eighteen

MICHAEL TURNER

Michael Turner

victories with the squadron between June and December 1941, including five Ju 87s in one fight on 5 December. He then led 112 Squadron, raising his score to twenty and a half, the first pilot to exceed Mason's score while flying in the Desert. Fellow-Australian John Waddy also first flew with 250, later serving with a number of other units and finishing up in a Spitfire squadron at the time of the Alamein battle. His total included twelve and a half victories on Kittyhawks and Tomahawks and three on Spitfires. His best day was 12 May 1942, when in a big combat with Luftwaffe transport aircraft over the Mediterranean he shot down two Ju 52s and two Bf 110s.

John 'Jack' Frost, the top-scoring pilot of the South African Air Force (though not top-scoring South African) also flew Tomahawks in Libya. Earlier in 1941, he flew Hurricanes in East Africa during the Allied invasion of Ethiopia, where he claimed eight and one shared victories in the air and twenty-one aircraft destroyed on the ground; his successes included three Caproni Ca 133 bomber-transports and one CR 42 fighter shot down on 3 February. At the head of 5 SAAF Squadron in summer 1942, he increased his total to fifteen and five sixths before he was reported missing late in June.

Billy Drake replaced Clive Caldwell at the head of 112 Squadron in April 1942, claiming some fifteen victories by the end of the year to add to the four and a half he had gained over France in 1940. He later led a Spitfire wing during the invasion of Sicily to increase his final score to twenty-four and a half, together with nine probables and thirteen destroyed on the ground.

Throughout the period of the Desert campaigns the island of Malta was under constant siege, the heaviest attacks being launched by the Germans and Italians during 1942. Spitfires reached the island in March of that year—the first of these fighters to serve outside the United Kingdom—and many pilots from all parts of the Commonwealth, as well as a number of Americans, became aces there. Several of these later went on to increase their scores elsewhere, while a few experienced pilots who already had substantial scores added further successes in defence of the island.

One of the first to score well was an Englishman, Peter Nash, who claimed ten and a half with 249 Squadron to add to two earlier victories; he was killed late in May. In the same unit early in 1942, Ray Hesslyn, a New Zealander, claimed twelve, 'Buck' McNair, a Canadian, got eight, and Rhodesian 'Johnny' Plagis also claimed eight, adding three more after being posted to 185 Squadron. In the latter unit, Australian John 'Slim' Yarra claimed eight German and four Italian aircraft to become one of the island's top-scorers.

Reinforcements of Spitfires during the summer brought a new generation of pilots,

including Henry 'Wally' McLeod, who before his death in action in 1944 was destined to be the RCAF's official top-scorer of the war with twenty-one victories. On Malta, serving with 603 and 1435 Squadrons, he made thirteen successful claims between June and October, this scoring making him second to only one pilot on Malta.

This was another Canadian, though not a member of the RCAF. George 'Screwball' Beurling joined the RAF after the RCAF had rejected him on educational grounds. Serving with 41 Squadron in May 1942 in England, he twice broke away from formation to shoot down Fw 190s, but his 'lone wolf' mentality did not endear him to his superiors and he was posted to Malta in June. This suited him well, for he was a dedicated fighter pilot. Serving with 249 Squadron, he quickly became the great ace of Malta. On 6 July he shot down three fighters, and when he claimed three more on the 11th, his score stood at nine since arriving on the island. More victories soon followed, including four on 27 July, and by the beginning of October he had twenty and a half to his credit, all but two gained over the island. He was then commissioned, and during the final great 'Blitz' on the island in October, he added eight more victories before being shot down and wounded on the 14th. His score of twenty-six and a third over Malta was more than double that of his nearest challenger, McLeod. Late in 1943 he joined 412 Squadron, RCAF, in England, adding three more Fw 190s to his score by the end of the year. Off operations during the rest of the war, he was killed in 1948 in an aircrash in Italy.

The RAF's first great night fighter was Group Captain John Cunningham, later famous as de Havilland's chief test pilot. After claiming sixteen victories during 1941–42 while flying the Bristol Beaufighter, he later led a Mosquito squadron in 1943, bringing his final score to twenty, all but one by night.

page 77
By June 1939 the Nomonhan Incident between Japan and Soviet Russia on the Manchurian-Mongolian border had developed into a full-scale war. On 27 June, Russian aircraft launched repeated attacks on the landing ground used by the *11th Sentai* of the Imperial Japanese Army Air Force at Tamsag, on the Manchurian steppe. Intercepting these raids, Warrant Officer Hiromichi Shinohara claimed a total of eleven Russian fighters shot down during the morning, all his combats being watched from the ground. He is seen here about to attack a Polikarpov I-16 fighter which is escorting a formation of Tupolev SB-2 bombers.
By Michael Turner.

pages 78–79
A burst of cannon fire brings a French Curtiss Hawk 75A fighter crashing to the ground alongside a retreating Allied column in north-western France. The victorious pilot, *Hauptmann* Werner Mölders, had just become the first German pilot of the Second World War to claim twenty victories. It is 27 May 1940.
By Michael Turner.

opposite page
On 6 January 1940, *Kapteeni* Jorma Sarvanto of the Finnish Air Force's Fighter Squadron *HLeLv 24* intercepted a formation of seven Russian Ilyushin DB-3 bombers raiding a Finnish village. Sarvanto, in his little Fokker D.XXI fighter, single-handedly shot down six of the intruders in quick succession. The seventh fell to another pilot. Sarvanto was to emerge as top-scoring pilot of Finland's brief 'Winter War' with her giant neighbour.
By Michael Turner.

Of the more experienced pilots serving on Malta during 1942, one was William Rolls, who had claimed eight and a half victories flying from England during 1940–42 and who doubled this total in a few weeks as a flight commander with 126 Squadron. When he reached Malta, 'Mike' Stephens had fifteen victories to his credit, gained in France in 1940, in the Battle of Britain, and over the Desert. During October 1942, flying with 249 and 229 Squadrons, he made seven further claims to raise his total to twenty-two.

Malta also produced a number of night-fighter aces, most notable of whom was Canadian Robert 'Moose' Fumerton, who claimed twelve of his fourteen victories over the Mediterranean, the majority while flying a Beaufighter from Malta. Other Beaufighters were used by day for long-range fighter-intruder work. After two tours as a bomber pilot, John Buchanan started flying these aircraft with 272 Squadron from Malta in November 1942. On his first five sorties he shot down six aircraft—mainly transports ferrying men and supplies from Sicily to Tunisia and Tripoli. By the end of May 1943 he had shot down ten aircraft, shared in the destruction of four more, and destroyed a seaplane on the water. This was the most achieved by any Beaufighter pilot by day and brought Buchanan several decorations. In February 1944, flying a second tour at the head of 227 Squadron, flak damage brought him down in the Aegean Sea and he died of exposure before he was found.

The Mediterranean was also the hunting ground for some of the Royal Navy's top carrier pilots. In 1940 Stanley Orr flew Fairey Fulmar fighters with 806 Squadron from *HMS Illustrious*, claiming seven victories by the end of that year. Three more followed in 1941, while in 1944, over Norway, he gained his last victories while flying Hellcats from *HMS Emperor*. Richard 'Dickie' Cork was loaned to

the RAF in summer 1940, flying in Douglas Bader's 242 Squadron where he gained five victories during the Battle of Britain. In August 1942, flying Sea Hurricanes with 880 Squadron aboard *HMS Indomitable*, he took part in the escorting of a big convoy carrying supplies for Malta. During this operation he claimed six victories in two days, five of them on the 12th. In 1944 he was leader of the fighter wing on *Illustrious* in the Indian Ocean, but was killed in an aircraft crash in Ceylon on 14 April.

The arrival of many new Spitfire units in the Mediterranean area for the Tunisian campaign, which began late in 1942, and for the invasions of Sicily and Italy the following year, again allowed many RAF pilots to do well. Among the more successful at this stage were two wing leaders, Petrus 'Dutch' Hugo, a South African, and Colin Gray, a New Zealander. Both had flown during 1940, Hugo on Hurricanes and Gray on Spitfires, and both had scores running into double figures. Gray was to claim nine victories during the first seven months of 1943, raising his personal score to twenty-seven and a half, making him top-scoring New Zealand pilot of the war. Hugo flew two tours in the area, claiming nearly a dozen victories to bring his score to twenty-two.

Another New Zealander to do well at this time was Evan Mackie, who arrived in Tunisia during spring 1943. In a short space of time he claimed six and a half victories, gaining another six during the invasions of Sicily and Italy. Posted from 243 Squadron to lead 92 Squadron, he had raised his total to sixteen by February 1944. On his return to Europe, he flew Tempests during the last months of the war with 2nd Tactical Air Force, leading first 80 Squadron and then 122 Wing. At the end of the war his score stood at twenty-one and a half plus four destroyed on the ground.

Top-scorer in Tunisia was an Englishman, Neville Duke. Initial service in England in 1941 with 92 Squadron brought him his first two claims, following which he was posted to join 112 Squadron in the Desert. Here he claimed five and two shared victories before his tour ended. Rejoining 92 Squadron, now also in Africa, late in 1942, he claimed fourteen victories in three months over Tunisia. A third tour at the head of 145 Squadron in Italy in 1944 added six more victories by September to make him Desert Air Force top-scorer of the war, with twenty-six of his twenty-eight victories claimed in the Mediterranean. After the war he became famous as Hawker's chief test pilot, gaining the world speed record in a Hunter in September 1953.

Night fighters also did well in this area, one of the most successful units being 600 Squadron, which was equipped with Beaufighters. Alwyn Downing, with John Lyons as radar operator, shot down five Ju 52 transports in the early dawn of 30 April 1943 during his first combat. He

Mosquito Mark VI fighter-bombers of 487 (New Zealand) Squadron, a unit of 2nd Tactical Air Force, are seen here flying over Western Europe.

went on to raise his score to twelve over Italy by the end of January 1944. Desmond Hughes, an Irishman, was an ex-Defiant pilot who already had six and a half victories to his credit when he reached Africa. With 600 Squadron he claimed ten more, finally ending the war with eighteen and a half victories, all but two at night.

During July 1943 a detachment of Mosquitos from 256 Squadron in England arrived on Malta to aid in the night defence of the forces invading Sicily. John Watson achieved great success at this time, claiming five bombers shot down during the night of 15 July, and two in one night on two subsequent occasions. Altogether, he claimed thirteen bombers during July, nine German and four Italian, adding one more Italian aircraft the following month.

A pilot serving in the Mediterranean who should also be mentioned was Anthony Lovell. After eight victories during 1940, Lovell led 1435 Squadron on Malta in 1942, claiming several more victories here. He later led Spitfire wings from the island, and from Corsica during 1944, bringing his score to between nineteen and twenty by the time the war ended. Sadly, he was killed in an aircraft accident in England in August 1945.

Over Western Europe during the mid-war years, new aces were still appearing. Finucane had been killed in 1942 after thirty-two victories, and Malan was no longer flying operationally. The way was clear for new blood, and several of the notable pilots of the 1941 sweeps were to push their totals up to over twenty during this period, while a number of others who had flown in the Desert or on Malta also increased their scores. However, a new star had appeared in the person of 'Johnny' Johnson, who had begun operations during 1941 with 616 Squadron, claiming his first six victories during the summer of that year. In 1942 he led 610 Squadron, claiming further victories over

Dieppe on 19 August of that year. Early in 1943 he was promoted again to lead a Canadian Spitfire wing, and during the year claimed at least seventeen aircraft shot down, bringing his score to twenty-five. Rested from operations, he returned early in 1944 to lead another Canadian wing, and during the next six months claimed thirteen more victories. He ended the war as a group captain commanding a wing of the latest Spitfire 14s. With his total of thirty-eight, he was certainly the RAF top-scorer in Western Europe and remains officially No. 1.

Other successful pilots during this period included William Crawford-Crompton, a New Zealander with twenty-one and a half victories, Ray Harries, a Welshman with twenty and a quarter, J. J. 'Chris' Le Roux with seventeen, four of them in Tunisia, and Jack Charles, a Canadian with fifteen and a half. All these pilots flew Spitfires between 1941 and 1944, all but Le Roux surviving the war. John Baldwin was active throughout 1943–44, but he flew Hawker Typhoons, and was to prove the most successful ace on these aircraft, being credited with sixteen and a half. He led a wing during the invasion of Western Europe, but was later killed over Korea with the United Nations forces.

Roland Beamont, a 1940 Hurricane ace, was a great exponent of the Typhoon, but in the ground-attack role. In 1944 he commanded the first Tempest wing, claiming three victories during 1944 to bring his score to at least nine. During the summer he led the wing against V-1 flying bombs, personally shooting down thirty-two. Later in the year, after moving to Holland, he was shot down by flak and became a prisoner. He gained fame after the war as the test pilot of the English Electric Canberra bomber and Lightning fighter.

Although not an ace against manned aircraft, Joseph Berry was the most successful pilot against the V-1s. Flying Tempests, he shot down fifty-two and a half in about six weeks,

Group Captain J. E. 'Johnny' Johnson (left), RAF official top-scorer with thirty-eight victories. He is seen here with Major Eugene Roberts, USAAF, a P-47 Thunderbolt pilot with the 78th Fighter Group, who finished the war with nine victories.

including seven in one sortie on 23 July (he twice claimed five in a sortie). Posted to command 501 Squadron in August 1944, he brought his score to sixty and a third, together with four piloted aircraft, but was shot down and killed over Holland during October.

1944 and the invasion of Normandy gave new opportunities to the RAF, and top-scorer during this last phase of the war was a Canadian, Donald Laubman, who claimed fifteen between March and October flying a Spitfire with 412 Squadron, RCAF. Two others who did well at this time were Harold Walmsley and Warren Schrader. In the late stages of the war Walmsley claimed six and a half victories to bring his total to nine and one shared. Schrader was a Tempest pilot who claimed nine and a half during the last month of war to raise his score to thirteen. He ended the war at the head of 616 Squadron, the first unit to take the Meteor jet fighter into action.

Late in the war Mosquito units, carrying on Braham's early work of supporting Bomber Command's night offensive, gained some of the greatest night successes. Bransome Burbridge flew in 85 Squadron, gaining his first victory in February 1944. More victories followed during the year, and on 4 November he shot down four German night fighters in one sortie. By early January 1945 his score stood at twenty, sixteen of them over hostile territory, making him the RAF's top-scoring night-fighter pilot. The following April he claimed a final victory during a day-intruder flight over Denmark. In the same squadron was Alan Owen, who claimed eight in three months late in 1944 to add to eight earlier victories, six of which were claimed in Italy with 600 Squadron.

In the Far East, too, the Commonwealth Air Forces had been deeply involved in the fighting. Early in 1942 the first reinforcements from the United Kingdom began to reach Burma. One of these was Frank Carey, commander of 135 Hurricane Squadron, who already had eighteen victories to his credit during 1940. During the retreat from Burma he shot down at least five Japanese aircraft, including three in one sortie. His total victories against the Japanese are not known, but he got at least one more during 1943.

In the same unit was an Australian, W. J. 'Jack' Storey, who claimed five during the 1942 retreat, then three more in one day on 5 March 1943. Spitfires subsequently arrived, some of these replacing Hurricanes in 136 Squadron. A. C. Conway had claimed two during 1943 on the older aircraft, claiming five more with the Spitfire early in 1944.

Patrick Meagher claimed one victory over Western Europe in 1941, next seeing action at the head of 211 Beaufighter Squadron in Burma in 1943. Flying one of these heavy aircraft most aggressively, he managed to shoot down, or cause to crash, six Japanese aircraft, including at least four of the potent Nakajima Ki 43 fighters. He also destroyed several other aircraft on the ground.

Despite all the fighting over Burma and the Indian frontier, probably the most successful Commonwealth pilot against the Japanese gained all his victories elsewhere. Geoffrey Fisken, a New Zealander, flew as a young NCO on Singapore early in the Pacific war, claiming six victories during early 1942 while flying Brewster Buffalos. Evacuated home, he later flew Kittyhawks in the Solomons with 15

Squadron, RNZAF, claiming five more victories in two combats during summer 1943. In Northern Australia meanwhile, a wing of Spitfires led by Clive Caldwell had arrived from England for the defence of Port Darwin. Going into action early in 1943, the wing enjoyed a fair amount of success, Caldwell proving the most successful pilot with eight victories, becoming top-scoring Australian of the war.

Early in 1945 the British Pacific Fleet, with a strong force of carriers, reached the Far East to begin operations alongside the US Navy. Pilots of Hellcats, Seafires and Fireflies all did well, several claiming two, three or four victories. However, two Corsair pilots flying from *HMS Victorious* became the only aces, and only one of them gained all his victories in the Pacific. The other was one of the Royal Navy's few Marine fighter pilots, R. C. Hay. Flying throughout the war, Hay now added two and two shared victories against Japanese aircraft to his earlier victories gained on Skuas and Fulmars, bringing his total to five and one-third. His wingman, a Canadian named Donald Sheppard, shot down three and two shared during January 1945 over Sumatra, adding one more in May. He was probably the last Commonwealth pilot to become an ace during the war.

The leading Commonwealth aces :

+ Squadron Leader M. T. St. J. Pattle	South African	51 approximately
Group Captain J. E. Johnson	English	38
+ Wing Commander B. Finucane	Irish	32
+ Group Captain A. G. Malan *Died 1963*	South African	32 at least
+ Flight Lieutenant G. F. Beurling *May 1948*	Canadian	31⅓
Wing Commander J. R. D. Braham	English	29 (19 at night) *BLENHEIMS*
Wing Commander R. R. S. Tuck	English	29
Wing Commander C. R. Caldwell	Australian	28½
Group Captain F. R. Carey	English	28 approximately
Squadron Leader N. F. Duke	English	28
Squadron Leader J. H. Lacey	English	28
Wing Commander C. F. Gray	New Zealander	27.7
+ Flight Lieutenant E. G. Lock	English	25
Wing Commander B. Drake	English	24½
Flight Lieutenant G. Allard	English	23.83
Group Captain D. R. S. Bader	English	23⅓ at least
Wing Commander D. E. Kingaby	English	23
Wing Commander R. F. Boyd	Scots	22½
Wing Commander H. M. Stephen	Scots	22½
Wing Commander M. N. Crossley	English	22
Group Captain P. H. Hugo	South African	22
Wing Commander M. M. Stephens	English	22
Flying Officer W. Vale	English	22 at least
Flight Lieutenant V. C. Woodward	Canadian	21.83
Wing Commander W. V. Crawford-Crompton	New Zealander	21½
Wing Commander A. C. Deere	New Zealander	21½
Flight Lieutenant R. B. Hesslyn	New Zealander	21½
Wing Commander E. D. Mackie	New Zealander	21½
Squadron Leader H. J. L. Hallowes	English	21⅓
Wing Commander B. A. Burbridge	English	21 (20 at night)
+ Flight Lieutenant A. A. McKellar	Scots	21
Wing Commander J. E. Rankin	Scots	21
+ Squadron Leader H. W. McLeod	Canadian	21
Wing Commander R. A. Harries	Welsh	20¼
Group Captain J. Cunningham	English	20 (19 at night)
Group Captain W. D. David	English	20

The Bulgarians

While Bulgaria supported the Axis powers in their invasion of Yugoslavia and Greece in April 1941, declaring war on the Western Allies, she wisely refrained from joining the Germans in the war against Russia.

Initially the Bulgarian fighter units were equipped with Czech-built Avia B-534 biplanes, although a handful of Messerschmitt Bf 109Es and G-2s were supplied during 1942-43, allowing one *eskadra* (squadron) of

In Russia many Battle of Britain pilots continued to do well. Walter Oesau led *III/JG 3*, reaching eighty victories by 15 July 1941 and 100 on 26 October, the third pilot to reach this score. Awarded the Swords and Oak Leaves to the Knight's Cross, he returned to France to command *JG 2* in 1943, but was killed in combat with American fighters on 11 May 1944. His final score of 123 included eight in Spain, forty-four in Russia, and ten four-engined bombers.

Herbert Ihlefeld had also been an ace in Spain, gaining seven victories there. During 1940–41 he had claimed thirty-six British aircraft, including one over Crete, and early in the Russian campaign reached forty. His 100th came on 22 April 1942, making him the fifth pilot to reach this score, but thereafter he claimed few further victories although he led several *Geschwadern* on various fronts. His final score of one hundred and thirty, in over 1,000 sorties, included fifty-six against the Western Allies, about fifteen of them heavy bombers. Despite these early successes, losses were suffered, and one of the first to fall was Hermann-Freidrich Joppien. After forty-two victories in the West, he swiftly increased his score in Russia to seventy, but on 25 August

1941 lost control and crashed to his death during combat. However, new pilots were still available to take the place of the veterans, and as the campaigns on the ground brought up Russian aircraft in droves, new records were constantly being set. Gordon Gollob, an ex-*Zerströer* pilot, raised his 1940 score of six to forty-two by mid-September, and then doubled it in the next six weeks. Another run of successes during summer 1942 brought his total to one hundred and fifty, at which point he was taken off operations. His best day was 18th October 1941, on which he claimed nine during several sorties.

The lead was soon taken over by Hermann Graf of *JG 52*, who had been an instructor until August 1941. In a little over a year he was to claim 202 victories; claims no. 47–104 were made in a period of three weeks, while no. 127–202 were claimed in just four weeks of hectic fighting during the early autumn of 1942. Taken off operations at that point, he returned to lead *JG 52* at the end of the war, adding ten US bombers to his total.

Even as Graf was at his peak, the Luftwaffe's most famous Austrian, Walter Nowotny, was already making a name for himself, claiming seven victories on 4 August 1942 alone. Flying

Every Luftwaffe ace of the early war years who flew single-seater fighters flew the Messerschmitt Bf 109E. A *Rotte*, or pair, of these aircraft have been caught by the camera at the moment of take-off.

Veteran fighter leaders confer on the Channel coast early in 1941. From left to right: *Oberstleutnant* Galland, *Major* Lützow, *Major* von Maltzahn. *Generalmajor* Osterkamp, and *Oberstleutnant* Mölders. Osterkamp was a veteran of both World Wars, gaining six victories in 1940 at the head of *JG 51* before his promotion to *Generalmajor*.

Major Walter Nowotny, the first pilot to reach 250 victories. He was shot down and killed late in 1944 while leading the first operational test unit equipped with Me 262 jet fighters. Apart from his 258 confirmed victories, he listed a further twenty-two which were not confirmed.

Fw 190s with *JG 54* during 1943, he claimed forty-one victories during June, ten of them on the 24th. This rate of scoring continued, with forty-nine in August, forty-five in September, and then thirty-two in ten days in October, raising his score to over 250. He was killed in combat on 8 November 1944 in a Messerschmitt Me 262 jet fighter. He gained three victories with this revolutionary aircraft in a special test commando which he was commanding.

Against the enemy in the West–which by 1942 included the Americans–scores rose less rapidly. Galland had reached ninety-four by the end of 1941, but then became Fighter Inspector when Mölders was killed. He had few further chances to fly until 1945, when he was dismissed from his post in disgrace but was allowed to form a special unit of jet fighters with highly experienced pilots. With this unit his final total reached 104.

On recovery from his wounds, Wilhelm Balthasar led *JG 2*, raising his score to forty-seven before his death in action on 6 July 1941. His best day had been 6 June 1940, when he made nine claims at the height of the Battle of France. In *JG 26* Josef 'Pips' Priller claimed his fortieth victory during July 1941, increasing his score to sixty-five by October. His score had reached 100 by July 1944, though he added only one more before the end of the war. His total included sixty-eight Spitfires and eleven American four-engined bombers. Siegfried Schnell also did well in the West, claiming eighty-seven of his ninety-three victories during 1940–43 with *JG 2*.

Most successful of all against the Western Allies was Hans-Joachim Marseille. After seven victories during the Battle of Britain, Marseille served in North Africa with *JG 27* throughout 1941 until his death in an accident in September 1942. During this period he claimed 151 aircraft shot down, most of them fighters. Most of his claiming was done between December 1941 and his death, and he frequently made multiple claims, shooting down six South African Tomahawks in one combat on 3 June 1942, and claiming seventeen victories in three sorties on 1 September. Despite the almost unbelievable nature of this claim, careful checking of Allied records has shown that at least a dozen of the British aircraft Marseille attacked were in fact shot down and others were damaged. He was considered to be one of the most brilliant exponents of the difficult art of deflection shooting, and was also a most gifted pilot, with the ability to outfight more manoeuvrable British fighters in his Bf 109.

The deterioration of the situation in Africa brought new units from other fronts, a number of pilots increasing their scores very rapidly over Tripolitania, Tunisia and Sicily during the late 1942–early 1943 period. Joachim Müncheberg, after a period in Russia, raised his score from 103 to 135, but was then killed in combat on 23 March 1943 when at the head of *JG 77*. In this same unit Heinz 'Pritzl' Bär, a most popular and successful pilot, claimed over sixty victories in five months to raise his score to nearly 200. Ernst Wilhelm Reinert claimed fifty-one in an even shorter period early in 1943, raising his own score to 154. In *JG 53* Friedrich-Karl 'Tutti' Müller, who had claimed 100 in Russia, fifty of them in one month, went on to add about thirty more victories over the Mediterranean. He was killed early in 1944 in a crash in Germany with his total at 140. Bär and Reinert both survived the war, the former with sixteen victories on Me 262s, which made him the top-scoring jet pilot of the war with an overall total of 220, while the latter's score reached 174.

In Russia the race for the No. 1 spot continued;

from 1943 onwards it was *JG 52*–the Luftwaffe's top-scoring fighter unit–which made all the running. The unit was to produce four of the top six aces of the war, including the top three. The first to rise was Günther Rall, who claimed his 100th victory in October 1942 and his 200th on 29 August 1943. A brilliant marksman, he reached 250 by November 1943, after making forty claims during the previous month. He later commanded units on Home Defence, ending the war with 275 victories, all but three against the Russians.

Gerhard Barkhorn had flown 120 sorties before he shot down his first victim on 2 July 1941. Thereafter he claimed steadily, reaching 250 in February 1944, and an incredible 300 on 5 January 1945. His final score was 301, all of which were gained against the Russians. However, one man had reached 300 before him, Erich Hartmann, the world's top-scoring fighter ace of all time. 'Bubi' (Baby) Hartmann joined *JG 52* in October 1942 as a very young man, gradually finding his feet as a fighter pilot. By July 1943 he had claimed thirty-four victories, but then within two months his score shot up to 95. This continued to rise steadily as the enormous land battles following the Germans' unsuccessful Kursk offensive raged on the ground. By March 1944 he had reached 200, and by the following July 250. Throughout the summer of 1944, as the Red Armies pushed the Germans back into East Prussia and Hungary, he was constantly in the air, on one occasion claiming seventy-eight victories in four weeks, including eight on 23 August and eleven next day, to bring his score to 301.

Flying on the southern sector of the front, he also met American aircraft from Italy during 1944, seven of his victories being claimed against US P-51 fighters. His final victory came on 8 May 1945, the last day of the war, to bring his total to 352. During the war he was awarded the Knight's Cross with Oak Leaves, Swords and Diamonds, but was subsequently imprisoned by the Russians as a 'war criminal', not returning home until 1955.

Wilhelm Batz joined *JG 52* as a highly experienced instructor with 5,000 hours flying to his credit. This stood him in good stead, for in his first year at the front he gained 100 victories, doubling this score by August 1944. On 30 May 1944 he flew seven sorties, claiming a total of fifteen victories. He ended the war with 237 victories, five of them against the Western Allies. The unit also included another very successful Austrian, Franz Schall. Originally a flak gunner, Schall claimed 123 victories in Russia, including thirteen in one day, all claimed in just a year and a half. He later flew Me 262s in the West and, with fourteen victories, was second only to Bär as a jet ace. He was killed on 10 April 1945 when he ran into a bomb crater and blew up.

The second most successful *Geschwader* in

A Focke-Wulf FW 190 and a Yak do battle in the sky over the Eastern Front.

Oberstleutnant Hermann Graf, the first pilot to top 200, on 2 October 1942. He flew several missions against heavy bombers late in the war, claiming ten of these shot down. He remained in captivity in Russia until 1950.

The basic German operational formation was the *Schwarm*, or section, of four aircraft. These Messerschmitt Bf 109Es are flying a closer formation than would normally be the case if opposition was expected. They are aircraft of *III Gruppe*, *Jagsgeschwader 51*.

Hauptmann Hans-Joachim Marseille, the great Desert ace of *JG 27*. All Marseille's 158 victories were claimed against the RAF. He is seen here with his wingman, Reiner Pöttgen (seven victories).

Russia was *JG 54*, and the top-scorer of this unit was Otto Kittel. A slow starter, he had raised his score to 120 by late 1943, after over two years at the front. Like Hartmann, he was twice shot down in combat, and once escaped after being a prisoner for two weeks. He was killed in combat on 14 February 1945 after gaining at least 267 victories, all claimed in the East.

Other pilots in this *Geschwader* included Gunther Scheel, who achieved considerable fame during 1943. In seventy flights he made seventy-one claims, but on 16 July was killed when he rammed a Russian Yak-9 fighter over Orel. Emil 'Bully' Lang, an ex-Lufthansa airline pilot, also did well in 1943; on 21 October he made twelve claims to raise his score to seventy-three. In one period he claimed seventy-two in three weeks, including eighteen in a single day–no pilot has ever shot down more in one day. By spring 1944 his total stood at 128 when he moved with *III/JG 54* to the West. He was one of the most successful pilots during the Normandy invasion, claiming twenty-five British and American aircraft. His career came to an end when he was shot down and killed by P-47 fighters in a combat on 3 September with his score standing at 173.

On the northern front in Russia was *JG 5*, based mainly on airfields in Finland and northern Norway. Fighting in Arctic conditions, this unit produced many aces, the most successful of whom was ex-*Zeströer* pilot Theodor Weissenberger. With twenty-three victories on Bf 110s to his credit by late 1942, Weissenberger quickly went on to pass the century mark as a Bf 109 pilot. In June 1944 he led *I/JG 5* to the Normandy invasion front, claiming twenty-five victories in a few weeks and reaching 200. Leading a *Gruppe* of Me 262 jets in *JG 7* later in the war he claimed his final eight victories on these to raise his score to 208, thirty-three of which were gained against the Western Allies. He was killed in 1950 while racing cars at Nürburgring.

From mid-1943 onwards a new breed of ace appeared in the Luftwaffe–the destroyer of the US heavy bombers which were appearing over Europe in growing numbers. Many pilots built up good scores against these difficult opponents, but most successful of all was Herbert Rollwage of *JG 53*. After service in Russia and the

Mediterranean, he flew on Home Defence, his final total of 102 including no less than forty-four four-engined bombers.

Another great killer of these aircraft, and also one of the most successful pilots in the West, was Egon Meyer of *JG 2*. His fiftieth victory was claimed over Dieppe on 19 August 1942, (he had shot down sixteen in the previous three weeks). He became *Kommodore* of the *Geschwader* in July 1943, and on 5 February 1944 he became the first pilot to gain 100 victories on the Channel front – the hardest of all in the opinion of most German pilots. Twenty-five of his claims were against heavy bombers, and by March 1944 his total stood at 102. The award of the Swords to his Knight's Cross was then announced, but he did not live to celebrate it, for on the same day he fell in combat with P-47s of the 'crack' US 56th Fighter Group.

Desperate measures were needed against the bomber streams, and early in 1944 a special unit of heavily armed *Sturm* (Storm) fighters, led by Walter Dahl, was formed to combat them. Dahl was to claim thirty-six bombers among his 128 victories, two of them by ramming. Over Schweinfurt on 14 October 1943, he claimed no less than three B-17 Flying Fortresses shot down. His total also included seventy-seven Russian aircraft, twenty-five shot down over Stalingrad in 1942 and thirteen gained in ten days over Berlin during the closing weeks of the war.

Despite the great hopes held for the *Zerströer* units in 1939, few pilots actually did well in these cumbersome and vulnerable aircraft. The great exception was Eduard Tratt, who claimed twelve victories during 1940 with *ZG 1*, and then thirteen more in Russia with *SKG 210*. Late in 1943 he led *II/ZG 26* on Home Defence, flying Me 410s against the US heavy bombers. He shot down several of these, but was shot down and killed by escort fighters on 22 February 1944 with his score at thirty-eight – twenty-five of them against the British and Americans. He also claimed twenty-six aircraft, twenty-four tanks and many other targets destroyed on the ground. He was the only *Zerströer* pilot to receive the Oak Leaves to his Knight's Cross.

In 1944 the removal of fighter units from Russia to the West left the ground troops short of cover. The ground-attack units (*Schlacht-geschwadern*) had by then been re-equipped with Fw 190 fighter-bombers, and these frequently doubled as fighters. One pilot did particularly well on these operations over the Crimea during 1944. During this period *SG-2* claimed 247 victories, more than a third of them being claimed by August Lambert. At the height of the battle he claimed seventy in three weeks, gaining twelve, fourteen and seventeen victories in single days, while also attacking and destroying many ground targets. In May, having gained ninety victories, he was relieved and

Oberstleutnant Heinz 'Pritzl' Bär. One of the great 'characters' of the Luftwaffe fighter arm, he flew from 1939 until the end of the war, claiming 220 victories. His last sixteen victories were claimed while flying Messerschmitt Me 262 jet fighters, making him top-scoring jet pilot of the war.

became an instructor. He returned to operations in *SG 77* during spring 1945, but on 17 April his Fw 190 was one of a large number shot down by P-51s while taking off and he was killed. His final score was 116.

Throughout the war the Luftwaffe was also faced with combating the night attacks of RAF's Bomber Command. Gradually a highly effective night-fighter force was built up, producing the world's highest-scoring night fighters as well as day fighters. Many of the early night pilots began flying in *Zerströer* units, and one such was Werner Streib. After one day victory during May, Streib went up on the moonlit night of 20

The greatest of them all! *Hauptmann* Erich 'Bubi' Hartmann, top-scoring fighter pilot of all time. Joining *JG 52* late in 1942, Hartmann became the first man to reach 300 in August 1944. His last victory was gained on the final day of hostilities, bringing his score to 352, including 260 fighters – seven of them American Mustangs shot down over southern Hungary and the Alps.

On an airfield on the Channel coast of Western Europe, yellow-nosed Bf 109Es of *III/JG 53* are prepared for a mission during the Battle of Britain. The *Geschwader's* emblem, the *Pik-as* (Ace of Spades) can be seen on the noses of these fighters.

Oberstleutnant Egon Meyer, the first pilot to reach 100 victories entirely on the extremely tough Channel front. He flew with *JG 2* from December 1939 until March 1944, becoming *Kommodore* of the unit in July 1943. He reached 100 in February 1944, but was killed in combat with American P-47s on 2 March 1944.

July 1940 to shoot down a Whitley—the first night victory for his unit, which had just become *I/NJG 1* (*Nachtjagdgeschwader 1*).

Streib soon became the Luftwaffe's first night ace, and by early 1943 his score had reached forty-two. In June that year he flew the first operational test of the Heinkel He 219 fighter,

shooting down five Lancasters in a single sortie. During 1944, with his score at sixty-six, he became Inspector of Night Fighters; sixty-five of his victories were gained at night.

Helmut Lent of *I/ZG 76* had claimed the Luftwaffe's first victory of the war over Poland on 2 September 1939, and by the end of 1940 had raised his score to eight. His unit then became *II/NJG 1*, and by mid-1942 he had claimed thirty-five more victories at night. He passed Streib's night total in August 1943, and during the night of 15–16 June 1944 claimed three Lancasters to reach 100. He was killed in a flying accident in daylight on 5 October 1944.

By 1943 many other pilots were running up big scores by night, one of the most notable being a nobleman, Heinrich Prinz zu Sayn-Wittgenstein. Previously a cavalryman and then a bomber pilot, he flew Ju 88s with *III/NJG 2*, claiming twenty-five victories in his first three months with the unit. Transferred to the East at the head of *I/NJG 100*, he claimed twenty-nine more in forty-five nights, including seven in one night. Returning to the West, he claimed six bombers in one hour on New Year's Day 1944 to raise his score to seventy-two. During the night of 21–22 January he shot down five bombers to reach eighty-four, but his aircraft was then badly hit; he ordered his crew to bale out and tried to save the aircraft, but crashed and was killed.

Gustav Francsi also did well with *I/NJG 100* in the East, where he was reputed to be most successful night fighter against the Russians.

Not all his victims were Russian, his total of fifty-six including four RAF Lancasters in one night.

The greatest night fighter ace of them all was Heinz-Wolfgang Schnauffer. First claiming in June 1942, he had passed twenty by August the following year. On 16 December 1943 he shot down four Lancasters in bad weather and low cloud. Leading *IV/NJG 1* during 1944, he claimed his fiftieth on 25 March, one of five Lancasters claimed by him during a quarter of an hour. On 29 October he was the second night fighter to claim 100, and by the end of the year he had overtaken Lent, his score standing at 106.

The Focke-Wulf FW 190 was the most widely used German fighter after the Bf 109E. First introduced in 1941, it proved more than a match for the Spitfire V. Operating in both France and Russia, it was later used as a fighter-bomber. These aircraft are carrying bombs beneath their fuselages, while that in the foreground has under-wing, long-range fuel tanks.

To combat heavy American daylight raids over the Reich in 1943, the Messerschmitt Bf 110 was employed on day interception operations. However, when escort fighters appeared over Germany a few months later, the Bf 110s suffered heavy losses and were withdrawn. Note the under-wing rocket tubes and extra under-fuselage gun packs of these Bf 110s of *II/ZG 26*.

An Me 262 jet of *III/JG 57*, photographed in Zurich just two days before the end of the war.

In February 1945, as *Kommodore* of *NJG 4*, he shot down two Lancasters during the early hours of the 21st. When darkness fell again that evening he was back in the air, claiming seven more in seventeen minutes. At the end of the war his score had reached 121, and his Bf 110 was subsequently put on show in London's Hyde Park. The victory-marked rudder of this aircraft is on view to this day in the Imperial War Museum, London.

The leading German day-fighter aces	
Major Erich Hartmann	352
Major Gerhard Barkhorn	301
Major Günther Rall	275
Oberleutnant Otto Kittel	267
Major Walter Nowotny	258
Major Wilhelm Batz	237
Major Erich Rudorffer	222
Oberst. Heinz Bär	220
Oberst. Hermann Graf	212
Major Heinrich Ehrler	209 at least
Major Theodor Weissenberger	208
Oberst. Hans Philipp	206
Oberleutnant Walter Schuck	206
Oberleutnant Anton Hafner	204
Hauptmann Helmut Lipfert	203

The leading German night-fighter aces	
Major Heinz-Wolfgang Schnauffer	121
Oberst. Helmut Lent	110
(8 of these by day)	
Major Heinrich Prinz zu Sayn-Wittgenstein	84
Major Wilhelm Herget	71
(14 of these by day)	
Oberst. Werner Streib	66
(1 of these by day)	
Hauptmann Manfred Meurer	65
Oberst. Günther Radusch	64
Hauptmann Heinz Rökker	64
Major Rudolf Schönert	64
Major Paul Zorner	59
Hauptmann Gerhard Raht	58
Hauptmann Martin Becker	57
Oberleutnant Gustav Francsi	56
Hauptmann Josef Kraft	56
Hauptmann Heinz Strüning	56

Twenty more pilots had scores between 150 and 197, while seventy had between 100 and 146. Nine more night fighters claimed between fifty and fifty-five. Altogether, approximately 360 day and night fighter pilots claimed between forty and 100 victories, while something of the order of 500 more claimed from twenty to forty. At least twenty-seven day pilots claimed twenty or more four-engined bombers, and at least twenty-two claimed five or more victories while flying jet or rocket-propelled aircraft.

The Greeks

Like the Dutch, the Greeks produced no aces as such during the war. In 1940–41 a small fighter force equipped mainly with Polish-built PZL P-24 high-wing monoplanes, together with a few French Bloch 151s and later some Gladiators handed over by the RAF, fought a courageous battle against the Italians and later the Germans. Altogether, Greek fighters were credited with about sixty-eight victories, three against the Luftwaffe, the rest against the *Regia Aeronautica*. Few details of claims are available,

but one of the more outstanding pilots was Lieutenant Marinos Mitralexis of the *22 Mira* (Squadron). On 2 November 1940 he was part of a force that intercepted an Italian formation over Salonika, shooting down one Cant Z.1007bis trimotor bomber. Having run out of ammunition, he managed to cut the tail off another bomber with the propeller of his P-24, before carrying out a successful forced-landing.

Later in the war two Free Greek fighter squadrons were formed within the RAF in the

Middle East, but these had little opportunity to engage in air combat, and claims were minimal. In England, however, one pilot of Greek descent who served with the RAF and did become an ace was Basilios Vassiliades. As an NCO in 19 Squadron, he flew Mustangs during 1944, claiming six and two shared, victories and receiving a DFM. Shot down by flak, he evaded capture and returned to join 3 Squadron in Holland early in 1945. Now an officer, he flew Tempests, claiming a further three victories by March. On the 22nd of that month he was hit by flak and killed. He had also destroyed one aircraft on the ground.

The Hungarians

Like Hitler's Germany, the new state of Hungary built up a secret air force during the 1930s in contravention of the Armistice terms of 1919. The Hungarian Government laid early claim to the Ruthenian area of Czechoslovakia, and late in October 1938 one Czech aircraft was shot down by Hungarian CR 32 fighters during a border incursion in the area. Following the German occupation of Czechoslovakia and the creation of the independent Slovakian republic, the Hungarians decided to annex Ruthenia, moving into the country during March 1939.

At once aerial warfare broke out on a limited scale, the squadrons of the 1/I Fighter Group, equipped with Italian Fiat CR 32 biplanes, achieving an early ascendancy over the Slovakian Avia B-534s. When fighting ceased at the end of March with the occupation accomplished, First Lieutenant A. Negro and Sergeant S. Szojak of 1/I Fighter Squadron had been the most successful pilots, claiming two victories each.

In June 1941 the Hungarians joined Germany in the invasion of Russia, the 1/I Fighter Group accompanying the Hungarian Fast Corps to the front; it was now equipped with Fiat CR 42 biplanes and a test batch of Reggianne Re 2000 monoplanes. There was little opportunity for air combat for the Hungarian pilots at this time, but three CR 42 pilots each claimed three aircraft. Szojak claimed a further victory and György Ujszaszy, later to become an ace, got two.

The group was subsequently withdrawn, and late in 1942 its place was taken by 5/I Group with a Hungarian-built version of the Re 2000, known as the *Heja*, plus one squadron of Messerschmitt Bf 109Es. Commanded by Aladar de Heppes von Bebnyes, the unit remained in Russia until its airfield was overrun, and then withdrew to convert to Bf 109Gs. With these it returned to the Kharkov area in April 1943, fighting over Russia for a further year. The group then returned to Hungary where it was re-formed and expanded as the 101 'Puma' Fighter Regiment, under Lieutenant Colonel Heppes, for the defence of the main cities against an increasing incidence of American air attack.

It was in the 5/I Group and 101 Regiment that the majority of Hungarian aces served and gained the greater part of their victories. The most successful was Deazsö Szentgyörgyi. After gaining six victories in Russia during 1943, he was to raise his score to thirty-four by the end of the war. György Debrödy had claimed eighteen Russian aircraft shot down when he became involved in home defence. His close friend, Miklos Kenyeres, had also claimed eighteen when in February 1944 Debrödy's aircraft was badly hit by a Russian Yak-9 and came down in enemy territory. Kenyeres shot down the Yak and then landed alongside Debrödy, taking off again under fire, with his friend squashed into the narrow cockpit with him. Two days later Kenyeres was shot down by ground fire and taken prisoner.

For Debrödy it was the second time he had gone down in Russian territory. Once before in September 1943 he had made his own way back, swimming the River Dnieper in doing so. After returning to Hungary, he shot down six American and two more Russian aircraft, but was then badly wounded. He returned to the regiment as a captain just before the end of the war, but saw no further combat.

Another very successful pilot in this unit was Laszlo Molnar, who claimed eighteen Russian and seven US aircraft. He was one of only two Hungarian pilots to receive the Gold Medal for Bravery (the other being Debrödy). He was killed in action with American fighters on 7 August 1944. Lajos Toth was close behind him with twenty-four victories, but he was shot by the Communists after the war, while the veteran Lieutenant Colonel Heppes survived to live in the USA, having notched up a final score of eight victories.

Unlike most of the Eastern European allies of the Germans, the Hungarians did not capitulate during the big Russian advances of summer 1944, fighting on alongside their allies until the last days of the European war.

The leading Hungarian aces

Second Lieutenant Dezsö Szentgyörgyi	34
Captain György Debrödy	26
Lieutenant Laszlo Molnar	25
First Lieutenant Lajos Toth	24
Lieutenant Mikos Kenyeres	19
Sergeant Istvan Fabian	13
Lieutenant Ferenc Malnasy	12
Lieutenant Jozsef Malik	10

The Icelanders

Iceland was not officially involved among the combatants during the Second World War, though its attitude towards the Western Allies was sympathetic, British and American units being based on the island. However, one Icelander did join the RAF as a volunteer and he went on to become an ace. As an NCO, Thor-stein Jonsson flew Spitfires with 111 Squadron during the North African campaign, where he won a DFM and claimed four victories. In 1944 he served in 65 Squadron, a Mustang unit in England. Now an officer, he claimed a further four victories during the summer to bring his total to eight.

The Italians

Early experiences of aerial operations over Ethiopia during the 'thirties added nothing to the store of knowledge of Italian fighter pilots, and although the *Regia Aeronautica* was developed into a large and highly trained organization by Benito Mussolini, the Fascist dictator, this development in many cases followed the wrong lines. The lessons of the First World War were remembered by Italy's fighter pilots, who stressed manœuvrability at all costs. As a result the biplane remained in service as major front-line equipment for a longer time than with other major European powers.

The opportunity to test combat material in Spain during the Civil War did nothing to alter the Italian view, for the Fiat CR 32 biplane supplied to the Spanish Nationalists, and used also by the Italian volunteer legion, achieved very considerable success against the obsolescent French types and the Russian Polikarpov fighters by which they were opposed. Several Italian fighter pilots did well in Spain, the most notable being *Colonello* Mario Bonzano. This pilot initially commanded a *squadriglia* in the *Asso di Bastoni Gruppo*, returning to Spain a second time late in the war at the head of a *squadriglia* equipped with Fiat G-50s, Italy's first production monoplane fighters. Bonzano is credited with about fifteen victories in Spain. He later served in the Libyan Desert during the Second World War, commanding the *20° Gruppo*, flying G-50bis fighter-bombers.

Capitano Enrico Degl'Incerti also flew with the *Legionaria*, claiming five individual victories in his CR 32 during 1937, together with shares in others. He did not live to see service in the Second World War, being killed in a flying accident near Rimini in July 1938. Other pilots who became aces in Spain included Carlo Romagnoli, with nine, and Franco Lucchini.

The whole question of the scores of Italian pilots during 1940–43 is clouded by the fact that the Italian Air Ministry did not encourage the keeping of personal score tallies, so that where pilots did not survive the war detailed confirmation of their reported scores has proved difficult to obtain. *Capitano* Lucchini provides a good example. After his service in Spain with

A Fiat G-55 Centauro, perhaps the best Italian fighter of the war, although only about 105 were built. Both Mario Bellagambi and Ugo Drago gained some of their victories with *2° Gruppo* of the *RSI* flying these aircraft.

the famous *Asso di Bastoni Gruppo*, he served with the *4° Stormo* throughout the three years of Italian involvement in the Mediterranean war. Initially flying a CR 42 biplane, he took part in the first combat to be recorded with British aircraft in Africa on 14 June 1940, subsequently flying in the Desert and over Malta for many months. By July 1943 he was reputed to have added twenty victories to his score in Spain, and to have assisted in the destruction of fifty-two more aircraft–probably most of the latter on the ground.

On 5 July 1943, on his 294th mission, he took off from Sicily in his Macchi 202 to intercept a raid by American heavy bombers. It was reported that he shot down one escorting fighter before falling victim to the guns of a Flying Fortress. At the time of his death his score of twenty-six made him the Italian top-scorer.

A notable pilot during the early years of war was Mario Visentini, who flew CR 42 biplanes with the *412ª Squadriglia* in Italian East Africa. Flying against a heterogenous collection of elderly aircraft employed over this area by the British and South Africans, he was the most successful pilot of the campaign, being credited with about seventeen aerial victories. He also took part in three successful attacks on British airfields, during which thirty-three aircraft were claimed destroyed on the ground. His most famous achievement came during one of these attacks when his commanding officer, *Capitano* Raffi, was forced to land in British territory after his aircraft had been hit by fire from the ground. Visentini landed alongside and discarded his parachute; Raffi leapt into the cockpit, and Visentini took off again, sitting on his passenger's knees to fly the fighter back to base. For this spirited rescue he received his country's highest decoration for bravery, the

Top-scoring *Regia Aeronautica* pilot to survive the war was *Capitano* Franco Bordoni-Bisleri, seen here with his Macchi fighter in 1943. In the background is an SIA 207 light fighter, only a few of which were produced. Flying over Libya and later in the defence of Rome, Bordoni had claimed nineteen victories by September 1943, when the armistice was signed between Italy and the Allies.

Medaglio d'Oro (Gold Medal). A few days later he was killed when he flew into the side of a mountain during bad visibility while searching for two of his pilots who had force-landed.

Leonardo Ferrulli flew in Spain during 1937, claiming his first victory there. Throughout the second half of 1940 he was very active over Libya, flying a CR 42 with *4° Stormo*. After a return to Italy to convert to Macchi 202 aircraft, he flew some sorties over Malta during early 1942, followed by a second tour in the Desert. July 1943 found him involved in the air defence of Sicily with some twenty victories reputedly to his credit, but on 5 July he was shot down and killed. Last seen in combat with some thirty

Macchi Mc 202s of *374ª Squadriglia* of *153° Gruppo* in Sicily in early summer 1943. These fine aircraft were plagued by the scarcity of the Daimler-Benz engines built by Alfa-Romeo. Nevertheless, about 1,500 Mc 202s operated on all fronts from Russia to the Mediterranean.

page 113
Guards Major Aleksandr
Pokryshkin, a leading Russian
ace, in action in the early
summer of 1942 over the
Caucasus in southern Russia.
Flying a Lease-Lend Bell P-39
Airacobra at the head of the
16th Guards Fighter Regiment,
he makes a devastating attack
on a formation of Ju 88A
bombers.
By Michael Turner.

hostile fighters, he was believed to have shot down two of his attackers before his own aircraft went down.

Ferrulli's score of twenty-two was matched by Teresio Martinoli, who also flew both in Africa and over Malta from 1940 to 1943. Flying in the *4° Stormo*, the first unit to receive the modern MC 202 fighters late in 1941, he claimed four victories in a period of about six weeks over Malta during October and November of that year. Later in the year he was awarded a *Medaglio d'Oro* for a reported twenty-two victories, together with shares in others. Following the armistice in September 1943, Martinoli joined the Co-Belligerent Air Force to fly alongside the Allies, but was killed in a flying accident at Naples the following summer in a P-39 Airacobra.

The highest-scoring pilot of the *Regia Aeronautica* to survive the war was Franco Bordoni-Bisleri. 1940 found him flying CR 42 biplanes with the *56° Stormo*, his first operational flights being undertaken over the English Channel from bases in Belgium as part of the Italian legion which supported the Luftwaffe during the final stages of the Battle of Britain. At the beginning of 1941 his unit was ordered to Libya, where the Italian forces were in dire straits, and here he claimed his first five victories during the spring of 1941, four of them being British Blenheim bombers.

Posted home to Italy, he saw no further action until late the following year, when he joined *18° Gruppo* of *3° Stormo* to fly MC 202s in Africa at the time of the Battle of El Alamein. During this period, despite the Axis retreat, he was able to claim six fighter-bombers and a light bomber shot down, but during late November he was badly injured in a road accident and was invalided home once more. On his recovery, he rejoined the unit, now based at Cerveteri for the defence of Rome against US bombing attacks, and during the summer of 1943 claimed seven bombers shot down in a little over a month. Five of these were claimed while flying the excellent new Macchi 205 fighter, and all

but one were four-engined Flying Fortresses. His last claim was made on 5 September, only four days before the armistice, bringing his score to nineteen.

Following the armistice, some Italian pilots obeyed their new government and joined the Co-Belligerents, while others made their way to northern Italy where a new Fascist state, the *Republica Sociale Italiana*, was being set up. The government of the *RSI* spared no efforts to form a new air force, and eventually three fighter *gruppi* were formed, several pilots who had already achieved both experience and success with the *Regia Aeronautica* serving in these units.

Like Bordoni-Bisleri, Luigi Gorrini had flown in *18° Gruppo* in Africa and Italy. He claimed two victories in spring 1941 while flying CR 42s in Libya, two over Tunisia flying MC 202s early in 1943, and then eleven more over the Rome area flying MC 205s during the summer of 1943, but was then wounded. Joining *1° Gruppo* of the *RSI* on recovery, he continued to fly MC 205s during the early months of 1944, claiming a further four victories to equal Bordoni's score of nineteen. He was then shot down and wounded for a second time in June 1944, his injuries preventing any further flying.

Adriano Visconti is reported to have gained nineteen victories flying MC 202s in Libya and Tunisia and then MC 205s over Sicily by the time of the 1943 armistice. He served later with *1° Gruppo* of the *RSI*, becoming the unit's commander during 1945. During this period he claimed a further seven victories to equal Lucchini's score of twenty-six. However, as the war drew to a close in April 1945 he was killed by Italian pro-Allied partisan forces in Milan.

The second *RSI* unit, *2° Gruppo*, was to produce the two top aces of this force. Mario Bellagambi and Ugo Drago had both flown in the *Regia Aeronautica*, where it is believed that Bellagambi gained several victories. Flying Fiat G-55s and later Messerschmitt Bf 109 Gs with the *RSI*, both pilots claimed eleven victories during 1944-45 over northern Italy.

pages 114-115
Over Eleusis Bay, Athens, a
great fighting career is just about
to be snuffed out. In his
Hawker Hurricane, Squadron
Leader M. T. St. J. Pattle, top-
scorer of the Royal Air Force
during the Second World War,
goes to the aid of a fellow pilot
who is under attack. Seconds
later Pattle's own aircraft went
crashing into the waters of the
Bay, shot down by two
Messerschmitt Bf 110Cs of
II/ZG 26. Pattle was at this
time commanding 33 Squadron
in Greece, where he had claimed
the great majority of his
victories.
By Michael Turner.

The leading Italian aces

Capitano Franco Lucchini	26 (including 5 in Spain)
Maggiore Adriano Visconti	26 (including 7 with the *RSI*)
Sottotenente Leonardo Ferrulli	22 (including 1 in Spain)
Sergente Maggiore Teresio Martinoli	22
Capitano Franco Bordoni-Bisleri	19
Sergente Luigi Gorrini	19 (including 4 with the *RSI*)
Capitano Mario Visentini	17 approximately
Colonello Mario Bonzano	15 at least (all in Spain)
Colonello Duilio Fanali	15
Tenente Luigi Giannella	12
Tenente Adriano Mantelli	12 (all in Spain)
Capitano Mario Bellagambi	11 at least (all with the *RSI*)
Capitano Ugo Drago	11 at least (all with the *RSI*)
Capitano Vasco Magrini	11
Capitano Angelo Mastrogostino	11

MICHAEL TURNER

MICHAEL TURNER

Michael Turner

The Japanese

Although they played a relatively minor role in the First World War, it was not until after that conflict that the Japanese began to provide military aviation services for their armed forces. Despite their late start, the Japanese were quick to appreciate the advantages of air power, particularly when it was exercised in conjunction with a force of aircraft carriers at sea. As Japan was one of the world's leading naval powers this was of considerable importance. Separate army and navy air forces were set up, and while at first foreign assistance was sought, by the early 'thirties a thriving home-based aviation industry had been organized which was turning out aircraft of excellent design. As a result of their study of the First World War, the Japanese stressed manœuvrability as the supreme virtue in their fighter aircraft. They also decided that a very high level of training was of paramount importance.

After 1918, successive Japanese governments, prodded by powerful army elements, pursued an expansionist policy in the Far East which soon led to friction with neighbouring Soviet Russia in the north, and China to the south. It was at the expense of China–torn by internal strife and instability–that most Japanese moves were made. Inevitably, hostilities broke out from time to time, and it was during one of these clashes, in February 1932, that the first Japanese air victory was claimed. A single Boeing 218 demonstration biplane fighter had been delivered to China, and this was being flown for the Chinese by an American pilot, Robert Short, in defence of Shanghai. It was finally brought to bay and shot down on 22 February by three Nakajima A1N (licence-built Gloster Gamecock) biplane fighters of the Japanese navy flying from the aircraft carrier *Kaga*, Short being killed. One of the victorious pilots was NAP3/C (Naval Air Pilot 3rd Class) Toshio Kuroiwa, later to become one of the leading aces of the Sino-Japanese conflict.

No further combat took place for over five years, by which time Japan had two highly trained air forces which were in the process of re-equipment with monoplane aircraft of advanced design. The navy had just begun exchanging its Nakajima A3N biplanes for Mitsubishi A5M monoplanes, while the army was about to start to supplement its Kawasaki Ki.10 biplanes with Nakajima Ki.27s. These new monoplane designs featured fixed, spatted undercarriages and only light armament, but they were supremely manœuvrable.

In July 1937 the Sino-Japanese Incident flared up in North China and an undeclared war began which was eventually to merge into the Second World War, fighting in China not

ceasing until eight years later. In mid-August the fighting spread to Shanghai, where various nations maintained a military presence for the protection of the International Settlement and its trading interests. On 14 August Chinese troops attacked Japanese army elements around the city, which were supported by a small force of army aircraft and by naval aircraft flying from carriers off-shore and the land base at Taipei.

At once naval land-based bombers from Taipei and Kyushu, one of the Japanese home islands, began attacking Chinese targets, suffering severe losses at the hands of Chinese fighters. Japanese attack aircraft from the carrier *Kaga* also suffered heavily, eleven from a formation of twelve failing to return from a raid on Hangchow on 17 August. Chinese raids on Japanese shipping at Shanghai brought up the navy's fighters from *Ryujo*, Yoshio Fukui claiming three victories on the 22nd, and Masaichi Kondo two more next day. It was abundantly clear, however, that the A3N was basically outclassed by the fighters opposing it, while it had neither the range nor the performance to escort the bombers.

As a result *Kaga* was despatched to Japan to load up with new A5Ms, while part of the land-based 2nd Air Flotilla was ordered to Shanghai, including the 13th Air Corps with its 13th Fighter Group, which also flew these fighters. One of the first victories for the new aircraft was claimed by one of *Kaga*'s pilots, Watari Handa, who shot down a Curtiss Hawk biplane over Shanghai on 7 September. A few days later the fighters of the 13th Group, led by Lieutenant Mochifumi Nango, flew their first mission, escorting a raid over Nanking. This unit's first big fight came next day over the same area, and here three future aces each claimed two victories, these being Kiyoto Koga, Toshiyuki Sueda and Tadashi Torakuma. The following day it was again the turn of *Kaga*, Handa claiming three victories, while on the 21st Koshiro Yamashita, flying one of the old A3Ns from *Ryujo*, claimed one and one shared over Canton.

The Chinese were greatly surprised to meet the A5M as far afield as Nanking, and during the rest of 1937 there were frequent fighter battles over this city, the Chinese fighter force being all but wiped out by early December. On the 2nd of that month ten of the new Russian Polikarpov I-16 monoplanes were claimed shot down, and soon after this the Chinese withdrew their air units to Nanchang in central China, beyond the range of the A5M. Nanking fell to Japanese troops just before the turn of the year.

Meanwhile, Kiyoto Koga had become the first Japanese ace on 6 October, claiming three

opposite page
America's Ace of Aces, Major Richard I. Bong, returned to the US as a hero early in 1944, having claimed twenty-eight victories over the New Guinea area. He is seen here in October 1944, after his return to the Far East for a second tour. Covering the landings in the Philippine Islands, he was to claim twelve more victories to raise his total to forty. He and his wingman, in their Lockheed P-38G Lightning fighters of the 49th Fighter Group, are attacking a pair of Nakajima Ki 43 Hayabusa fighters of the JAAF over the island-studded Philippine Sea.
By Michael Turner.

further victories to bring his total to seven. By 9 December he had increased his score to thirteen in six combats, retaining his lead as top-scorer for some months. He was later to be killed in a flying accident during 1938. Other 13th Fighter Group pilots who did well included Kuniyoshi Tanaka with twelve victories, Isamu Mochizuki with nine, Kanichi Kashimura with eight, and Tadashi Torakuma with seven. Kashimura became a national hero on 9 December 1937; during a dogfight over Nanchang, he collided with a Chinese aircraft which cut off the outer one-third of his port wing. Despite this damage he managed to nurse his A5M back to Shanghai and land safely. His crippled fighter was subsequently put on permanent display in Japan as an inspiration to young trainee pilots.

Early in the new year of 1938 the 12th Fighter Group, part of the 2nd Air Flotilla's 12th Air Corps, arrived to join the 13th, having completed re-equipment with A5Ms. Refuelling arrangements had now been made for the fighters at Kuangte, near the front line, this allowing them to stage on to Nanchang, where the Chinese believed their own badly mauled fighter units were out of range of the deadly A5Ms.

On 25 February 1938 both groups engaged Chinese fighters over Nanchang with devastating results. Mamoto Matsumura of the 13th Group claimed four and three probables in one combat, while Sadaaki Akamatsu, who had joined the unit during December 1937, also claimed four. However, honours went to a pilot of the newly arrived 12th Group, Tetsuzo Iwamoto claiming five victories on his first operational sortie to become Japan's first ace-in-a-day. This brilliant performance was no flash in the pan, for Iwamoto went on to claim a total of fourteen victories in eighty-two sorties, returning to Japan in September as top navy ace of the Chinese campaigns.

He was closely followed by Toshio Kuroiwa, one of the victors of the original 1932 combat, who claimed thirteen victories in three months with the 12th Fighter Group during early 1938. Akamatsu, with the 13th, pushed his score up to eleven by September 1938, and other pilots also enjoyed some notable successes. In March, Matsumura was posted from the 13th to the 12th Group, and on the last day of the month claimed three victories over Hankow, his score in China rising to ten during the year.

Meanwhile army fighters had also taken an active part in the fighting, though not on as large a scale as those of the navy. Three units operated over the fighting in North China, while one more, the *10th Chutai*, was sent to Shanghai in September 1937. All four units initially flew Ki. 10 biplanes. The first army victories were claimed on 19 September by the *33rd Sentai*, a flight led by Yoshio Hirose catching six Chinese biplane bombers and shooting down four of them. During the following month this unit withdrew to Manchuria, seeing no further

action for some considerable length of time.

The other units each enjoyed their occasional successes, but these were generally few and far between. Only the *2nd Hiko Datai* enjoyed consistent success, claiming eighty-six victories between October 1937 and May 1938. On 30 January this unit claimed thirteen I-15 biplane fighters shot down; on 25 March nineteen more victories; and twenty-four on 10 April. During the combat of 10 April the first Ki. 27 monoplanes to reach China entered action, one being flown by the unit commander, Major Tateo Kato, who claimed three I-15s. He had already claimed six victories during the two previous battles while flying a Ki. 10, and he now became top-scoring army pilot in the 1937–1941 campaigns in China. In doing so he passed the total of Kousuke Kawahara, who had claimed eight and one shared but had been killed in action on 25 March. Another pilot who became an ace on 10 April was Yonesuke Fukuyama, whose seven victories were all claimed while flying Ki.10s. Subsequently two more of the unit's pilots also became aces, but these five members of the *2nd Datai* were the only army pilots to achieve such scores in China before 1942.

By the end of 1938 most Chinese units had withdrawn deep into the interior, and through 1939 many Japanese bombing raids were made, these suffering a steady series of losses to the Chinese fighters. The Japanese fighter units could do nothing but engage the occasional aircraft that strayed within range of their bases and cooperate with the ground forces.

Fresh action was forthcoming however, and after the navy's successes in South China the Army Air Force was now about to have its day. Manchuria in the late 'thirties was a major sphere of Japanese influence, and powerful forces were stationed there. Friction over an ill-defined border with Mongolia had led to fighting with Soviet-Mongolian forces during summer 1938, but without the participation of Japanese air units. In May 1939 further troubles here led to a severe outbreak of fighting, both Russia and Japan rushing air units to the area. At first air fighting developed only slowly, but by late May strong forces of opposing fighter aircraft were clashing regularly.

The fighting lasted until mid-September, and for the Japanese was an all-army affair. While war was not officially declared, the Nomonhan or Khalkin Gol Incident, as it was variously known, had all the aspects of a full-blown campaign. Overshadowed by events in Europe, it received no publicity in the West, but air battles during the later stages of the fighting were frequently every bit as big as those which would occur a year later during the Battle of Britain.

On the ground the Japanese suffered two severe defeats, but in the air the story was very different. Although outnumbered, the highly

trained and experienced army pilots in their manœuvrable Ki.27s proved more than a match for the Russians, who were to a large extent novices. The area favoured aerial combat; both sides were based close to the front, allowing several sorties to be flown each day, while the flat steppe allowed forced-landings to be made with minimal difficulty when aircraft were damaged in combat. In many ways the situation of the Japanese fighter pilots resembled that in which their German opposite numbers found themselves when in Russia a few years later. Some pilots' scores rose meteorically, and on numerous occasions huge multiple claims were put in for single combats or single days. Such claims were not made by the Japanese in China, nor later in the Pacific War. They were only repeated against the Russians by the Germans and Finns, and later against the Japanese themselves by the Americans.

Most claims were made in whirling fighter dogfights where the opportunities for inadvertent overclaiming are greatest, but the actual Russian losses will probably never be known. Suffice it to say that while well over fifty Japanese pilots became aces during this short undeclared war, only a handful of Russians are known to have made claims of any size at all.

Three Japanese fighter units bore the greatest part of the fighting, the *1st*, *11th* and *24th* *Sentais*, though they were joined in the closing

weeks by the *64th* (formed from the successful *2nd Datai* from China), the *59th*, and the *33rd*. The *11th* enjoyed the most success, producing at least thirty of the aces to the *1st*'s twelve and the *24th*'s ten. As combat fatigue and improved Russian tactics began to tell, casualties among formation leaders mounted, fourteen of the aces – including ten from the *11th Sentai* – were

Fierce fighting over the border between Manchuria and Mongolia during the summer of 1939 brought many victories for the fighter pilots of the Imperial Japanese Army. The fighter which they employed was the Nakajima Ki. 27 Type 97 (Allied code-name 'Nate'), which was highly manœuvrable. This is an aircraft of the *1st Chutai* of the *64th Flying Sentai*, piloted by Sergeant Shigeru Takuwa.

Leading pilots of the *1st Chutai*, *11th Flying Sentai*, in Manchuria during the Nomonham Incident of 1939. On the far left, barely in the picture, is Sergeant-Major Bunji Yoshiyama (twenty victories); behind his left shoulder is Corporal Moritsugu Kanai, who claimed eight victories during the Incident, but later added twenty-six more during the Second World War; next is Second Lieutenant Tomoari Hasegawa (nineteen victories); on the far right, in the polo-neck sweater, is the Japanese Army Air Force top ace, Warrant Officer Hiromichi Shinohara (fifty-eight victories). Shinohara and Yoshiyama were both killed during the final phase of the Incident, shortly after this photograph was taken.

killed, and several others were wounded or died in flying accidents.

Top ace of the conflict was Hiromichi Shinohara of the *11th Sentai*, who was credited with fifty-eight victories, more than twice the number claimed by the next most successful pilot. On his first combat on 27 May Shinohara claimed four Russian fighters, adding six more next day and no less than eleven on 27 June. This latter series of combats took place over his own base and was witnessed by a considerable number of onlookers.

The terrain allowed several rescues of downed pilots to be made by both sides. The first opportunity for the Japanese occurred on 27 June when Bunji Yoshiyama (twenty victories) landed to pick up E. Suzuki and take off again with Suzuki stowed in the fuselage. At least five other such rescues would follow, two involving the picking up of senior officers. The most eventful day was 25 July when the leading ace, Shinohara, was brought down after he had gained four victories. Yutaka Aoyagi (ten victories) landed to rescue him, but his own aircraft was damaged by fire from Russian tanks and he was slightly wounded. Koichi Iwase (ten victories) then also landed, taking off again with both pilots aboard. However, on 27 August, after shooting down his three final victims, Shinohara was himself shot down in flames and was killed. His score was never to be approached by another army pilot.

Thirteen more pilots claimed twenty or more victories during the Incident, while many others

who would later do well during the Second World War gained their first experience of combat and notched up their first few claims. Several pilots showed their dedication during the conflict by ramming Russian aircraft when cut off by large numbers of opponents, but the most bizarre event was probably that which occurred on 7 August. Daisuke Kanbara (nine victories), having shot down a Russian fighter which had crash-landed, landed alongside and cut down his opponent with a Samurai sword, which many Japanese pilots took into combat in their cockpits with them.

Meanwhile in China the inability to reach the Chinese fighters which were savaging the bombers over Chungking and Chengtu demanded urgent action. In summer 1940 the navy was supplied with the first few examples of the superb new Mitsubishi A6M, the famous 'Zero'. The 12th Fighter Group received these aircraft and took them to China, where the aircraft had the range to reach the bombers' target areas and take on the opposing interceptors. On 13 September the I-15s and I-16s were first brought to bay, all of twenty-seven engaged being claimed shot down, Koshiro Yamashita claiming five of them personally.

Thereafter the Zeros swept the sky clear of Chinese fighters whenever these were met, claims for three and four in a combat frequently being made by this 'crack' unit's pilots. On 14 March 1941 twenty-four more were claimed over Chengtu, and on this occasion Masayaki Nakase claimed five and a probable. In September all navy units withdrew from China, the Zeros having claimed ninety-nine destroyed and four probables during their first year of action, losing no aircraft to Chinese fighters.

In China and Manchuria the Japanese had gained much valuable experience, and their fighter pilots were now undoubtedly among the best in the world. Many of the aces of the two conflicts would add to their scores against the Western Allies, but as with the Luftwaffe following its Spanish Civil War experience, not many of the earlier aces were to lead the field again. Among the thirty or so pilots who became aces in China, only three were to claim ten or more further victories in the Pacific war, while of the Nomonhan aces, five were to add substantially to their scores.

Top-scorers in these two conflicts were:

Navy pilots in China		*Army pilots in China*		*Army pilots in Manchuria*	
Tetsuzo Iwamoto	14	Tateo Kato	10	Hiromichi Shinohara	58
Watari Handa	13	Kosuke Kawahara	9	Mitsuyoshi Tarui	28
Kiyoto Koga	13	Mitsugu Sawada	7	Kenji Shimada	27
Toshio Kuroiwa	13	Yonesuke Fukuyama	7	Tomio Hanada	25
Kuniyoshi Tanaka	12			Shogo Saito	25
Sadaaki Akamatsu	11			Shoji Kato	23
Motonari Suho	11			Saburo Togo	22
Momoto Matsumura	10			Zenzaburo Ohtsaka	22
				Hitoshi Asano	22

On 7 December 1941 Japan attacked American, British, Dutch and Australian forces and possessions in the Pacific and South East Asia, and a new air war began which was to last until the summer of 1945. At first the experienced Japanese pilots found their opponents easy prey, the navy pilots in their Zeros and army men in their new Nakajima Ki.43 Hayabusas cutting a swathe through all opposition.

This time the navy was supreme, carrier-based fighter pilots enjoying considerable success in their early clashes with US Navy aircraft, while the pilots of the land-based flotillas achieved even greater success. The latter operated over the Philippines, the Dutch East Indies, and then over New Guinea. In the Tainan Fighter Group, which ended up at Lae in western New Guinea, four of the top eight navy pilots of the Pacific war gained many of their victories.

Later, as losses at Midway, in the Solomons, and in New Guinea began to tell, the quality of new pilots started to fall away. At the same time the numbers, quality of equipment and training of the American and Australian air forces improved, and by 1943 the navy units were mainly on the defensive. Many aces fought on New Britain in defence of the great naval base at Rabaul. Others saw service late in the war in the Philippines, Okinawa, and in the defence of the home islands.

The navy's top-scorer was also Japan's Ace of Aces. Hiroyoshi Nishizawa flew in the East Indies campaign in 1942, and then at Lae with the Tainan Fighter Group. On 7 August 1942 he was credited with six victories in a day over the critical island of Guadalcanal, and by November of that year his score stood at thirty. He subsequently served at Rabaul and in the Philippines, claiming his last two victories while escorting a force of *Kamikaze* suicide bombers on 25 October 1944. He was killed next day

when a transport aircraft in which he was a passenger was shot down by American fighters. Although his final score is listed as eighty-seven, some sources have given it as 102 or even higher.

Tetsuzo Iwamoto, top-scorer in China, only narrowly missed Nishizawa's 'top spot'. Carrier-based on *Zuikaku* until August 1942, he later served at Rabaul, Truk, and in the Philippines. During a single month he claimed twenty victories, including five probables. At the end of the war his score stood at over eighty, more than sixty-six of these victories having been claimed in the Pacific area. He was the highest-scoring Japanese pilot to survive the war.

Japan's fourth-ranking ace is also probably the most famous. Saburo Sakai claimed his first victory in China, then flying in the Tainan Fighter Group. He claimed the first American aircraft to be shot down over the Philippines on 8 December 1941, subsequently operating over Java and New Guinea, where he raised his score to a total reported to be in excess of fifty. Badly wounded during a combat over Guadalcanal, he flew back to Lae, but was then invalided home. He subsequently shot down a number of aircraft over the home islands late in the war, his final score being listed as sixty-four.

One of the 'grand old men' of the navy's fighter force was Sadaaki Akamatsu, who was over thirty when the Pacific war broke out. He flew fighters for fourteen years, putting in more than 6,000 hours in the air. After doing well in China, he fought over the East Indies and later on home defence, his total being of the order of twenty-seven when the war ended.

Kenji Okabe made a name for himself on 8 May 1942 during the Battle of the Coral Sea, the first all-carrier operations naval battle in the world. The previous month Okabe, a pilot on *Shokaku*, had claimed his first victories against British fighters defending Ceylon. Now he

This group of fighter pilots of the *25th Sentai*, seen at Hankow in China in 1944, includes the most successful pilot in that theatre, Second Lieutenant Moritsugu Kanai (front right). After eight victories over Manchuria in 1939, Kanai added twenty-six more in China to become one of the army's top-scorers.

Japan's Ace of Aces, the naval pilot Hiroyoshi Nishizawa. Flying at Lae, New Guinea, he first built up his score during the summer of 1942 in the fierce fighting there. Later in the year he operated over Guadalcanal, where on 7 August 1942 he was credited with six victories in one day; by November his score had reached thirty. Later over Rabaul and the Philippines he pushed his total higher, getting his last victories on 25 October 1944. Next day he was killed when a transport aircraft in which he was a passenger was shot down. His final score is listed at eighty-seven, though it has been quoted variously as high as 102 as the result of the inclusion of 'probable' victories.

claimed eight American naval aircraft from one of the attacking waves, including three probables. He was later land-based at Rabaul, in the Philippines, and at home, ending the war with a score of fifteen.

There were few Japanese night-fighter aces, but one who did well was Sachio Endo. Flying first as a torpedo-bomber pilot and then as pilot of a reconnaissance aircraft, he became a night fighter in March 1944, flying a modification of his reconnaissance Nakajima Gekko aircraft (known by the Allied codename 'Irving'). On 20 August he shot down two B-29 Superfortresses over Kyushu Island, Japan, claiming a third probable and two more damaged. By 14 January 1945 he had shot down seven of these big bombers by night. His final victory was gained by day, but in the same combat he was shot down in flames and killed. Altogether more than ninety navy pilots claimed ten or more victories during the Pacific war, an unknown number claiming between five and ten.

The army played a part in the initial attack on the Philippines and East Indies, and subsequently aided in the fighting over New Guinea. However, its main activities during the first half

of the war were centred on China and Burma. As in the navy, attrition gradually cut down the quality of both pilots and equipment, and many of the men reaching the units late in the war could scarcely be considered trained at all. From 1944 onwards many units fought in the Philippines, where several were wiped out. Others were heavily involved in the defence of the home islands, fighting B-29s and US carrier aircraft. Late in the war the difficulty of successfully intercepting Superfortresses with the equipment available led to the introduction of ramming tactics, which enjoyed some success but resulted in the death of a large percentage of the pilots involved.

Throughout the war at least forty-four army pilots gained ten or more victories, but scores generally were never as high as those in the brief Manchurian fighting, and of these forty-four only about five claimed in excess of twenty victories. It is noteworthy, however, that all five of these leading pilots gained all, or a major part, of their victories in Burma.

Satoshi Anabuki emerged from the war as top-scorer with fifty-one victories. His first were claimed over the Philippines flying the Ki.27, but his unit, the 50th Sentai, then moved to Burma, where in eighteen months he flew 173 sorties and was credited with at least thirty victories, his personal claims during this period numbering forty-eight. He was the first pilot in Burma to shoot down an American B-24 Liberator four-engined bomber, but his most famous combat occurred on 8 October 1943. After claiming two B-24s and two P-38 Lightnings shot down, he rammed a third B-24 and then crash-landed. For this action he received an individual citation – hitherto unknown in the Japanese army for a living pilot. In 1944 he returned to Japan as an instructor, but claimed six more victories while ferrying fighters to the Philippines later in the year, and another over Japan during 1945.

Serving in the 50th Sentai at the same time were two more notable pilots, Isamu Sasaki and Yukio Shimokawa. Sasaki claimed thirty-two victories over Burma by April 1944, later adding six B-29s while flying in defence of Japan. He received the Bukosho, a gallantry decoration introduced late in the war and awarded to only a small number of servicemen. Shimokawa's score in Burma was fifteen, but he was shot down three times himself. On the third occasion, late in 1943, he lost an eye and was invalided home. He shot down a single Hellcat fighter over Japan in 1945 to bring his score to sixteen.

Lieutenant Colonel Tateo Kato has been listed in the past as the army's top-scoring pilot with fifty-eight victories, but in fact his score was eighteen. Famous as the first great army ace in China, he was also a fine leader. After action in China, he led his unit, the 64th Sentai, during the invasion of Malaya, over Sumatra and Java, and then in Burma. On 22 May 1942 he was shot down by the gunner of an RAF Blenheim bomber and crashed into the sea. His wingmen returned to report that he had shot down the bomber before going down himself. It has been reported that he achieved a large number of victories over Manchuria in 1939, but he did not actually fly there. It is thought that he was confused with Shoji Kato, who achieved twenty-three victories there, and that this accounts for the high total previously credited to him by some sources.

Another great leader who served with the *64th* was Yasuhiko Kuroe. After gaining two victories in the Nomonhan fighting with the *59th Sentai*, he led a special test unit equipped with new pre-production Nakajima Ki.44 Shoki fighters during the invasion of Malaya and Singapore, claiming three more victories to become an ace. In spring 1942 he joined the *64th Sentai* in Burma, rising to command of the unit. After twenty-two more victories he returned to Japan to become a test pilot. Here in 1945 he shot down three B-29s in an experimental fighter to bring his total score to thirty.

The top three aces in China were 1st Lieutenant Moritsugu Kanai (twenty-six), Lieutenant Colonel Nakakazu Ozaki (nineteen) and Lieutenant Colonel Yukiyoshi Wakamatsu (eighteen plus). Kanai already had eight victories in Manchuria when he joined the *25th Sentai*, after officer training, in late 1943. In just one year he added twenty-six more, surviving the war. Ozaki led the *2nd Chutai* of the *25th Sentai* during 1943, his unit claiming fifty victories; he was credited with nineteen of these, including six B-24s. On 27 December 1943 over Suichwan, just after becoming a captain, he rammed an

aircraft that was attacking his wingman but was killed in so doing. He was promoted posthumously.

Wakamatsu also received posthumous promotion after his death on 18 December 1944. Flying with the *85th Sentai* from July 1943, he became notorious among the Allied forces as the 'red nose' ace because of the red spinner on his aircraft. The Chinese Nationalist Government is said to have put a price on his head. He was noted as a very good shot, most of his victories being claimed against American fighters.

The most successful army pilot outside the China-Burma area is believed to have been Major Shogo Takeuchi. After service over Malaya and the East Indies with the *64th Sentai*, he flew in New Guinea with the *68th Sentai*. He was the most successful pilot in the unit during 1943, but on 21 December of that year was killed in a landing accident after bringing his score to at least nineteen, sixteen of these being claimed with the *68th*.

Another pilot who did well in New Guinea was Lieutenant Colonel Shigeo Nango, brother of the navy ace of the China campaign, Lieutenant Commander Mochifumi Nango. Leading the *59th Sentai* from March 1942 until early 1944, Shigeo Nango's score was estimated at fifteen when he was shot down and killed over Wewak on 23 January 1944.

One of the most successful Japanese aircraft against American heavy bombers was the twin-engined Kawasaki Ki.45 Soryu, known to the Allies as 'Nick'. Probably its greatest exponent was Captain Totaro Ito, who flew with the *5th Sentai*. Operating initially over Java, he shot down four B-24s over Ambon Island on 17

It was unusual for Japanese pilots to mark their victories on their aircraft, but this Kawasaki Ki. 61 *Hien* fighter (Allied codename 'Tony') is the mount of Major Teruhiko Kobayashi (twelve victories), commanding officer of the *244th Sentai*. Kobayashi claimed all his victories late in the war on home defence, and it will be noted that the silhouettes of fourteen aircraft, all but two of them heavy bombers, are painted beneath the cockpit to indicate his claims – including probables and damaged.

January 1944, making frontal attacks on all of them. Returning to Japan in September, he then shot down at least nine B-29s, although twice having to force-land himself. He was one of the few pilots to receive the Bukosho award.

Late in the war some bomber pilots converted to fighters, and one of these was Major Teruhiko Kobayashi, who made the change in June 1944. The following November he took command of the new *244th Sentai* as the army's youngest unit commander. Flying the Kawasaki Ki.61 Hien (Tony) fighter, he was shot down by return fire from a B-29 on his first combat on 3 December 1944. Escaping unscathed, he returned to ram one of the bombers on 27 January 1945, ending the war with a score of twelve, and a Bukosho. Another home defence Bukosho-holder was Captain Isamu Kashiide. As an NCO he had gained his first two victories in the Manchurian fighting of 1939. After officer training, he served with the *4th Sentai*, flying the twin-engined Soryu, and was involved in intercepting B-29s over Kyushu from mid-1944. By the end of the war he had shot down seven of these bombers, including two on 20 August 1944 and three on 27–28 March 1945. The list below contains the top-scoring Japanese aces from both services in all conflicts.

The leading Japanese aces

Imperial Japanese Navy Air Force

Warrant Officer Hiroyoshi Nishizawa	87
Lieutenant(jg) Tetsuzo Iwamoto	about 80 (14 in China)
Petty Officer 1st Class Shoichi Sugita	about 70
Lieutenant(jg) Saburo Sakai	64 (2 in China)
Petty Officer 1st Class Takeo Okumura	54 (4 in China)
Petty Officer 1st Class Toshio Ohta	34
Warrant Officer Kazuo Sugino	32
Petty Officer 1st Class Shizuo Ishii	29 (3 in China)
Ensign Kaneyoshi Muto	28 (5 in China)
Lieutenant(jg) Junichi Sasai	27
Lieutenant(jg) Sadaaki Akamatsu	27 (11 in China)
Lieutenant Naoshi Kanno	25
Warrant Officer Nobuo Ogiya	24
Lieutenant(jg) Shigeo Sugio	20+

Imperial Japanese Army Air Force

Warrant Officer Hiromichi Shinohara	58 (All in Manchuria, 1939)
Master Sergeant Satoshi Anabuki	51
Lieutenant Mitsuyoshi Tarui	38 (28 in Manchuria, 1939)
Warrant Officer Isamu Sasaki	38
Major Yasuhiko Kuroe	30 (2 in Manchuria, 1939)
Captain Kenji Shimada	27 (All in Manchuria, 1939)
Lieutenant Goichi Sumino	27
Warrant Officer Rikio Shibuta	27 (14 in Manchuria, 1939)
Lieutenant Moritsugu Kanai	34 (8 in Manchuria, 1939)
2nd Lieutenant Shogo Saito	26+ (25 in Manchuria, 1939)
Lieutenant Isamu Hosono	26 (21 in Manchuria, 1939)
Warrant Officer Goro Furugori	25+ (20+ in Manchuria, 1939)
Master Sergeant Tomio Hanada	25 (All in Manchuria, 1939)

The Norwegians

When Norway was invaded by the Germans in April 1940, just one Norwegian fighter squadron, equipped with Gloster Gladiator biplanes, was in existence. Those pilots able to get into the air put up a good fight, but within two days every aircraft was damaged beyond repair. A large number of Norwegian personnel escaped to England, either at the time of the surrender or subsequently. Many were sent to Canada for training, and a number of Free Norwegian squadrons were set up in the RAF, including two fighter units, 331 and 332 Squadrons, both equipped with Spitfires.

No less than fifteen Norwegian fighter pilots became aces, several also reaching high rank. The greatest leader was undoubtedly Helge Mehre, who commanded 331 Squadron on its formation in summer 1941, having first served with an RAF unit. Flying regularly for two years, he claimed five victories, while rising to the leadership of 132 (Norwegian) Wing early in 1943. He was awarded the OBE, DSO and DFC by the British, and after the war became a general in the Royal Norwegian Air Force.

Another leader of great merit was Werner Christie. He first joined 332 Squadron in 1942, becoming commanding officer at the start of 1944. Later in the year he commanded 331

Squadron, but following a rest from operations was posted to lead an RAF Mustang squadron. During the final months of the war in Europe he led the RAF's Andrews Field Mustang Wing, ending the war with eleven victories, a DSO and a DFC.

Initially, the most successful pilot was Marius Eriksen, who joined 332 Squadron as a sergeant in 1942. Within less than a year he had claimed nine victories, at which point he was the leading Norwegian fighter ace. However, on 2 May 1943 he was shot down and became a prisoner of war. His place was then taken by Svein Heglund, who served with 331 Squadron from spring 1942 until autumn 1943, becoming a flight commander and claiming the destruction of eleven and a half German fighters, five probables and several damaged. After a rest he joined the RAF's 85 Squadron to try his hand at flying Mosquito night fighters in support of the bomber streams over Europe. In one month he shot down three German night fighters to bring his final score to at least fourteen and a half. He was decorated three times by the British for his outstanding achievements.

Helmer Grundt-Spang served with Heglund in 331 Squadron, claiming six German fighters and a seventh shared during the same period. He returned for a second tour late in 1944, and on 29 December shot down three Messerschmitt Bf 109s during a series of combats over the Ardennes area of Belgium. One more victory followed to bring his score up to double figures, ten and a third.

The leading Norwegian aces

Captain Svein Heglund	$14\frac{1}{2}$
Lieutenant Colonel Werner Christie	11
Captain Helmer G. E. Grundt-Spang	$10\frac{1}{3}$
Major Martin Y. Gran	$9\frac{1}{2}$
Captain Marius Eriksen	9

below, left
Norway's leading ace, Flight Lieutenant Svein Heglund is seen here with his Spitfire 9 after a combat during 1943. He had just shot down a Focke-Wulf FW 190, but debris from his victim had damaged his own aircraft, as can be seen here.

below
The destruction of a Focke-Wulf FW 190 over Western Europe, recorded by the camera-gun of a Norwegian pilot.

125

The Poles

The German attack on Poland in September 1939 found that country with a small but efficient air force, which was well trained but equipped with mainly obsolescent aircraft. Contrary to popular belief, the Polish air force was not destroyed on the ground during the first hours of the war. Although outnumbered by aircraft of generally superior performance, it put up a splendid resistance, taking a heavy toll of the Luftwaffe. Flying their elderly high-wing PZL P-XI monoplanes, the Polish fighter pilots claimed 126 victories, the most successful being Stanislav Skalski of 142 Squadron, who was credited with four individual and one shared victories, including two Dornier Do 17 bombers shot down on the second day of the war. After the war a review of claims was undertaken by the Polish authorities, and Skalski was then credited with a further two victories.

When all was clearly lost, a large number of Polish pilots escaped via Rumania to France. Others made their way to the Mediterranean and thence to Paris or London. In France a special Polish fighter unit was set up, while other pilots were attached in flights to normal *Armée de l'Air* units, or formed local factory defence units known as 'Chimney Flights'. During the *Blitzkrieg* of May–June 1940 these Poles, equipped with second-rate aircraft, were able to claim only a few further successes, although they fought with great tenacity. However, many of them escaped the holocaust and made their way to the United Kingdom.

As with other foreign nationals, those who were already trained were initially posted to ordinary RAF squadrons, while special Polish units were formed as a Free Polish Air Force existing within the body of the RAF. Poland's two top-scorers both began their service in England with RAF units in this way, Witold Urbanowicz flying Hurricanes with 145 Squadron, while Skalski flew similar fighters with 501 Squadron, claiming four more victories with this unit during summer 1940, becoming the first official Polish ace of the war.

Urbanowicz claimed two victories with his unit, but was then posted to command a flight in 303 Squadron, the first Polish fighter squadron to enter action. Entering the fray late in August, this famous unit, known by the name *Kosciuszko*, quickly made a great name for itself, the dashing and aggressive Poles swiftly building up one of the highest unit scores of the Battle of Britain.

The top-scoring pilot of this unit initially was the Czech Josef Frantisek; on 26 September Frantisek's Battle of Britain score stood at fourteen, Urbanowicz's at nine. Next day Frantisek added two more, but Urbanowicz claimed four, and on 30 September, when Frantisek claimed his last victory, bringing his score in England to seventeen, the Pole again claimed four to equal him. Heavily decorated by Polish and British authorities, he was rested until 1941, when he undertook a second tour leading the Polish Wing at Northolt. Bored with lack of activity over Western Europe during the mid-war years, he volunteered to fly for the Americans in China. His offer was accepted, and at the age of thirty-eight he claimed victories over three Japanese fighters during 1944 to end the war as Poland's greatest ace with twenty victories (although the reassessment of Skalski's score after the war was to push him into second place). After the war he became a US citizen.

Six other pilots became aces with 303 Squadron during 1940, including Zdislaw Henneburg, Jan Zumbach and Eugeniusz Szaposznikow, all with eight victories apiece, and Miroslaw Feric with seven. Three other pilots did particularly well with RAF squadrons: flying Hurricanes with 501 Squadron, Anthoni Glowacki claimed eleven, including three Stukas on 15 August, and five aircraft–three Bf 109s and two Ju 88 bombers–during three sorties on 24 August; another Hurricane pilot was Jozef Jeka, who claimed five and one shared with 238 Squadron, while Fadenaz Nowierski claimed a similar score flying Spitfires with 609 Squadron. All three pilots survived the war, Jeka later raising his score to eight and a half.

Throughout 1941 and 1942 Poles played a major role in the cross-Channel sweeps and fighter battles, several pilots running up their scores at this time, though casualties began to mount. While Zumbach pushed his score up to over twelve by late 1942 Henneberg and Feric were both shot down and killed. Another pilot to be lost during 1942 was Wing Commander Marion Pisarek; credited with two and one shared victories in Poland and four during the Battle of Britain, Pisarek's score had risen to twelve and a half by the end of 1941, during which year he led 308 Polish Squadron. Promoted to lead the Polish No. 1 Wing during April 1942, he was killed in action only eleven days later.

Meanwhile Skalski had claimed four more victories during 1941 with 306 Squadron, followed by another during 1942 at the head of 316 Squadron. Early in 1943 a special unit of veteran Polish volunteer pilots was formed to go to Tunisia as part of the Desert Air Force to fly some of the first Spitfire 9s to reach the Mediterranean area. Skalski led this unit in the air, and with him was a young pilot, Eugeniusz Horbaczewski, who had been credited with three victories during 1942 with 303 Squadron, but who had fallen foul of his commanding officer, Squadron Leader Jan Zumbach.

Operating over North Africa during the last weeks of the fighting, the Polish Fighting Team achieved considerable success, Horbaczewski and Skalski emerging as the two most successful pilots with five and four victories respectively. Both pilots volunteered to remain with Desert Air Force when the Team was disbanded in June 1943, becoming the first Poles to command RAF units, Skalski leading 601 Squadron and Horbaczewski 43 Squadron. During the Salerno landings in September of that year, the latter was to claim three more victories to bring his score to eleven.

After a rest from operations, both pilots joined 133 Polish Wing at Northolt, flying Mustang 3 long-range fighters, Skalski as Wing Leader, Horbaczewski as commanding officer of 315 Squadron. Operating over Normandy during the invasion of June 1944, Skalski claimed his final two victories on 24 June to bring his score to nearly nineteen then, and

nearly twenty-one subsequently. Horbaczewski also added further victories, and on one occasion landed near the front to pick up a wounded fellow-pilot and fly him back to base. During July and August he intercepted and shot down a number of V-1 flying bombs, and by mid-August his score of aircraft stood at thirteen and a half. On the 18th he led his unit over France in a very successful dogfight in which a large number of Fw 190s were claimed shot down. He was seen to account personally for three, but his own aircraft was then shot down and he was killed – the only pilot lost by the Poles in this fight.

Several Polish pilots volunteered to fly with the USAAF during 1943, most of them flying P-47 Thunderbolts in the 56th Fighter Group of the 8th Air Force. Several Polish aces claimed victories while flying with the Americans, among them B. M. Gladych, who claimed an Me 262 jet shot down. By the end of the war at least forty-three Poles had become aces.

Wing Commander Stanislav Skalski was the only Polish pilot to become an ace during the fighting in September 1939 – though this was not known at the time, as two of his early claims were not confirmed until the records were re-examined after the war. He served with the RAF from 1940, both in England and later in North Africa. In 1944 he led one of the Polish Mustang wings, raising his total to over twenty as top Polish ace of the war. He is seen here in his Mustang 3 in 1944, his score marked beneath his cockpit.

The leading Polish aces

Wing Commander Stanislav F. Skalski	$20\frac{11}{12}$ ($6\frac{1}{4}$ in Poland)
Wing Commander Witold Urbanowicz	20 (3 in China)
Squadron Leader Eugeniusz Horbaczewski	$16\frac{1}{2}$ + 4 V-1s
Major Boleslaw M. Gladych	14 (at least 2 with the USAAF)
Wing Commander Marion Pisarek	$12\frac{1}{2}$ ($2\frac{1}{2}$ in Poland)
Squadron Leader Jan E. L. Zumbach	$12\frac{1}{3}$
Squadron Leader Anthoni Glowacki	$11\frac{1}{3}$
Pilot Officer Michael K. Maciejowski	$10\frac{1}{2}$
Wing Commander Henryk Szczesny	$10\frac{1}{3}$

The Rumanians

Rumania proved to be one of Germany's major allies on the Eastern Front, fighting alongside Hitler's forces on the southern sector of the front from June 1941 to September 1944 when the Red Army poured across the Rumanian frontier, forcing an armistice. Throughout this time units of the Rumanian air force were operational at the front, initial equipment of Messerschmitt Bf 109Es, Heinkel He 112Bs and PZL P-24s gradually being replaced by Bf 109Gs and home-designed and built IAR 80s and 81s.

Following the first American bombing attack on the Ploesti oil refineries in August 1943, the defence of this target, and of the homeland itself, necessitated the withdrawal of many units from Russia, and much of the later aerial combat experienced by the Rumanians was against the US 15th Air Force, which operated from southern Italy.

Regrettably, less is known about the Rumanian fighter pilots than about those of any of the other European powers, and little information

can be given. The top-scorer appears to have been Captain Prince Constantine Cantacuzene, credited with some sixty victories, the majority apparently gained while flying the Bf 109. When the downfall of his country became inevitable he flew south to give himself up to the Western Allies in Italy.

Another Messerschmitt pilot of note was Captain Alexandre Serbanescu, who first flew in Russia and subsequently commanded a unit at Pepira, Rumania, for the defence of Ploesti. He was shot down and killed by American aircraft on 18 August 1944, after claiming his fiftieth victory. One of his pilots operating from Pepira was Lieutenant Florian Budu, believed to have been credited with over forty victories.

The leading Rumanian aces provisional list

Captain Prince Constantine Cantacuzene	60
Captain Alexandre Serbanescu	50
Lieutenant Florian Budu	40+
Lieutenant Jon Milu	18

The Russians

Like several other nations, the Soviet Union became engaged in an almost unceasing succession of aerial combats from 1936 until 1945. When civil war broke out in Spain, early assistance to the Nationalist insurgent forces by Germany and Italy was swiftly matched by Russian aid to the Spanish Republican Government. By the end of 1936 substantial numbers of Polikarpov I-15 biplane and I-16 monoplane fighters had been despatched to Spain, together with bomber and reconnaissance aircraft and volunteer aircrews.

While most of the new aircraft were initially flown by Russians, some I-15s were supplied for use by the Spanish and foreign volunteer pilots already at the front, and arrangements were made to train numbers of Spanish aircrew recruits in the Soviet Union. At this stage the main opposing fighter type in Spain was the German Heinkel He 51 biplane, and both Soviet fighter types proved to be well able to master this aircraft. As early as November 1936, one of the Russian pilots, Lieutenant Palancer, had shot down four of the Heinkels in a relatively brief period, and by early 1937 the German and Spanish pilots flying these aircraft were forced to avoid combat and concentrate on ground attack. When opposed by the Italian Fiat CR 32 biplane, both Russian aircraft were found to be fairly evenly matched, pilot quality and luck then being the deciding factors.

Throughout 1937 the Russian pilots continued to bear the brunt of the Republicans' aerial activity, and several of them began to build up good scores. The first pilot to receive the Hero of the Soviet Union award for activities in Spain was Boris Turshanski, the son of a former Polish nobleman. Flying the I-16 monoplane, this pilot was credited with some six victories, but was wounded in combat and lost one eye. Returning to Russia, he was rapidly promoted to the rank of Brigade Commander, but was shot in one of the Stalinist purges in 1938.

In 1938 the flow of Spanish pilots trained in Russia allowed many of the Soviet volunteers to be replaced, while the continued Nationalist successes began to blunt Russia's enthusiasm for continuing to support what was now clearly becoming a lost cause. By this time a number of pilots had emerged as the top-scorers, the most successful being A. K. Serov, with sixteen victories. Close behind him was P. V. Rychagov with fifteen, I. T. Yeremenko with fourteen, S. P. Denisov and Vladimir I. Bobrov with thirteen each, and Ivan A. Lakeiev with twelve plus shares in several others. Of these six pilots, Serov, Denisov and Lakeiev later reached the rank of general, but Serov was killed during

a flying accident in May 1939. Like Turshanski, Rychagov was later shot. Lakeiev later added one further victory to his total during the Khalkin Gol Incident in 1939, flying against the Japanese.

While the fighting over Spain was raging, Russian aid was being channelled elsewhere. Although the Soviet Union and Chiang Kai-Shek's Nationalist Government in China had never enjoyed cordial relations, Japan was considered a much greater threat to Russian security, and the beginning of the Sino-Japanese 'Incident' in July 1937 led to the supply of Russian fighter aircraft to the Chinese during the autumn of that year. Volunteer units of Russian fighters and bombers followed close behind the initial aid.

The most successful Russian pilot over China appears to have been Piotr K. Kozachenko, who became a Hero of the Soviet Union after shooting down eleven Japanese aircraft. He subsequently commanded a fighter regiment during the Second World War, and is believed to have gained several more victories before being killed over Berlin during April 1945. The Russian volunteers in China were able to gain a number of successes against Japanese bomber formations, but found the pilots of the Imperial Navy, in their nimble Mitsubishi A5M monoplanes, extremely dangerous opponents.

During summer 1938 fighting with the Japanese flared up on the borders of Mongolia and Manchuria, Russian fighters and bombers operating over the area but meeting no opposition in the air. The following May came the Khalkin Gol, or Nomonhan Incident, border fighting escalating into a major undeclared war which lasted four bitter months. Three full regiments of fighters were employed by the Russians, several of the unit commanders and formation leaders being pilots with experience in Spain or China, while others were ex-test pilots. However, most of the pilots involved were relatively inexperienced, and losses in some of the big dogfights that occurred are believed to have been quite severe. Several pilots who would later become notable during the Second World War fought here.

One of the leading pilots of this short war was Grigori P. Kravchenko. After service as a test pilot, Kravchenko flew in China, where he claimed at least three victories, though he was shot down himself on one occasion by four Japanese fighters and had to bale out. He then led an I-16 unit in Mongolia which enjoyed considerable success; he became a Hero of the Soviet Union for his leadership here, and was also reputed to be the most successful individual pilot, with a score of some fifteen victories. He later reached the rank of Lieutenant General, but was killed in action against the Germans on 22 February 1943.

As the fighting with the Japanese army was drawing to a close in September 1939, other Russian fighters took part in the occupation of eastern Poland following the signing of the Russo-German Non-Aggression Pact. No opposition was encountered in the air, since the Polish air force had already been destroyed in the desperate battles with the Luftwaffe further to the west.

A little under three months later there were fresh hostilities, this time over the Karelian Isthmus, following a refusal by Finland to cede territory and bases required by the Soviet Union for the defence of Leningrad. Expecting little resistance, the Russian units committed for this operation were generally inexperienced. However, the sustained and vigorous reaction of the small but efficient Finnish armed forces led to a long, hard winter campaign. Further units of first-line fighters were moved to the area, and some quite severe combats with Finnish Fokker D.XXIs, Gladiators and other aircraft took place, peace not being restored until an armistice was signed in March 1940.

There followed fifteen months of relative quiet, while efforts were made to re-equip the Soviet aviation units with more modern aircraft, including such fighter types as the Yakovlev Yak-1, Mikoyan MiG-1 and 3, and Lavochkin LaGG-3. During the late 'thirties, however, the purges launched by Stalin had robbed the armed forces of many of their most promising and energetic officers, the air force being no exception. As has already been mentioned, at least two of the leading aces from the Spanish war, together with many others who had gained invaluable experience there, were removed and liquidated. This undoubtedly had an adverse effect upon the efficiency and training of the forces as a whole, and caused many other officers to bury their personal initiative and behave in a most circumspect manner.

On 22 June 1941 came the sudden German invasion, and within days the Soviet Union found herself beset not only by Germany but also by Rumania, Hungary and Italy, while Finland, too, was soon brought into the war. In the background hovered the spectacle of the threat of a second front in Mongolia, should the Japanese decide to support their fellow-members of the Anti-Comintern Pact and launch an attack.

The shock and fury of the initial onslaught hit the Russians very hard. Large numbers of aircraft were destroyed on the ground, while many of those pilots who did manage to get into the air found themselves outclassed both in aircraft performance and individual experience by the confident Messerschmitt pilots of the Luftwaffe. Despite these disadvantages, many

pilots managed to survive and fight on. As they gradually improved their own performance and received better aircraft, they were able to face their opponents on more equal terms.

Initially there were many examples of selfless gallantry, as Russian pilots threw themselves into the attack with almost reckless abandon, many cases of ramming being reported during the German drives on Moscow and Leningrad. By a supreme effort, war production was withdrawn almost entirely to the east of the Ural Mountains, beyond the range of German air attack, and superhuman efforts were made to increase the production of new fighter and ground-attack aircraft.

At first Russia's only ally was Great Britain. Despite their own peril, the British despatched Hurricane fighters to Russia in 1941, later allowing shipments of American Lease-Lend Bell Airacobras and Curtiss Tomahawks and Kittyhawks to be diverted to the Soviet Union. Once the first German advances finally came to a halt and winter arrived, a massive front stretching from the Arctic to the Black Sea came into being, manned by millions of soldiers, supported by tens of thousands of tanks, guns and aircraft.

With each spring came new offensives, many of these being launched in the south, precipitating huge air battles during which aircraft fell in their hundreds. In 1942 the Germans retained the initiative until the desperate struggle at Stalingrad (September 1942–February 1943) saw the tide begin to turn. After another grim winter, the Germans staked everything in a last supreme effort at Kursk. They were decisively beaten, and from then onwards it was a matter of time, the Russians steadily driving the

A veteran of the Spanish Civil War, the Russo-Finnish war, and the fighting with the Japanese in China and Manchuria, the Polikarpov I-16 was still the most numerous Soviet fighter at the time of the German invasion in June 1941. Many Russian aces flew these fighters early in the struggle, gaining successes despite their obsolescence. These aircraft are late production I-16 Type 24s, with more powerful engines and increased armament.

The highly respected fighter pilot and test pilot, Lieutenant Colonel Stepan Suprun, who claimed eight victories against the Japanese over China and Manchuria, and then four against the Germans at the start of the Great Patriotic War in June 1941. He was killed in combat on 4 July 1941, receiving a second award of the Hero of the Soviet Union posthumously.

invaders back across Eastern Europe and into the territory of the Reich.

Gradually the quality of new pilots arriving at the front improved, and from 1943 onwards increasing numbers of excellent Yak-3, Yak-9, La-5 and La-7 fighters reached the front. During 1944 the steady withdrawal of German fighter units for the defence of the Reich weakened German resistance in the air. Numbers were made up by the re-equipment of dive-bombers, but most of the pilots were not properly trained for air fighting, while the general decline in the quality of Luftwaffe pilot training allowed the Soviet fighters to wrest aerial superiority from the Messerschmitts and Focke-Wulfs. Only on isolated occasions, when special efforts were made to gain local superiority for a brief period, were the Germans able to achieve some semblance of their previous dominance. It was, however, always a tough fight for the Russians, and those who survived to build up big scores were undoubtedly among the finest fighter pilots in the world.

Certainly the continued intensity of combat on the Eastern Front allowed the Russian pilots to emerge with the highest personal scores of all the Allied nations during the Second World War. As in most air forces, however, some of the most outstanding and respected pilots, although aces, were not among those with the highest scores. One such case was Lieutenant Colonel Stepan P. Suprun, a fighter pilot of long standing at the start of the war. In 1938 Suprun led two *eskadrilli* of I-16s to China, where he fought as a volunteer. It appears that he also served in Mongolia the following year, and his total score against the Japanese air forces is reported to have been eight. Immediately following this active service, he became a test pilot, and in 1940 was made a Hero of the Soviet Union for his work testing the new I-180 and Yak-1 fighters. The outbreak of war in June 1941 found him commanding a special volunteer fighter unit, the *401st Polk* (a *Polk* was a fighter regiment), equipped with the latest MiG-3s. He was very active during the first weeks of the war, apparently claiming a further four victories at least at this time, but on 4 July he was killed while defending an airfield in the Tolochinsk region. On 22 July came the posthumous award of a second Hero of the Soviet Union medal, Suprun being the first pilot in the Great Patriotic War to receive such a second award. His final score is believed to be of the order of twelve to fifteen.

Major Arsenii V. Vorozheikin, one of Russia's most successful fighter pilots, also enjoyed a long and varied career of active service. During 1939 he flew with an I-16 unit in Mongolia as commissar, claiming six Japanese aircraft shot down to become one of the Soviet top-scorers in this campaign. Subsequently he served in Finland in 1940, and 1941 found him still flying

I-16s with the *728th Polk*. His unit retained this obsolescent equipment for some time, and it was not until mid-1943 that it finally re-equipped with modern Yak-7Bs. Now Vorozheikin's score rose quickly, and during 1944 he twice received the Hero of the Soviet Union award. His score at the end of the war stood at fifty-two, forty-six of these claimed during the Great Patriotic War.

1941 found Aleksandr I. Pokryshkin a flight commander in the *55th Polk*, flying MiG-3 fighters. At this time he little realized that he would soon be looked upon with reverence as the father of Soviet fighter tactics and their greatest exponent. On 23 June, the second day of the war, while engaged in escorting SB-2 bombers, he shot down a Messerschmitt Bf 109E of *Jagdgeschwader* 77 near Jassy. Flying a reconnaissance mission over the Beltsy area in his MiG on 20 July 1941, his aircraft was hit by anti-aircraft fire and he had to come down in German territory. Evading capture, he made his way back to his own lines, this being the first of four occasions on which he was shot down during the war. He volunteered for another lone reconnaissance on 20 November 1941, and on this occasion discovered von Kleist's Panzers approaching Rostov in a snowstorm. His timely warning to the defenders earned him the Order of Lenin.

His score continued to rise steadily, and at the same time he was instrumental in devising and introducing many of the fighter tactics which became standard for the Red Air Force throughout the war. On one occasion he led his *eskadril* to attack two formations, each of eight Stukas, and personally claimed the destruction of four of these. By early 1943 his score had risen to nearly twenty, and he now commanded an *eskadril* of P-39 Airacobras in the *16th Guards Polk*, part of the 216th Fighter Division.

Heavily involved in the fierce battles over the Caucasus during 1943, he proved to be a great leader and teacher. No less than thirty of the pilots who served under him were to become Heroes of the Soviet Union, and between them were to claim some 500 Axis aircraft shot down. By mid-1944 Pokryshkin had become a Colonel and commander of the 9th Guards Fighter Division. The Germans held him in great esteem and credited him in their intelligence sources with far higher scores than did the Russian authorities. During the fighting over the Kuban, whenever the German radio listening services ascertained that he had become airborne, warnings were broadcast to Luftwaffe aircraft: 'Achtung! Der As Pokryshkin in der Luft!' (Attention! The Ace Pokryshkin is in the air!).

Having been top-scoring Soviet ace during much of the war, Pokryshkin was pushed into second place early in 1945 by Ivan Kozhedub; nevertheless, he retained a very special place in Russian hearts. Three times a Hero of the

Soviet Union, he also received the Order of Lenin and the Gold Star three times, as well as numerous Allied decorations, including the American DSC. Although he ended the war flying a Yak-9, forty-eight of his fifty-nine victories were claimed while flying the Airacobra.

Lieutenant Commander Boris F. Safonov was a pilot in the Red Naval Air Force, commanding the *72nd Fighter Polk*. Initially flying I-16s, he claimed his first victory, a Heinkel He 111 bomber, in the Murmansk area on 24 June 1941. This was the first Axis aircraft to be shot down on the northern front. After nearly three months' combat with the I-16, his unit became the first to receive foreign aircraft, converting to the Hawker Hurricanes which had been brought to Archangel by the RAF's 151 Wing.

These British fighters were used for about six months, and then in the spring of 1942 further re-equipment took place, this time with American Kittyhawks. By May Safonov's score had risen to over twenty, and he was one of the leading Russian aces. However, on 30 May he was struck down. Three Soviet fighters were providing cover to PQ 18, an Arctic convoy from the United Kingdom, when a large force of Ju 88s, escorted by Messerschmitts of *Jagdgeschwader 5*, attacked. Four bombers were claimed shot down, two by Safonov, in the first interception. He then attacked a third, hitting its engines, but was seen to go down into the icy sea.

There is some confusion surrounding his fate, some records indicating that he crashed after being hit by the bomber's defensive fire, others that he was shot down by the great German ace of *JG 5*, Rudolf Müller. It has also been suggested that he was flying a Yak-1 during this last mission, rather than a Kittyhawk, but no confirmation of this has been found. At the time of his death he was credited with at least twenty-five victories (some sources have indicated a total as high as forty-one) and had become a Hero of the Soviet Union. He was posthumously awarded a second HSU, the first pilot to receive two awards during the Great Patriotic War. He was also the first of the great Russian aces to die.

Guards Major Vladimir D. Lavrinenkov was an instructor in June 1941, but managed to get himself posted to the front some months later. Joining the *69th Polk*, he flew I-16s initially on the Bryansk front, gaining four victories here. He then operated over the River Volga during 1942, and when he shot down a Bf 109 on 26 August of that year, his score had risen to nine. By now he was flying Yak fighters in defence of Stalingrad, often escorting Ilyushin Il-2 *Sturmovik* ground-attack aircraft over the front.

His score rose rapidly, and during one month of fighting he claimed sixteen victories. By the end of April 1943 he was credited with twenty-six, becoming a Hero of the Soviet Union on May Day. He had just shot down an Fw 187 reconnaissance aircraft over Matveyeyer Kurgana on 23 August 1943 when his own aircraft was hit, forcing him to bale out. Having been taken prisoner, he managed to escape with another officer by leaping from a moving train. He crossed the River Dnieper, joined a partisan band and spent some months with it, making raids behind German lines. The advance of the Russian armies in spring 1944 finally allowed him to return to the Red Air Force, and he was soon back in the air. On 1 July 1944 he was promoted to command a fighter regiment, and at the same time became a Hero of the Soviet Union for the second time. He ended the war with thirty-five victories and shares in eleven others, subsequently becoming a Lieutenant General during the early 'sixties.

Another pilot who served with Lavrinenkov in the *69th Polk* was Guards Colonel Aleksei V. Alelyukhin. His first victories were gained while flying an I-16, and during fighting over Odessa he claimed three Ju 87s shot down and five more shared. His unit converted to Yak fighters for the Stalingrad fighting during the summer and autumn of 1942, while early 1943 found him in action over Rostov. Here he took part in the destruction of ten Axis bombers, and by August 1943 his score stood at eleven individual and six shared victories; at this stage he gained his first Hero of the Soviet Union award. He claimed fifteen more victories during the next two months, receiving a second HSU award during October. Following this early fighting, he later became a very successful unit commander, showing considerable qualities of leadership. When the war ended, his score stood at forty, with shares in a further seventeen.

A number of the most successful Soviet fighter pilots flew in Pokryshkin's 9th Guards Fighter Division for a substantial part of their time at the front. After flying I-153 biplanes and I-16s, Captain Grigori A. Rechkalov operated Airacobras with the 9th, claiming forty-four of his fifty-eight victories while piloting these aircraft, including nineteen during the Kuban battles of 1943. Captain Aleksandr F. Klubov first flew in the 'crack' *16th Guards Polk* on I-153s and then MiG-3s, once taking on six Bf 109s in one of the latter and shooting down two. He did very well on Airacobras, particularly during the Jassy battle of early 1944, emerging as top-scorer with nine victories in five days. Between 10 August 1943 and November 1944 he flew 457 sorties and claimed thirty-one victories to bring his score to fifty, but during the latter month he was killed in a crash while converting with the rest of the unit from Airacobras to La-7s.

Commanding one of the *eskadrilli* of the 9th was Vladimir I. Bobrov, the one pilot with a high score in Spain who also did well during the Great Patriotic War. From 1941 to the end of

Top-scoring Russian fighter pilot and leading Allied ace of the war, Ivan Kozhedub, who first saw action over the Kursk battlefield in July 1943. His final total was sixty-two.

Colonel Aleksandr Pokryshkin was leading Russian ace throughout much of the war, and was looked upon as the 'father' of Soviet fighter tactics. A great leader as well as a great fighter pilot, he trained many of the other Russian high-scorers.

Guards Colonel Kirill Yevstigneyev was one of the later aces of the war. Flying Lavochkin fighters with the 13th Guards Fighter Division, he claimed twelve in nine combats during October 1943, continuing to score fast during 1944. He twice became a Hero of the Soviet Union, the second time during February 1945, and ended the war with fifty-two victories.

the war he claimed thirty more victories and became a Lieutenant Colonel, though he was one of the few high-scorers not to become a Hero of the Soviet Union. Another successful Airacobra pilot was Major Nikolai D. Gulayev, who had four victories to his credit in June 1941 from one of the earlier conflicts. He twice successfully led small formations against much larger numbers, on the second occasion personally claiming five of the eleven aircraft shot down. His final total was fifty-seven, of which thirty-six were claimed while flying Airacobras.

The Airacobra, so vilified by other Allied pilots yet so effectively employed by the Russians, was also flown by a pair of famous brothers, Dmitri and Boris Glinka. Dmitri was one of the first great aces of the war, initially flying MiGs and Yaks. Flying with Ivan I. Babak as his wingman, he had claimed thirty victories by the end of the Kuban battles of 1943, Babak having also claimed nine, and Dmitri's brother Boris having claimed twenty. Babak later flew as an element leader himself, raising his score to thirty-eight. Boris reached thirty and Dmitri brought his final score to fifty, twenty-seven while flying Airacobras. Both brothers twice became Heroes of the Soviet Union, and on one occasion, shortly after Dmitri's second award, they shot down seven bombers between them in a single day.

Guards Colonel Kirill A. Yevstigneyev flew Lavochkin fighters with the 13th Guards Fighter Division. During October 1943 he came to the fore when he claimed twelve aircraft shot down during nine combats. He later did very well over the Jassy area during 1944, receiving his second HSU award in February 1945. With 300 sorties and 120 air battles in his logbook, his final score was fifty-two.

Several of the Soviet Union's earliest aces were naval fighter pilots in the north, one of these being Major Aleksei S. Khlobystov. The fiery Khlobystov gained particular fame for claiming three of his thirty victories by ramming. On the first occasion he got too close to an He 111 in his Curtiss Tomahawk and hit its wing with his propeller, whereupon the bomber crashed. Later, when his guns froze up and refused to fire, he deliberately used his propeller to cut off his opponent's tail. On another occasion he was attacked by a number of Bf 109s; after shooting down two Bf 109s, his Tomahawk was hit and set on fire. He then deliberately rammed a third before baling out. Other naval pilots who did particularly well included Senior Lieutenant Nikolai F. Kuznetsov, who claimed thirty-six victories, many of them while flying a Curtiss Kittyhawk.

Russia was the one nation to make full operational use of women as aircrew, both fighter and bomber regiments being manned by female personnel. At least two of the ladies were to become aces, the most successful being 2nd Lieutenant Lilya Litvak, a member of the

73rd Polk. Flying 130 sorties over the Rostov and Stalingrad areas in a Yak-1, she took part in sixty-six combats and claimed twelve or thirteen victories in one year. She became a Heroine of the Soviet Union, but was killed in action over Orel on 1 September 1943 at the age of twenty-one.

The greatest ace of the Soviet Union, Ivan N. Kozhedub, proved to be almost too good a pilot. Because of his skill during training he was retained as an instructor, and was unable to get to the front until June 1943. Joining the 16th Air Army, he flew La-5s during the great Kursk battle of July 1943. Indeed, his first battle was almost his last, for he was badly shot up by German fighters. On 6 July he recorded his first victory, over a Ju 87, and soon he was given command of an *eskadril.* During autumn 1943 he claimed eleven victories in ten days over Kiev.

During 1944 he served in a 'crack' regiment, which was switched from front to front as the situation demanded. His score rose fast, and when his unit converted to the latest La-7s, he had claimed forty-five victories. By the end of 1944 his score stood at fifty-seven, but by then German aircraft were becoming scarce on the Eastern Front. On 12 February 1945 he shot down two Fw 190 fighter-bombers, equalling Pokryshkin's score of fifty-nine. Three days later he spotted an Me 262 jet, the first to be seen in the East, and managed to surprise it and shoot it down. On 19 April he scored again, he and another pilot bouncing forty unsuspecting Fw 190Ds, allowing Kozhedub to add his last two victories to his score. With sixty-two victories, he was top-scoring Russian and Allied ace of the war. He was the only fighter pilot other than Pokryshkin to become a Hero of the Soviet Union three times.

While the story of Douglas Bader, the RAF's gallant legless pilot, is well known, far less familiar are the stories of the Russian pilots who also lost limbs and returned to fight again. These were Major Alexei P. Maras'ev, who claimed nineteen victories, and naval pilot Zakhar A. Sorokin, who claimed eighteen. Maras'ev was flying Yak-1 fighters during early 1942, and his score stood at six by April of that year. Escorting Il-2s to attack a German airfield, he then shot down two Junkers Ju 52 transport aircraft which were taking off, but was shot down by ten Bf 109s and crashed. Although he managed to emerge from the wreckage alive, both his feet were crushed and he was only able to crawl through the snow in an effort to return to Russian lines. By a tremendous force of will, he kept going for nineteen days, living on berries, ants and hedgehogs. On one occasion he had to shoot a bear with his revolver. Finally he was picked up by partisans and air-evacuated. By this time gangrene had set in, and both legs had to be amputated. Despite this tremendous handicap, he was back with his unit by July 1943, in time for the Kursk battles, now flying an La-5. On his first flight, on 6 July, he shot down one of twenty Stukas. Next day in a big combat with Fw 190s, he claimed three shot down, and again claimed three in a day on the 14th.

The terrible bloodbath of the Eastern Front claimed thousands of pilots of both sides. It is not known how many Russians became aces, but at least fifty claimed thirty or more victories, while another 153 got between twenty and twenty-nine. Between them these 203 pilots received 173 awards of the Hero of the Soviet Union Gold Star for their gallantry and sacrifice during the Great Patriotic War.

The leading Russian aces

Ivan N. Kozhedub	62	Ivan M. Pilipenko	48
Aleksandr I. Pokryshkin	59	Vasilii N. Kubarev	46
Grigori A. Rechkalov	58	Nikolai M. Skomorokhov	46
Nikolai D. Gulayev	57	Vladimir I. Bobrov	43
(including 4 prior to June 1941)		(including 13 in Spain)	
Arsenii V. Vorozheikin	52	Georgii D. Kostilev	43
(including 6 in Mongolia, 1939)		Sergei N. Morgunov	42
Kirill A. Yevstigneyev	52	Vitalii I. Popkov	41
Dmitri B. Glinka	50	Aleksei V. Alelyukhin	40
Aleksandr F. Klubov	50		

The Spaniards

While the Spanish Civil War attracted pilots from many countries, the top-scorers at the end of the long and bitter conflict were those involved most deeply and for the longest period – the Spaniards themselves.

At the outbreak of war the greater number of aircraft were retained by the Government forces, although the majority of the trained pilots joined the insurgents. The standard Spanish Air Force fighter at the outbreak of the war was an export version of the elderly French sesquiplane, the Nieuport-Delage NiD 52, and it was in aircraft of this type that the initial combats were fought.

The first Republican aircraft to be shot down was a Vickers Vildebeest bomber, claimed over Granada on 29 July by Miguel Guerrero, while on 12 August another of these aircraft fell victim to Joaquin Garcia Morato, soon to emerge as the Nationalists' outstanding pilot of the war. During this same month the first German Heinkel He 51 fighters became available in small numbers, Garcia Morato converting to this aircraft and at once shooting down two more Republican types on 18 August and another on 2 September. A few days later he was able to try out the Italian Fiat CR 32; preferring this to the Heinkel, he became the first Spanish pilot to fly it in combat, also becoming the first Nationalist ace on 11 September, claiming his third victory over a Republican NiD 52. At this time he was only marginally ahead of Guerrero, who claimed four victories on the NiD 52, but then ceased flying fighters for some months. At this point Garcia Morato joined forces with two other pilots, Julio Salvador and Bermudez de Castro, forming the *Patrulla Azul* (Blue Patrol), which was to gain fame as Spain's most successful fighting team. Other pilots who did well early in the war included Angel Salas and Garcia Pardo.

Throughout the remainder of 1936 and into 1937 these pilots fought alongside German and Italian units, as more Spaniards were trained to add to the strength of Franco's indigenous air force. In a little over two months Garcia Morato added eleven more victories to his total, including three of the new Russian fighters which began appearing late in 1936. On 29 October Salas shot down the first of the fast new Tupolev SB-2 bombers which were proving so difficult for the CR 32s and He 51s to intercept. He claimed a second of these aircraft during November, while on 3 January 1937 Garcia Morato managed to shoot down two of them in one combat.

The strength of the *Patrulla Azul* had gradually crept up to an *escuadrulla*, and in July 1937 a full *gruppo*, 2-G-3, was formed under Garcia Morato's command. By this time his own score stood at twenty-three, that of Salas at seven, and Salvador's at five and a probable. As the problems of command occupied more of his time, Garcia Morato enjoyed fewer opportunities to engage in combat over the front, but while leading 2-G-3 he claimed a further nine victories in a year, on three occasions claiming two in one day. A further fighter *gruppo* was then formed from a nucleus provided by 2-G-3, this new unit being 3-G-3; together the two *gruppi* formed 3 *Escuadra*. Garcia Morato was promoted to lead this unit, leaving Salas in command of 2-G-3. During the summer of 1938 he claimed four more Republican fighters, and on Christmas Eve of that year enjoyed his greatest success, shooting down three Polikarpov R-5 reconnaissance-bomber biplanes. His last victory came in January 1939, bringing his total to forty, well ahead of all other pilots engaged in the Civil War.

Salas continued to add to his score, claiming ten more victories by the end of 1938, one of which was shared. His greatest day came on 2 September 1938, when he shot down three SB-2s and a Polikarpov I-16 fighter over the Badajoz area. In this same period, however, he was overtaken by several pilots, Salvador claiming eighteen more victories with *2-G-3*, while Manuel Vazquez claimed twenty-one and one shared, and Aristides Garcia brought his score to seventeen. Garcia claimed one early in the war while flying a He 51, followed by sixteen more with *3 Escuadra*. Miguel Guerrero also returned to fighter flying with *2-G-3*, claiming nine more victories, while Miguel Garcia Pardo claimed a total of twelve, one while flying NiD 52s, ten on CR 32s, and one as commander of *5-G-5* while flying a Heinkel He 112B monoplane fighter late in the war. Top-scoring pilot of *3-G-3* was Joaquin Velasco, who claimed about eleven victories.

Nineteen Spanish pilots became aces while flying in the units of *3 Escuadra*, the majority in *2-G-3*. The only foreign pilot to become an ace while serving with this unit was the Belgian, de Hemricourt de Grunne. However, these successes were not achieved without loss, Manuel Vazquez being killed in January 1939, and Miguel Garcia Pardo during the last week of the war in April 1939. Immediately after the end of hostilities, the great Joaquin Garcia Morato was killed in an air crash while stunting in his CR 32 for the benefit of newsreel cameramen.

Following the German attack on Russia in June 1941, a Spanish volunteer legion was sent to the Eastern Front to fight alongside Franco's former ally, this force including a fighter *escuadrulla*, named the *Escuadrulla Azul*. Flying Messerschmitt Bf 109E fighters, the unit was attached to *Jagdgeschwader 27* as *15/JG 27* during the autumn of 1941, and was led by Angel Salas, who claimed the unit's first two victories on 4 October. During the next few weeks he brought his score in Russia to seven, also destroying two more aircraft on the ground. Other notable pilots in the unit included Aristides Garcia and Carlos Bayo, who had claimed eleven victories during the Civil War.

Bayo was to add two more to his total while in Russia, but Garcia was reported missing on 27 October 1941 after a strafing attack, and was believed to have been shot down and killed by flak.

Subsequently the personnel of the unit were rotated back to Spain, and a new batch sent out, some four *escuadrullas* serving in Russia in succession until early 1944. When the units of *JG 27* in this area left for Africa, the Spanish *Escuadrulla* was attached to *JG 51*; the first three of these units flew Bf 109Es and Fs, the final unit flying Fw 190s. At least nine aces of the civil war flew in Russia, and at least one of these was credited with more victories here. Additionally, several other pilots with lower scores in Spain added further victories here, while at least four pilots who had not previously scored became aces on the Eastern Front, including Gonzalo Hevia with twelve victories and Mariano Cuadra with ten. The top-scoring surviving ace, Julio Salvador, also flew in Russia, some sources crediting him with a further fifteen victories here, although this has not been confirmed.

On the other side of the lines during the Civil War, a number of Spaniards are reputed to have become aces flying with the air force of the Republic. The most famous of these was Andres Garcia Lacalle, credited by some sources with eleven victories during the early months of the war while flying NiD 52 fighters and, possibly, the lone Boeing 281 supplied to Spain. It is reported that on one occasion he gained five victories in one day.

From late 1936 until well into 1937 the main weight of the Republican air effort was borne by Russian aircrew, but Spaniards trained in Russia gradually took over from them, and by 1938 the Republican air force was manned almost entirely by Spanish nationals. Apart from Lacalle, four pilots at least are thought to have claimed in excess of ten victories: Jose Bravo, who initially flew NiD 52s; Miguel Zamudio, who flew I-15 biplanes; and Manuel Zarauza, together with a pilot called Ramirez, who both flew I-16 monoplanes. Most Republican pilots fled the country after the war, Lacalle settling in Mexico, Zamudio in France, Zarauza and Bravo in Russia. Zarauza was later reported killed in a flying accident, while Bravo flew in the Red Air Force during the Second World War, returning to his native Spain in 1948.

The leading Spanish Nationalist aces

Commondante Joaquin Garcia Morato y Castano	40
Commondante Julio Salvador Diaz Benzumea	23 (possibly plus others in Russia)
Commondante Angel Salas Larrazabal	22 (including 7 in Russia)
Capitano Manuel Vazquez Sagaztizobal	22
Capitano Aristides Gracia Lopez	17
Capitano Carlos Bayo Alexandri	13 (including 2 in Russia)
Capitano Miguel Guerrero Garcia	13

Capitano Gonzalo Hevia	12 (all in Russia)
Capitano Miguel Garcia Pardo	12
Teniente Joaquin Velasco Fernandez	11

The leading Spanish Republican aces provisional list

Andres Garcia Lacalle	11+
Jose Bravo Fernandez	10+
Miguel Zamudio Martinez	10+
Manuel Zarauza Clavier	10+
? Ramirez	10+

The Yugoslavs and Croats

Several Yugoslav pilots flew with the Republican forces in Spain during the civil war, and one of these, Bosko Petrovic, is reported to have claimed seven victories before he was shot down and killed over Madrid in 1937.

The Axis invasion of Yugoslavia on 6 April 1941 swiftly overwhelmed the defences of that gallant country. Before the outbreak of hostilities the Yugoslavs had built up a relatively small, but none the less efficient and modern air force, the fighter elements of which were equipped with German Messerschmitt Bf 109Es, British Hawker Hurricanes and Furies, and nationally designed and constructed IK-2s and 3s.

As most Yugoslav airfields were rapidly threatened by the swift German *Blitzkrieg*, few pilots enjoyed much opportunity to take part in sustained aerial fighting. Weather also took a hand, preventing operations over most of the country on 9 and 10 April. Nevertheless, Yugoslav Bf 109Es and IK-3s flew a number of sorties in defence of Belgrade, the capital city, shooting down about fourteen aircraft. The most successful pilot during these brief operations appears to have been Milisav Semiz, who made seventeen sorties in IK-3 fighters of the *51st Grupa* between 6 and 11 April, claiming four victories. Elsewhere IK-2s, Furies and Hurricanes were also in action, a few further claims being made.

Even as the invasion was underway, the Croats, one of the ethnic minority groups making up Yugoslavia, who had often proved hostile to the ruling Serbs, broke away from the parent nation, setting up their own pro-Axis state of Croatia. Subsequently the intensely Roman Catholic Croats provided units to aid the Axis forces fighting in Russia, including two air groups, one of them equipped with Fiat G-50bis fighters provided by the Italian Government. Most of the flying personnel were ex-members of the Yugoslav air force; attached to the Luftwaffe's *JG 52*, and flying on the southern sector of the front in Russia, a number of them achieved considerable successes.

During 1942 the unit suffered quite heavy casualties, but re-equipment with modern Mes-serschmitt Bf 109G-10 aircraft eventually took place. The strength of the Croat air force steadily fell, and by 1944 the remaining aircraft were back on Yugoslav soil, opposing British and American air raids. At least eighteen pilots became aces, including the commanding officer, Fanjo Dzal, and his brother Zisko. Dzal claimed thirteen victories, but was later hanged by the new Yugoslav régime of Marshal Tito after the war.

Of the other Croatian pilots, Cvitan Galic was the most successful, with thirty-six victories. He was closely followed by Mato Dubovac with thirty-four and Jan Gerthofer with thirty-three. Galic, who had claimed thirty-four of his victories by May 1943, was killed in 1944 when his aircraft was destroyed on the ground by strafing American Mustang fighters just as he was about to take off from Sarajevo airfield. The first ace to be lost in combat was Veva Micovic, who was shot down during July 1942. Two more of these pilots were killed when shot down by anti-aircraft fire during low-level attacks, while another two were subsequently shot while prisoners. The remainder survived, although several were imprisoned for long periods after the war.

The leading Croat aces

Leutnant Cvitan Galic	36
Oberleutnant Mato Dubovak	34
Oberleutnant Jan Gerthofer	33
Feldwebel Isidor Kovaric	28
Feldwebel Jan Reznak	26
Oberleutnant Mato Culinovic	18
Leutnant Dragutin Ivanic	18
Oberleutnant Benectic	16
Oberleutnant Jergowitsch	16
Leutnant Boskic	13
Oberst Fanjo Dzal	13
Hauptmann Stipic	12
Stabsfeldwebel Tomislav Kauzlavic	10
Oberfeldwebel Veva Micovic	10

Only Yugoslav ace

Bosko Petrovic during Spanish Civil War	7

THE JET AGE
1946-1974

The Jet Age
POSTWAR CONFLICT
1945-1953

No sooner was the First World War at an end than pundits the world over were prophesying that the day of the individual fighter pilot and of the dogfight was over. With the close of the Second World War and the entry into general service of the jet aircraft, such predictions were resumed. Human beings would not be able to stand the stress of gravity during high-speed combats; the very speed of the aircraft would give the pilot no chance to fire a telling burst at an opponent, thus making the gun obsolete in fighter design; the automated missile, incapable of human error, would sweep manned aircraft from the skies. These were the theories, yet every conflict since air fighting began has served only to underline the basic rules which had been so swiftly and completely understood by those early aces on the Western Front. Height advantage, speed, gunnery, turning circle and acceleration have remained the constants in air combat. However, jet conflict has hammered home as never before the paramount importance of experience, morale and training on the part of the pilot.

When the Second World War ended in 1945, the tremendous advantages offered to a fighter pilot by the hard school of experience had not been fully understood. Those nations where this valuable lesson had been most thoroughly learned – Germany, Japan, Finland – were among the vanquished and, not surprisingly, the victors were more impressed by their own recent experiences than by those of their foes.

For six years few shots were fired in anger high in the sky, the only aerial activity during this period being recorded in China, where Communist and Nationalist forces still fought each other, and in the Middle East. In the Far East activity was limited to attacks on ground forces by the aircraft still in the hands of Chiang Kai-Shek's air force after the war with Japan. Not until after the Nationalists had been driven from mainland China to their sanctuary on Formosa (or Taiwan, as it came to be known) was the Chinese Communist Air Force born.

May 1948 saw the creation of the state of Israel when British forces withdrew from Palestine after a difficult spell of peace-keeping under a United Nations mandate. The Arab world was extremely hostile to the establishment of a new Jewish independent presence in its midst, and from the very moment of independence proceeded to attack the emergent nation. Egyptian Air Force Spitfires made attacks on

Israeli targets, and also twice attacked Ramat David airfield, near Haifa, where British aircraft were still based. Several aircraft were destroyed on the ground, but during the second attack the Egyptians were intercepted, and lost three aircraft.

Meanwhile the Israelis were putting together the rudiments of an air force, including Avia C.210 fighters. These latter were basically re-engined Messerschmitt Bf 109Gs, which had been built since the war in Czechoslovakia and were now sold to Israel. The first Israeli air victory was claimed on 3 June 1948, when Mody Allon, an ex-RAF pilot, shot down two Egyptian Dakota transports which had been modified as bombers and were attempting to raid Tel Aviv. On 18 July, Allon shot down an Egyptian Spitfire over the same area; the following October he was badly wounded by anti-aircraft fire and was killed when he force-landed on return. Although not an ace as such, he was the first Israeli fighter pilot to achieve success, and became a national hero.

A brief cease-fire enabled the Israelis to acquire more aircraft, including Spitfire 9s from Czechoslovakia, but during July 1948 fighting flared again, this time Syrian and Jordanian forces joining in. By the beginning of 1949 the Israeli fighters had claimed fifteen victories, the most successful pilot being Rudi Orgarten, who shot down three Egyptian Spitfires and a Fiat G.55 while flying a Spitfire. Then during two combats on 7 January 1949, Israeli Spitfires shot down four RAF Spitfire 18s and a Tempest over the Suez Canal Zone – ostensibly mistaking them for Egyptian aircraft. The threat of British intervention, together with United Nations efforts to secure an armistice, resulted in the Israelis giving up territory they had captured. Thereafter, an uneasy peace settled over the area, lasting for nearly eight years while both sides began building up their forces from every possible source.

Elsewhere the rest of the world was rapidly dividing itself into two camps dominated by opposing ideologies. No sooner were the common enemies defeated in 1945 than Josef Stalin made clear Soviet Russia's basic hostility to the Western democracies, and the struggle was on for spheres of influence. Steadily control of all the East European nations passed into the hands of governments sympathetic to Russia, thus providing that nation with the buffer zone she had long desired between her frontiers and those of the industrial nations of the West.

It was in the Far East that the confrontation of the Cold War first burst into flames. After years of foreign domination of Korea, it had been proposed in 1945 that an independent republic with a freely elected government should be formed. However, the northern part of the country had been occupied by Russian forces at the close of hostilities, and while the requisite elections took place in the South, north of the 38th Parallel a Communist People's Republic was set up.

After some guerrilla activity across the border with the South, the North Korean forces, strong and well trained, exploded across the frontier on 25 June 1950, the relatively weak forces of the South falling back before them. At this stage the first concern of the US government was to evacuate American advisers and their dependants, but attacks on South Korean airfields by North Korean Yak fighters quickly showed that air cover would be necessary for the transport aircraft undertaking part of the evacuation.

This cover was given, not by jets but by conventional piston-engined aircraft – North American F-82 Twin Mustang night fighters from Japan. Two days later five of these aircraft intercepted five Yaks over Seoul and shot down three of them. The tenor of the fighting which was to follow was set in this combat by Major James W. Little, who was not the young twenty-one-year-old of legend, but a Second World War veteran and an ace in that earlier war, with five victories. During the afternoon of the same day, four of eight Ilyushin Il-10 attack aircraft were shot down over Kimpo by F-80C Shooting Stars for the USAF's first jet victories, Lieutenant Robert E. Wayne being credited with two of them.

It was not the intention of the United States that South Korea should be abandoned to its fate, and when the United Nations decided to oppose the North's aggression, US forces from Japan were sent in on behalf of the international organization in an effort to stabilize the situation. The US ground forces were soon joined by representative elements from the British Commonwealth and other nations, and good use of available air power was made to assist in bringing

the Communist forces to a halt. Much use was initially made of F-51 Mustangs and the F-80, which possessed a much shorter range. The USAF elements were reinforced by Australian and South African squadrons, while carrier-borne aircraft of the US Navy and the Royal Navy were soon available off-shore, and US Marine air units were also sent over.

By the late summer the North Korean attack had been held and turned back, while during September an invasion at Inchon, on the west coast, helped further in driving the defeated Communist forces from South Korea. North Korean aircraft made desultory appearances, and a few more were shot down, but the numbers used were small and many were destroyed

Captain Manuel J. Fernandez, who finished the Korean war with fourteen and a half victories to his credit.

Several other air forces flew alongside the Americans in Korea, and these F-86 Sabres are from a South African squadron. The Sabre, an outstanding aircraft, went on to become the standard fighter in the air forces of about thirty countries.

on the ground. United Nations forces then moved on into Northern territory with the intention of re-uniting the whole country and imposing elections for the whole of Korea as one state. With all falling before them, the victorious troops swept on towards the Yalu River on Korea's northern frontier, almost the entire country being occupied by mid-November 1950.

It was at this stage, however, that numbers of Chinese Communist troops–apparently volunteers at first–began to appear at the front, while in the air a resurgence of opposition was encountered. On 1 November six swept-wing jet fighters of superior performance attacked a flight of F-80Cs; they were Russian-built MiG-15s. Thereafter these aircraft, together with piston-engined Yak fighters, regularly attacked American aircraft in the area south of the Yalu, though the Yaks were clearly not up to the task and seven were swiftly shot down. On 8 November MiGs and F-80s engaged in the world's first decisive jet-versus-jet combat, in which Lieutenant Russell J. Brown of the 51st Fighter-Interceptor Wing shot down one of the attackers.

Late in November a United Nations offensive designed to complete the occupation of Korea was counterattacked by a massively strong Chinese Communist army that had been moved into Korea. In a matter of days the American, British and South Korean troops were in full retreat. All North Korea was given up by the end of the year, and not until late January 1951 were the Communist forces held. By this time Seoul, the South Korean capital, and other areas of the country had been lost.

Air attack was employed on a large scale to slow down the Communist advance, terrible losses being inflicted by United Nations fighter-bombers and by B-26 and B-29 conventional bombers. However, the MiGs posed the main threat. Although they were bested in individual dogfights by both Shooting Stars and the US Navy's new Grumman F9F Panther, it was clear that they were superior in performance to both types by a considerable margin. To resolve the situation, two more fighter wings were rushed to the area from the US, one equipped with Republic F-84E Thunderjets, the other with North American F-86A Sabres. The former was a straight-wing aircraft, and while its initial combats with the MiGs produced some favourable results, it was clear that this was due more to pilot quality than to performance. Consequently, the Thunderjets were soon relegated to fighter-bomber duties, the air-superiority role falling to the Sabres. The F-86A unit was the 4th Fighter-Interceptor Wing, which was an extremely experienced unit containing many pilots with battle experience gained during the Second World War, several of them having been aces in that war. One of these was the unit's commanding officer, Lieutenant Colonel John C. Meyer.

The first encounter came on 17 December 1950, when four Sabres attacked an equal number of MiGs, Lieutenant Colonel Bruce H. Hinton shooting down one of the MiGs. Quickly the shape which the rest of war in the air was to take began to appear. The MiGs were based on airfields to the north of the Yalu, in Manchurian territory, and United Nations pilots were strictly forbidden to enter this air space. As long as the MiGs were tied to these airfields, their limited range prevented them operating anywhere other than over the north-western part of North Korea, which became known as 'MiG Alley'. Thus over the battle front and the supply lines immediately behind it, United Nations aircraft could attack their targets unmolested by MiGs, as long as the latter remained based north of the Yalu. The striking power of the United Nations air force was the main factor allowing the relatively small ground army to contain the great preponderance of numbers facing them. So long as the Sabres could protect United Nations bombers and fighter-bombers raiding Communist airfields south of the Yalu, it was not safe for the MiGs to move to them and threaten the ground-support aircraft over the battle zone. So everything depended upon the Sabres retaining the initiative against the MiGs over north-eastern Korea.

Experience quickly proved that special tactics were necessary. In the combat zone the Sabres had to maintain a very high flight speed if they were to have any chance of catching MiGs, which usually attacked from higher altitude and then fled for the Yalu. At the height and speed at which combats now took place, large formations such as those flown over Europe during the earlier war became unmanageable and a liability. The optimum formation became the four aircraft flight flying in the classic 'finger four' formation.

The two opposing fighters were in many ways equally matched, each possessing some advantages and some disadvantages. The deciding factor seemed undoubtedly to be the greater experience and superior training of the Americans. It was very often clear that many of the pilots by whom they were opposed were extremely new and inexperienced, and their propensity for fleeing for home allowed most 'kills' to be gained in a direct stern chase position, so that deflection shooting was a rarity in Korea. Some MiG pilots proved to be considerably more dangerous opponents, and these were believed to be formation leaders or instructors. They became known to the American pilots as 'honchos'. It was also very apparent that large numbers of pilots were being given experience over Korea, for no sooner did one batch start to perform in a more polished manner than they were replaced by a new batch of 'rookies'. At first the opponents were clearly Chinese and North Korean pilots, but it was believed on

Still displaying its North Korean markings, this MiG-15 was flown to an American air base by a deserter. Comparison between the MiG and the Sabre showed the former to be superior in climb and manœuvrability, although American pilot experience did much to outweigh this.

good evidence that pilots from other Communist nations in Europe also appeared from across the Yalu.

From the start the Sabres were almost always outnumbered, but despite this they gained a marked ascendancy. By the end of December 1950, after little more than a fortnight in combat, the 4th's pilots had claimed eight MiGs shot down for no loss. However, the loss of airfields occasioned by the retreat led to the withdrawal of the one squadron of F-86s in Korea to rejoin the rest of the wing in Japan. This reduced the availability of aircraft over the Yalu, and early in 1951 the bombers and fighter-bombers operating in this area began to suffer more sustained MiG attacks. Early in March, Sabres began refuelling at Suwon airfield, to allow them to resume their patrols. Counterattacks by the ground forces were steadily regaining lost ground at this time, and by April the 38th Parallel had once more been crossed. Steadily the 4th Wing's score rose, and by the end of the month Captain James Jabara had claimed four of the opposing jets shot down. He should then have returned to Japan when his squadron was rotated with another in the wing, but the understanding USAF–better attuned to the propaganda value of the fighter ace than are many other air forces–allowed him to stay on. For some weeks there was no sign of the MiGs; on 20 May, however, some were encountered and a big fight began which eventually attracted fifty MiGs and three dozen Sabres. Three MiGs were claimed without loss, two by Jabara, who thus became the first ace of the Korean war. At the time it was believed that he was the first jet ace in the world, but the exploits of the Luftwaffe's Me 262 pilots were not then general knowledge. Shortly after this success his tour ended, and he returned to the United States with his score standing at six, though he had previously been credited with another one and a half victories during the Second World War.

During mid-June 1951 three hectic battles were fought with some well-flown MiGs, during which six were claimed shot down and several more damaged. Two Sabres were lost in these combats, bringing the number shot down at this time to three. These partial successes apparently persuaded the North Koreans to reintroduce their conventional aircraft to the front, and on 20 June eight Il-10s and six Yak-9s were engaged by F-51 Mustangs, which shot down two of the former and one of the latter. Escorting MiGs shot down one Mustang, but the rest were driven off by Sabres.

During May 1951 the Chinese and North Koreans had launched their biggest offensive, but this time the United Nations were ready and the attack was driven off, the Communists being forced to withdraw and the United Nations troops moving forward into North Korea again. Realizing that they were not going to break through, the Chinese now requested a cease-fire, and while this was not granted, peace talks did begin. A two-year stalemate followed, during which the positions on the ground remained almost unchanged, while each side strove to gain such military advantage as would strengthen its bargaining position at the talks. One of the major factors remained the control of the air, and as a result the struggle for air superiority continued throughout the whole of this period.

Steadily MiG strength in Manchuria was built up, but despite an overwhelming preponderance of strength in their favour, the Communists remained unable to master the deadly Sabres. In July F-86Es began to arrive in Japan, but at this time there were only about ninety Sabres available against an estimated strength of 445 MiG 15s. With increasing numbers of Russian advisers available, the MiG pilots attempted numerous changes of tactics, at the same time committing increasingly strong formations to battle.

During September 1951, 911 MiGs were engaged, fourteen being claimed for the loss of three Sabres, and one more was claimed by an F-84 pilot. On 2 September two more American pilots, Captains R. S. Becker and D. Gibson, each achieved their fifth victory. The construction of new airfields in North Korea led to increased efforts to prevent the Communists from using them, and October erupted with fierce fighting, culminating in a record claim of nine MiGs shot down on the 16th. On the 23rd some 100 MiGs broke through the Sabre screen to shoot down three B-29s from a formation of eight, damaging all the others and also shooting down one of fifty-five escorting Thunderjets. Two of the attacking MiGs were claimed by the Sabres, but it was a bad defeat.

By the end of October twenty-four MiGs had been claimed by Sabres, and eight by bomber gunners and their escorting Thunderjets, which were now joined by Australian Meteor 8 jet fighters. However, seven Sabres, five B-29s, two F-84s and an RF-80 reconnaissance-fighter had been shot down in the fighting, and the Superfortresses had to be withdrawn from daylight operations. Encouraged, the Communists began moving MiGs to bases south of the Yalu and preparing other aircraft for further action. At the same time the improved MiG 15bis began to appear, prompting urgent requests from the USAF for more Sabres in Korea. In November the 51st Fighter-Interceptor Wing began an emergency conversion in the field to F-86s, and Colonel Francis F. Gabreski, the top-scoring surviving USAF ace of the Second World War, who was serving as deputy commander of the 4th Wing, was transferred to command this unit.

On 27 November four MiGs were claimed by the 4th Wing, two of these falling to Major George A. Davis Jr. This pilot was to become the most colourful and extraordinary ace of the Korean war, enjoying a brief but meteoric career. During the Second World War he had flown P-47 Thunderbolts with the 5th Air Force over New Guinea and the Philippines, and had claimed six Japanese fighters shot down over the latter area in just three combats during December 1944.

Following his first victories over Korea, he found himself in a formation of thirty-one Sabres which took part in one of the most unusual interceptions of the war. Conventional North Korean aircraft had been attacking garrisons on some of the off-shore islands; a patrol was flown in the area on 30 November 1951, engaging a formation of twelve Tupolev Tu-2 twin-engined bombers, sixteen Lavochkin La-9 fighters, and sixteen MiGs. Eight Tu-2s, three La-9s and a MiG were claimed without loss, Davis accounting for three of the bombers and the MiG to become the fifth ace of the war, while Winton 'Bones' Marshall got a Tu-2 and an La-9, becoming the sixth.

The following month Davis was twice engaged, claiming two MiGs on the first occasion and four on the second, raising his score to double figures. Success then eluded him until February 1952, when on the 10th he led eighteen Sabres to cover fighter-bombers near Kunni-ri. Seeing contrails far away over the Yalu, he and his wingman broke away to give chase, attacking two MiGs at 32,000 feet and shooting both down. He was about to attack a third when another, flown by one Chiang Chi-Wei, got on his tail and shot him down. With his score at fourteen, Davis died as top-scorer by a good margin, and was subsequently awarded the Congressional Medal of Honor–the only Sabre pilot to receive this supreme award.

Meanwhile during January 1952, the 51st Wing, equipped entirely with new F-86Es, had done very well, claiming twenty-five MiGs against the veteran 4th's five. The following month Major William T. Whisner, an 8th Air Force Second World War ace with fifteen and a half victories, became the first jet ace of the 51st. The quality of the MiG pilots continued to improve, and while thirty-nine MiGs were claimed during March and April, six Sabres and three fighter-bombers were lost to them. Francis Gabreski claimed his fifth MiG on 1 April, and three other pilots achieved ace status during the month. The arrival of Communist aircraft on North Korean airfields allowed several strafes to be undertaken by the Sabres at this time, a number of aircraft being destroyed on the ground.

Five more Sabres and four fighter-bombers fell to the MiGs in May, but twenty-seven were claimed in return and another four pilots became aces, including the 4th Wing's current commander, Colonel Harrison R. Thyng. This pilot had flown Spitfires and Mustangs in the Mediterranean and Far East during the Second World War, his six victories in that conflict including Vichy French, German and Japanese aircraft–a greater diversification of nationalities than that claimed by any other American ace.

June 1952 saw the arrival of the F-86F, an improved Sabre which was able to handle the MiG-15bis with little difficulty. Only one new ace appeared during the month, but he was unusual in being the archetype of earlier wars. Second Lieutenant James F. Low began flight training in July 1950 and became an ace with the 4th Wing only six months after graduating as a pilot. His score finally rose to nine.

Throughout the summer and autumn the Sabres continued to claim about twenty to thirty MiGs a month, and by the end of September twenty American pilots had become aces in Korea. On 17 November the 4th Wing's latest commander, Colonel Royal N. Baker, a Second World War Spitfire pilot with three and a half victories in the Mediterranean area to his credit, became an ace in Korea. By March 1953 his score had risen to thirteen, and he had become top-scorer still at the front.

January 1953 proved a good month for the Sabres, with thirty-seven MiGs and one Tu-2 shot down for only one loss, while during February two pilots who were to make big names for themselves, Joseph McConnell Jr of the 51st Wing and Manuel Fernandez of the 4th Wing, both became aces. Meanwhile the 18th

Fighter-Bomber Wing had been converted from F-51s direct to Sabres and flew some counter-air missions as an introduction to jet operations. Flying these missions in March, Major James P. Hagerstrom became an ace—the wing's only ace of the war. Hagerstrom was another veteran, claiming six victories in the 5th Air Force during the Second World War. He would add eight and a half MiGs before the fighting ended. A second fighter-bomber unit, the 8th Wing, also converted to F-86s from F-80Cs, but produced no aces.

During April another leading ace was lost, Captain Harold E. Fischer, with ten victories to his credit; he was shot down and taken prisoner. McConnell was also shot down, but parachuted into the sea and was picked up by helicopter. Immediately after his return to action he claimed his tenth MiG.

After April the quality of the MiG pilots deteriorated noticeably, and it was believed that Russian advisers and instructors were no longer present. With four wings of Sabres available, the Americans were let loose on the opposition. Between 8 and 31 May fifty-six were claimed for one loss, Manuel Fernandez overtaking Davis's long-standing score by reaching fourteen and a half. The race was now on, and before the month was out McConnell had claimed six more to leap into first place with sixteen, equalling Heinz Bär's Me 262 record. At this stage both pilots were relieved from combat, leaving the way clear for Major James Jabara, who had returned for a second tour and had pushed his score up to nine during the month.

June was the best month of all, seventy-seven confirmed and eleven probables being claimed. On 30 June sixteen were shot down in one combat, a record number, Jabara bringing his own score to fourteen with two victories on that date. Five new aces appeared, including thirty-seven-year-old Lieutenant Colonel Vermont Garrison, a Second World War 8th Air Force ace with seven and one shared in that war. Lieutenant Henry Buttelmann claimed five in twelve days to become the youngest ace of the war at twenty-four.

Monsoon weather during July 1953 reduced combat, but thirty-two MiGs were claimed for the loss of two Sabres. Jabara claimed his last victory, securing the No. 2 position with fifteen, while several more new aces appeared, including a US Marine, Major John F. Bolt, flying with the 51st Wing on attachment. Bolt had claimed six and a half victories in the Second World War, flying Corsairs in 'Pappy' Boyington's squadron; he now added six MiGs to his total. The thirty-ninth and final ace was Major S. L. Bettinger, who shot down his fifth on 20 July. He was then shot down and taken prisoner, so that his final victory could not be confirmed until after his release. Two days later Lieutenant Sam P. Young of the 51st Wing claimed his first MiG. It was also the Sabres pilots' last. The final

victory came on the last day of the war, 27 July, when Captain Ralph S. Parr shot down an Il-12 transport to bring his score to ten.

During the war US Navy, Marine and Air Force night fighters also saw combat, but only one pilot, Lieutenant Guy B. Bordelon of VC-3, reached the magic total. Loaned to the 5th Air Force, whose jet night fighters were having trouble intercepting the slow piston-engined aircraft employed at night by the Communists, Bordelon in his F4U-5N Corsair shot down five in three nights during June–July 1953. Other Navy pilots claimed eleven victories during the war, one on attachment to a USAF Sabre Wing, while the Marines claimed thirty-five and a half, twenty-one and a half by pilots flying on attachment with the USAF, like Bolt, and at least ten at night. Three of the other pilots who scored had been aces in the Second World War.

USAF Sabres claimed 829 of the total United Nations air combat claims of 900 aircraft shot down; 811 of these claims were MiG-15s. In

Major George A. Davis, who gained a posthumous award of the Congressional Medal of Honor. He was shot down in a combat on 10 February 1952, having disposed of two MiGs and while attacking a third. His final total in Korea was fourteen.

combat the United States lost 139 aircraft, seventy-eight of them Sabres. Whether any North Korean or Communist Chinese pilots became aces during this period is an open question, but in the circumstances it seems relatively unlikely. Of the thirty-nine Sabre pilots who became aces, thirteen had already gained at least one victory during the Second World War, and the average scoring F-86 pilot had put in eighteen missions during the earlier war. Apart from those who actually became aces in Korea, twelve more Second World War aces added to their scores, including Major Walker M. Mahurin, who added three and a half to his twenty-one before becoming a prisoner, Colonel John C. Meyer, with two added to his twenty-four, and Lieutenant Colonel Glenn T. Eagleston, with two to add to his eighteen and a half. Two pilots who were aces in neither conflict had sufficient combined victories from the two to bring their aggregate scores to five or more. A number of pilots from other United Nations countries also flew on attachment with the Sabre Wings, notably from the RAF and RCAF. One Canadian pilot, Flight-Lieutenant Ernest A. Glover, was credited with three MiGs destroyed, while two Canadian aces of the Second World War, Squadron Leaders James D. Lindsay and J. McKay, each added to their scores.

The leading USAF aces of the Korean war

Captain Joseph McConnell Jr	16
Major James Jabara	15 (plus 1½ in the Second World War)
Captain Manuel J. Fernandez	14½
Major George A. Davis Jr	14 (plus 7 in the Second World War)
Colonel Royal N. Baker	13 (plus 3½ in the Second World War)
Major Frederick C. Blesse	10
Lieutenant Harold E. Fischer	10
Lieutenant Colonel Vermont Garrison	10 (plus 7⅓ in the Second World War)
Colonel James K. Johnson	10 (plus 1 in the Second World War)
Captain Lonnie R. Moore	10
Captain Ralph S. Parr Jr	10

Major Walker M. Mahurin who added three and a half victories in Korea to his Second World War total of twenty-one before being shot down and taken prisoner.

The Jet Age
CONFRONTATION 1955-1974

After the Korean War an uneasy peace was established. Nevertheless, it was soon clear that in the Middle East it would be impossible to forestall another clash between Israel and the Arabs, and this was emphasized by Egypt's nationalization of the Suez Canal in 1955.

Rearmament had proceeded apace, Israel having purchased Mustangs from Sweden, Meteor 8s from the United Kingdom, and Dassault Ouragans from France. An attempt to acquire Canadian-built Sabres failed in 1956, but the French stepped in again to supply a splendid replacement in the shape of Dassault's swept-wing Mystère IVA. After acquiring Vampires and Meteors from Britain, Egypt had reached an agreement with the Soviet Union leading to the supply of MiG-15s and other combat aircraft, while during 1956 a few of the more modern MiG-17s were also received. On Israel's northern border, Syria had also acquired MiG-15s.

During late 1955 and early 1956, the first jet fighter battles took place over the Sinai, Egyptian Vampires being intercepted while infringing Israeli airspace on two or three occasions, three or four of the jets being shot down by Ouragans and Meteors. By the autumn of 1956 it was clear that the Arabs were preparing to attack Israel, while Israel was planning a preemptive strike. On 30 October the Israeli attack on Egyptian forces in the Sinai Desert began, and at once Egyptian aircraft appeared over the battle area. During the first two days several combats took place, Ouragans and Mystères shooting down a number of Egyptian aircraft variously reported as seven or eleven, but apparently including four MiG-15s, one MiG-17, four Vampires and two Meteors. Most of these fell to the air superiority of the Mystères, and the most successful pilot was a Captain Yac, who shot down two of the MiGs in one combat.

Thereafter, France and Britain – with Israeli pre-knowledge – seized the opportunity to regain their control of the Suez Canal by threatening to occupy it if the combatants did not cease fighting and withdraw to positions ten miles from either side of it. French fighters had already moved to Israeli soil, and at the start of November French and British aircraft attacked Egyptian airfields and other targets, following which paratroops were dropped on the Canal Zone, bringing the conflict to an end. Subsequently United Nations (and particularly American and Russian) pressure forced the French and British to withdraw, but their action had prevented more Egyptian aircraft from being employed against the Israeli army, which had undertaken a brilliant lightning campaign, seizing the greater part of Sinai, much of which the Israelis retained.

French F-84F Thunderstreaks caught twenty Ilyushin Il-28 jet bombers on the ground and wiped them out before they could become operational, but otherwise these aircraft, together with Mystère IVAs and Aeronavale Corsairs, plus British Hunters, Sea Hawks, Venoms and Wyverns, saw no air combat. However, over Syria an RAF Canberra reconnaissance aircraft was intercepted and shot down by a Syrian MiG-15. While a number of Israeli aircraft had been lost to ground fire, the only loss in air combat was a single Piper Cub liaison and spotter aircraft, which was shot down by a MiG.

It was clear that the Mustang and Meteor were now outdated, but the Ouragan was still a very useful ground-attack aircraft, able to take on MiG-15s if necessary. More Ouragans were acquired from France in 1957, and twin jet swept-wing Vautour fighter-bombers the following year. Russia undertook the re-equipment of the Egyptians at the same time, supplying more MiG-17s, followed in 1958 by supersonic MiG-19s. To counteract the threat posed by the MiG-19s, the Israelis ordered Super Mystères from the French, these supersonic fighters arriving in 1959, while in 1962–63 they were followed by supplies of the superlative delta-winged Dassault Mirage III Mach-2 interceptor. At the same time MiG-21s were supplied to both Egypt and Syria to provide them with a counter to the Mirage. The stage was by then set for more trouble.

In the meantime, re-equipment of the Chinese Nationalist Air Force on Formosa with modern jet aircraft had allowed it to play a more aggressive role, and clashes with Communist MiGs over the Formosa Strait became quite common. In 1958 the Chinese Nationalists were supplied with American Sidewinder air-to-air missiles, becoming the first pilots in the world to use such heat-seeking weapons in combat. On 24 September 1958 six Nationalist F-86F Sabres, carrying Sidewinders and escorted by eight more Sabres without these weapons, became involved in a fierce dogfight with some twenty MiGs. Six Sidewinders were

First American pilot to claim more than two victories over Vietnam was a middle-aged veteran ace of the Second World War. More than twenty years before, Colonel Robin Olds had claimed twelve victories over Europe, flying P-38 Lightnings with the 479th Fighter Group of the 8th Air Force. In 1967, as commander of the 8th Tactical Fighter Wing, he shot down four MiGs in a few months. He was to remain top-scorer of the Vietnam conflict until 1972.

Wing Commander Mohammad Alam was the first ace of the Pakistani Air Force. He is also the only jet pilot known to have claimed five victories in a single sortie. Using basically the same F-86 Sabre operated by the Americans in Korea more than ten years earlier, he claimed nine victories over Indian aircraft during the brief war in Kashmir in 1965.

fired and four MiGs claimed shot down by them, two by one pilot; a further six MiGs were claimed with conventional gun armament, all for no loss. Further combats were not always so successful, and it is believed that at least one Chinese Communist pilot became an ace during these desultory engagements.

The mid-'sixties saw a growth of air fighting throughout the world, which has continued almost without a halt for over ten years. Once again it began in the Middle East, as clashes during border incursions became more serious. During the early part of the decade Super Mystères shot down two MiG-17s, but thus far no Israeli ace had appeared. The arrival of the Mirage soon changed this. The first clash involving the new aircraft occurred on 20 August 1963 when two Mirages shot down two Syrian MiG-17s from a formation of eight. A little over a year later came the first Mirage-MiG-21 encounter, two Mirages claiming one of the Russian-built super fighters shot down between them.

In 1965 fighting erupted almost simultaneously in two separate parts of the world. In the Far East the United States had become increasingly embroiled in supporting the régime in South Vietnam, first as military advisers and later by an increasing military presence. During the 'fifties the French had employed substantial air forces in the fight with the Communist Viet Cong, but as their opponents were a guerrilla army, they met no opposition in the air. Now the Viet Cong had their own country, North Vietnam, and as their guerrilla activities to the South became ever more severe, the Americans

steadily poured in both ground and air support. Finally in 1965 the USAF and US Naval air force began attacking targets in North Vietnam in an effort to prevent the passage of further men, arms and supplies across the border.

North Vietnamese troops, as a result of their earlier experiences with the French, were always well equipped with light anti-aircraft weapons, and losses to these were heavy throughout all the operations in Vietnam. Over the Communist homeland, however, the Americans found themselves faced by ground-to-air guided missiles of Russian manufacture and an increasing number of hostile interceptors. Initially the North Vietnamese were supplied with small numbers of MiG-17s, but later the supply was considerably stepped up and the latest MiG-21s were also brought in.

The first loss at the hands of Vietnamese MiGs occurred on 4 April 1965 when three Republic F-105 Thunderchief fighter-bombers were shot down. At this stage the Americans were preparing for combat operations. They made their first claims on 17 June when two MiG-17s were shot down by Navy McDonnell F4B Phantoms. Other claims followed, and the first MiG-21 to be shot down was recorded on 26 April 1966. By mid-May twelve MiGs had been claimed, but the last of these was reported by the Chinese to be one of their aircraft; each side claimed that the other had strayed across the border. Certainly American aircraft did stray into Chinese airspace from time to time, and by the end of 1966 four of their aircraft had fallen to Chinese fighters.

The big news came from North Vietnam, however, when it was announced that Captain Nguyen Van Bay had become the first ace of the war, having claimed seven victories, including four Thunderchiefs, an F-100 Super Sabre and two Phantoms—the latter both claimed during April—by the end of May 1966.

While the war in Vietnam was escalating into a major conflict, hostilities had also broken out on the Indian sub-continent between India and Pakistan over conflicting territorial claims to the territory of Kashmir. Throughout the first three weeks of September 1965 fighting raged fiercely, both in the air and on the ground. When international negotiation brought a return of peace, the results were not entirely conclusive. On the ground, the outnumbered Pakistan forces had suffered severe losses, and the Indian armour had undoubtedly won a victory. In the air, the small but efficient Pakistani air force appeared to have more than held its own.

Equipped mainly with Sidewinder-carrying F-86F Sabres, together with a few Lockheed F-104A Starfighters and B-57 Canberras of American construction, the Pakistanis were faced by a strong force of Hawker Hunters, Folland Gnats, Mystères, Ouragans, Vampires, and Canberras of British and French construction, plus a handful of MiG-21s, which had

MiG-19 fighters of the Pakistani Air Force as flown by Wing Commander Hatmi. The aircraft were supplied to Pakistan by the Chinese Government, and in 1971 were used to combat Russian-designed MiG-21s, Sukhoi Su-7s and other types of the Indian Air Force.

been supplied by the Soviet Union.

When fighting ceased on 23 September, each side had made conflicting claims regarding aircraft destroyed and their own losses. Claims in combat had, in total, been reasonably modest and much in line with admitted losses. It was in totals of aircraft shot down by ground defences and destroyed on the ground in strafing and bombing attacks that the greatest disparities appear.

The Indians employed the Mystères, Ouragans, Vampires and, to some extent, the Hunters mainly in the ground-attack role, relying largely on the nimble Gnat for air defence and counter-air operations. Of known Indian claims, all were against Sabres, at least five being made by Hunter pilots and six by Gnats. It was reported that both types were well able to handle the American-built aircraft, but the Gnats proved particularly superior, receiving the nickname 'Sabre-Slayer' by the end of the conflict.

Interested observers in the West waited with anticipation for the first clash between the F-104 and the MiG-21, as these were the current air-superiority fighters of the two power blocs in Europe. The expected clash never came, for the MiGs were not yet fully operational. Pakistani Starfighter pilots claimed five of the thirty-five victories reported by their air force, but the brunt of combat was borne by the faithful Sabres.

The outstanding pilot of the conflict was a highly experienced commander of a Pakistani squadron equipped with F-86Fs, Squadron Leader Mohammad M. Alam, who enjoyed the advantage of having flown Hunters while in England, thus possessing a keen awareness of their capabilities and weaknesses. On 6 September, a day on which Sabre pilots claimed nine of these aircraft shot down, Alam was credited with two. Next day Sabres and F-104s were scrambled to combat a raid on their airfield at Sargodha by Mystères and Hunters, and during this Alam attacked a formation of six Hunters reported to be flown by three squadron leaders and three flight lieutenants of the Indian Air Force. He fired his Sidewinders at one Hunter, the pilot of which ejected. He then attacked the other five with his guns; these all broke away in the same direction—a critical error—passing through his sights in a nose-to-tail procession. Alam was too experienced a pilot and marksman to let such an opportunity pass; loosing off rapid bursts of fire, he shot down four of them in rapid succession, witnessed by other Pakistani pilots nearby.

Squadron Leader Alam had become the first known jet ace-in-a-day, proving yet again that experience, training and morale are every bit as important as equipment; at the time of his success he was thirty-two years old. He had put in more than 1,400 hours flying Sabres and held the highest gunnery scores in his air force. He was not finished yet, however, for on 17 September he was to claim two more Hunters, bringing his score to nine in just three combats. While it will be recalled that most combats in Korea had been direct stern attacks, in which deflection firing skill was not necessary, Squadron Leader Alam has made the point that in this war combats were generally turning and banking

Wing Commander Sa'ad Hatmi also flew Sabres during 1965, claiming three victories. He finally became Pakistan's second ace in 1971, when at the head of a MiG-19 squadron he shot down two further Indian aircraft.

fights of the more classic dogfight type, where good deflection shooting was absolutely essential.

Sixteen other Pakistani pilots claimed during the brief fighting, three being credited with three victories apiece and three with two each. Altogether, the Sabres claimed nineteen Hunters, six Gnats, four Vampires, a Mystère and a Canberra, while the Starfighters claimed three Mystères and two Canberras.

In Vietnam and on the Israeli borders the fighting continued throughout 1967. Over Vietnam the Americans had claimed a total of thirty-eight victories by the end of March, most of the victims being MiG-17s. While eight claims were made by US Navy aircraft, the rest were credited to the USAF. By an incredible chance, two of the MiGs had fallen to old piston-engined Douglas A-1 Skyraiders of Korean War vintage.

North Vietnamese resistance was now stiffening, and between 19 April and 5 June 1967 a further thirty-nine claims against MiGs were made, while ten US aircraft went down in return. The majority of claims were gained by Air Force and Navy Phantoms, but substantial totals also went to the pilots of USAF F-105s and Navy F-8 Crusaders. So far only a few pilots had been able to run their scores up even to two, but during this period an outstanding

pilot emerged, and once more he was a mature veteran. Colonel Robin Olds had flown with the 8th Air Force over Europe more than twenty years earlier, claiming twelve victories. Between 2 January and 20 May 1967, he accounted for four MiGs, just missing becoming the first US ace since Korea. He was then rotated back to the States. Flying a Phantom, his successes were all gained with air-to-air rockets.

The struggle continued unabated, and by December 1967 US claims had risen to ninety-seven. The century was passed early in the New Year, and by February 1968 the score stood at 105, losses to MiGs in the same period being put at forty-seven. During April fighting diminished as the American Government put a standstill on bombing raids over the northern part of North Vietnam, while in November the bombing was halted altogether. At that time American claims stood at 110, but many aircraft had been lost to anti-aircraft fire, SAM missiles and MiGs, three former Korean War aces being among those known to have been taken prisoner. Following this end to the air fighting, a MiG-21 was displayed in Hanoi, the North Vietnamese capital, showing on its side thirteen victory stars and a MiG-17 sporting seven stars. It is believed that one of these was Captain van Bay's aircraft – possibly denoting further successes – and the other was probably the mount of Colonel Tomb, a second North Vietnamese pilot to become an ace.

In the Middle East, 1966 had seen an escalation of hostilities, mainly between Israeli and Syrian aircraft in the area of the Golan Heights. A MiG-21 was shot down by Mirages on 14 July, the Mirages accounting for another MiG on 15 August. On 13 November a Jordanian Hunter was shot down after a long fight lasting eight and a half minutes, while on the 29th of that month a pair of Egyptian MiG-19s were claimed, one by cannon-fire, the other by a Matra 530 air-to-air missile, the first of these to be launched in action by an Israeli Mirage.

The Mirages enjoyed their greatest success to date during a severe skirmish with Syrian forces on 7 April 1967, six MiG-21s being shot down during a number of combats. It is reported that the Jordanian Hunter was shot down by Lieutenant Colonel Ran, commanding officer of one of the Mirage units, and that later – probably during this 7 April combat – he shot down two MiG-21s, one with rockets and the other with his cannons.

War was once again about to break out. Finally, on 5 June 1967, the Israelis once again launched a lightning pre-emptive strike which had been brilliantly planned. Mirages, Super Mystères, Mystères, Ouragans and Vautours hit airfields in Egypt, Syria, Iraq and Jordan, destroying the greater part of the Arab air forces before they could get off the ground as a prelude to the famous Six Day War.

Some Arab aircraft did manage to get into the

First American pilot to become an ace over Vietnam was Captain Richard 'Steve' Ritchie (right), who claimed his fifth MiG on 28 August 1972. His weapons operator, Captain Charles 'Chuck' DeBellvue (left) was taking part in his fourth successful combat. He later joined in two more with other pilots. Both men served with the 555th Squadron of the 432nd Tactical Fighter Reconnaissance Wing.

opposite page
On 24 October 1944, during the Battle of Leyte Gulf, David McCampbell, leader of Air Group 15 flying from USS *Essex*, shot down nine Mitsubishi A6M Zeros in a long, running combat. He and his wingman, Roy Rushing, had intercepted some forty Zeros flown by inexperienced Japanese pilots who made no attempt to evade their attack. Rushing downed six Zeros in this combat. McCampbell's fighter *Minsi III* is a Grumman F6F Hellcat. By Michael Turner.

MICHAEL TURNER

MICHAEL TURNER

air, and of 452 aircraft claimed destroyed by the Israelis, seventy-nine were claimed in air combat. Israeli losses totalled forty, the majority falling to ground fire. It is known that Lieutenant Colonel Ran was involved in several strikes, during one of which on 5 June three MiG-19s were shot down as they were taking off. Another unnamed pilot flew three sorties on 5 June, shooting down two MiG-21s on the first and one on the third. Two days later he shot down a further pair of MiGs to bring his score to at least five.

Apart from MiGs of all varieties, Sukhoi Su-7 fighter-bombers and Hunters, a substantial Egyptian bomber force of Tupolev Tu-16 medium bombers and of Iraqui Ilyushin Il-28 light bombers was also put out of action, together with large numbers of helicopters. Supported by strong ground attack elements of the air force, Israeli troops then launched an advance in three directions, clearing the rest of the Sinai peninsula and Gaza Strip, taking Jordanian territory west of the River Jordan, including the Arab half of Jerusalem, and driving the Syrians off the critical Golan Heights. In just six days it was all over, and the Israelis had gained the security they desired and a considerable amount of territory.

Once again the Soviet Union began to re-equip the Arabs with modern warplanes. Soon the Egyptians and Syrians were almost up to their old strength with modern MiG-21s, Su-7s and Tu-16s. Israel ordered further

Mirage Vs from France, but after a guerrilla attack on Beirut airport, a reprisal for the hijacking of an El Al airliner by Palestinian guerrillas, General de Gaulle, the French President, forbade their export. In April 1969 the Egyptians began a war of attrition across the Suez Canal, shelling Israeli positions and launching small raiding parties. The Israelis replied with air-strikes, and once again fighting flared up.

By November 1969 thirty-four Egyptian aircraft had been shot down in combat and seventeen more had been lost to guns and Hawk rockets. In January 1970 the Israelis began a series of air attacks on strategic targets deep in Egypt, and though losses rose, so did claims. By the end of March over 100 aircraft had been claimed since the end of the Six Day War, eighty-five of them Egyptian and the remainder Syrian, for the loss of nineteen Israeli aircraft. The total continued to rise, and before long it was approaching the 150 mark. At the same time supplies of new aircraft were obtained from the United States to make good the loss of those ordered from France, both F4 Phantoms and A4 Skyhawk fighter-bombers reaching Israel during mid-1970.

It was at this time that photographs were released showing Mirages bearing victory scores on their noses, some with five or six, and one with as many as eleven. By the end of 1970 it was believed that at least one Israeli had reached a score of twenty, but it has always been Israeli

pages 150-151
Only one jet fighter pilot is known to have shot down five aircraft in a single mission. This was Squadron Leader Mohammad Alam of the Pakistani Air Force, who on 6 September 1965 intercepted six Hawker Hunters of the Indian Air Force over Kashmir, shooting down one with his Sidewinder missiles, and then claiming four more shot down with his guns as they curved in line astern across his sights. Squadron Leader Alam was Pakistan's first ace, claiming nine victories in just three combats. All were claimed whilst flying the rather elderly North American F-86F Sabre. By Michael Turner.

opposite page
Racing across the skies of North Vietnam, a Russian-built MiG-21 chases a Republic F-105 Thunderchief of the USAF. The North Vietnamese aircraft is emblazoned with victory stars on its nose, and is believed to be the aircraft flown by one of the two great Vietnamese aces of this conflict— either Captain Nguyen Van Bay, or Colonel Tomb. By Michael Turner.

previous page
Although Israel will not release the names of her successful jet fighter pilots for security reasons it is known that several Israelis have built up substantial scores. It is probable that Israeli Mirage and Phantom pilots are by now the top-scoring jet pilots of all time. Several are known to have scores around the fifteen mark, and at least one is believed to have a score in excess of twenty. This Mirage IIIC fighter is clearly the aircraft of an ace, showing ten victory markings against Arab aircraft on its nose.

Second Phantom team to become aces were members of Navy Fighting Squadron VF-96. Lieutenant Randy Cunningham and his operator, Lieutenant William Driscoll, also claimed five Vietnamese MiGs shot down during 1973.

policy to avoid revealing the names of their successful pilots until after they have ceased to fly operationally. The soundness of this policy in the particular circumstances in which Israel finds herself, though frustrating to the historian; can swiftly be observed on consideration. Surrounded as Israel is by enemies, any pilot shot down has a very substantial chance of becoming a prisoner. If reports are to be believed, the treatment of Israeli prisoners by the Arabs frequently leaves a very great deal to be desired, and for this reason the less known about a pilot by the enemy in advance, the better.

As the summer of 1970 passed, Phantoms and Skyhawks joined the assault on Egyptian targets to such good effect that during August of that year a cease-fire was called, allowing a temporary lull to descend once more.

Elsewhere in 1969 a war broke out which was probably one of the most ludicrous of all time. Following an unruly international football match between the South American states of Honduras and El Salvadore, the two countries briefly went to war! Old piston-engined Hon-

duran Vought F4U-5 Corsairs opposed even older F-47D Thunderbolts and F-51 Mustangs. When hostilities closed it was reported that eight Honduran and four Salvadorean aircraft had been shot down, about half of them in dogfights. An American who flew as a mercenary for one of these states has described to the author how on one occasion he shot down a light twin-engined aircraft belonging to the other state, watching it force-land on a beach. Out climbed the pilot, wearing Bermuda shorts and looking very much like another American mercenary, who proceeded to jump up and down in rage. Even the fighting had its ridiculous aspect, it seems.

More seriously, Pakistan and India went to war again on 3 December 1971, after a series of air and ground skirmishes in the disputed Kashmiri area. This time the fighting lasted only a fortnight, but was more intense, resulting in heavier claims and losses. Pakistan still relied heavily on the old F-86F Sabre, but had reinforced them with a batch of Canadair Sabre 6s–probably the best version of the

Sabre ever built. Apart from five squadrons of these aircraft, there were now three squadrons of MiG-19s, supplied by the Chinese, one squadron of Mirages, one of B-57s and a few flights of F-104As.

The Indian air force had been greatly strengthened and included large numbers of MiG-21s, many of them assembled in India, Su-7 fighter-bombers from Russia and home-designed HF-24 Marut fighters, together with the Indian-built Gnats and the older British and French aircraft. The Indians claimed ninety-four aircraft destroyed, including fifty-four F-86s, six Mirages and nine F-104s, admitting their own losses to be fifty-four. No breakdown was given on which claims were made in air combat, and which were claimed by ground fire.

The Pakistanis were more specific, claiming 104 Indian aircraft, fifty of them in combat. Eleven of these were claimed by the Canadair-Sabres of 14 Squadron in East Pakistan (now Bangladesh), which lost five of its own aircraft in the air before the remaining eleven had to be destroyed on the ground by their own ground crews in the face of the Indian advance. Other losses admitted were two Sabres, two F-104s and a MiG-19 in the West.

Among the Pakistani pilots making claims on this occasion were at least three who had been involved in the 1965 war. One of these, Wing Commander Syed Sa'ad Hatmi, had been a flight commander flying Sabres in the first conflict and had claimed two victories over a Hunter and a Gnat. Now leading a MiG-19 squadron, he claimed another Hunter and two Su-7s to become Pakistan's second ace. Squadron Leader Cecil Chaudhary, still flying F-86Fs, added a further victory to the three claimed in 1965.

On the Indian side, four Gnats of 24 Squadron claimed three of four Sabres shot down on 22 November, before the outbreak of war, while during December Hunters of 14 Squadron claimed four of the Canadair-Sabres of Pakistan's 14 Squadron shot down in the East. On 12 December the clash between the F-104A and the MiG-21 came at last, the Russian aircraft proving much more manœuvrable; one Starfighter was claimed shot down. Four days later MiG-21s and MiG-19s clashed, the Indians claiming one of the latter, while next day MiG–21s of 29 Squadron claimed three more F-104As in two battles. However, no Indian pilots have yet become aces.

Following a lull of nearly four years, fighting over North Vietnam was resumed with a vengeance early in 1972, as the United States strove to force a conclusion to stalemated peace talks taking place between the Governments of North and South. By March the total claimed since the beginning of the air fighting in 1965 had risen to 138, while on 10 May 1972 the biggest day's claim of the whole war was made, the destruction of ten MiGs being confirmed.

The total had risen to 160 by August, and on the 28th of that month the first American ace of the war was announced, Captain Richard S. Ritchie of the USAF. He was soon followed by another pilot, this time a member of a Navy unit, Lieutenant Randy Cunningham. Both men flew F4 Phantoms in all their combats. Cunningham's last victory was over a MiG 17 on 10 May 1972, which it was believed was flown by Colonel Tomb. At this stage Tomb was thought to be leading North Vietnamese ace, with at least thirteen victories.

When the fighting finally ended in January 1973 and the main American presence began to be withdrawn from Vietnam, 191 MiG claims had been confirmed, 135 being credited to USAF fighters (two when flown by Navy or Marine pilots on attachment), fifty-four to US

Flown by all the most successful Air Force and Navy MiG-killers over Vietnam, the big McDonnell F-4 Phantom is the Western world's main air-superiority fighter aircraft at the time of going to press. In Vietnam USAF aircraft were camouflaged in greens and browns, but Navy aircraft retained their gull grey and white finish, as seen on this F-4B of Fighting Squadron VF-114 from the carrier USS *Kittyhawk*. This aircraft, seen here heading for North Vietnam, is fully armed with Sidewinder infra-red homing missiles beneath the wings.

Navy pilots, and two to the rear-gunners of Boeing B-52 Stratofortress bombers.

During the Vietnam war the US authorities credited victories not only to pilots but also to the radar men in the rear cockpits of the Phantoms. Thus in the case of Phantoms, each MiG shot down was credited twice; when a final list of aces was prepared it included five names, three of these being 'back-seat men'. Ironically, the top-scorer was one of these. Working on the traditional ace basis of 'pilots only', it can be seen that just two Americans became aces during this conflict.

In the Middle East the tension began to rise again during 1973, and before long clashes between Israeli and Arab aircraft were once more being reported regularly. The climax came on 13 September, when Israeli fighters engaged a strong force of Syrian MiG-21s and claimed at least eight of them shot down.

The Israelis were aware that an Arab attack was inevitable, but the effect on world opinion of a third pre-emptive strike made such an operation politically unacceptable. Conse-

quently the initiative was left with the Arabs, and on 6 October 1973, the Jewish Day of Atonement (Yom Kippur), the Egyptians and Syrians struck on two fronts. This time the forces involved were much larger than in the past, and had employed several years of preparation. As a result the fighting lasted considerably longer than before, and the Israelis paid dearly for the loss of the initiative, their losses in the air and on the ground being much higher this time. Nevertheless, they managed by dint of hard fighting to push back the initial advances, retaking the Golan Heights, advancing into Syria, and then crossing the Suez Canal and outflanking the Egyptians, before a cease-fire arranged by the United Nations came into force.

Most Israeli air force losses were to radar-directed ground fire during ground-attack missions, and to ground-to-air guided missiles, the advanced SAM-IIIs at first proving most deadly, though later in the conflict the Israeli pilots seemed to be devising methods of avoiding them. Something in excess of 118 aircraft

An Israeli Mirage. Since 1962–63 the Israelis have relied heavily on this superb French fighter.

are believed to have been lost, though at least ninety-five of these are known to have fallen to missiles or guns. Greatest losses were suffered by the Skyhawk fighter-bombers (at least fifty-two), with the Phantoms following (about twenty-seven). These were, of course, the two most widely used types, and additional numbers of both aircraft were supplied by the US during the conflict.

As before, the Israeli fighters–Phantoms and Mirages, some of the latter re-engined with American J-79 engines–mastered the Arab air forces, inflicting a toll estimated by US observers to total about 440 (twenty-five by Hawk missiles) by the end of the conflict. Because the fighting was mainly over the fronts, few strikes on Arab airfields were made, and the vast majority of claims related to aircraft in the air. The cease-fire brought a halt to the major fighting on the ground, but outbreaks of fighting continued to occur for days afterwards, and in the air there were frequent clashes. Before the end of the year Israeli claims were announced, totalling 248 Egyptian and 221 Syrian aircraft, twenty and ten respectively having been claimed since the cease-fire came into effect. Twenty-one Iraqi aircraft are also known to have been destroyed.

As a result of the much higher level of losses to the various Arab defences on this occasion, Israeli aircrew casualties were far more severe than before. Many pilots fell into Arab hands, where it is known that they were very badly treated, newspapers reporting that at least one pilot, said to be an 'Israeli air force ace', had died as a result of torture during interrogation. It is feared therefore that some Israeli aces may well have lost their lives to one cause or another during this recent war. It seems highly probable, however, that some of their pilots must by now have very considerable scores, and it is to be hoped that one day in the future it will be possible for details to be released.

At the time of writing this book there has been one of the periodic lulls in air fighting throughout the world. In the Middle East the main antagonists have once again been brought up to strength by the super powers, and fears are being expressed of a further explosion. It is reported that apart from Phantoms and Skyhawks, the Israelis have also been able to obtain additional Mirages from the French. The Arabs have certainly received many of the latest models of the MiG-21; some of the latest MiG-23s may also have been supplied.

It is to be hoped that no more fighting will occur, but past experience of men's inability to settle their differences without recourse to violence would seem to make this an optimistic wish. Already Turkish fighters have attacked targets in Cyprus, though the lack of a defending air force here has precluded fighting in the air.

Israel's Mirage force had been supplemented by numbers of Phantoms by the time the Yom Kippur war broke out in 1973. Subsequently, many more of these aircraft have been delivered, and probably make up the greater part of the fighter force at present. This camouflaged Phantom, already marked with one victory tally on the nose, is typical of those which will probably bear the brunt of any further aerial fighting, should the war in the Middle East flare up again.

Jet fighter aces since 1953

USA (Vietnam)

Captain Charles B. DeBelleveu USAF	6 (Radar Operator)
Captain Richard S. Ritchie USAF	5
Captain Jeffrey S. Feinstein USAF	5 (Radar Operator)
Lieutenant Randy Cunningham USN	5
Lieutenant(jg) William Driscoll USN	5 (Radar Operator)

North Vietnam

Colonel Tomb	13 at least
Captain Nguyen Van Bay	7 at least (possibly 13 or more)

Pakistan

Squadron Leader Mohammad M. Alam	9 (1965 conflict)
Wing Commander Syed Sa'ad Hatmi	5 (2 in 1965, 3 in 1971)

Israel

Unknown but believed to be several, including one at least with a score in excess of twenty. List could now be substantial.

Acknowledgments

Photographic Acknowledgments
E. C. R. Baker 82; F. Bordoni-Bisleri 111 top; Bundesarchiv, Koblenz 19, 20, 21, 22 bottom, 53 top, 98, 99 top, 102 bottom, 103 bottom, 105 bottom, 106 top, 106 bottom, 107 bottom, 108, 111 bottom; Don Chalif 59 bottom, 86, 87 top, 87 bottom, 130; J. B. Cynk, London 53 bottom; E. C. P. Armées, Ivry sur Seine 15 bottom, 93, 94 top, 94 bottom, 95 top, 95 bottom, 96–97; Fox Photos Ltd., London 62–63; General Sikorski Institute 127; W. N. Hess, Louisiana 154; Imperial War Museum, London 4, 8–9, 12 top, 16 bottom, 24 top, 31 top, 31 bottom, 32, 33, 35 top, 35 bottom, 48–49, 54, 55 top, 62 top, 71, 72, 73, 74, 75 top, 83, 110, 125 right, 129; Israeli Embassy, London 153, 156, 157; Italian Air Ministry 51; Italian Air Staff, Rome 12 bottom, 41 top, 41 bottom; Yasuho Izawa, Tokyo 52, 55 bottom, 119 top, 119 bottom, 120, 121, 122, 123; Kalevi Keskinen, Helsinki 91 bottom, 92 bottom; Keystone Press Agency Ltd, London 63 top, 64, 66 bottom, 81, 84; A. S. Norsk Telegrambyra, Oslo 125 left; North American Aviation Inc. 139 bottom; Novosti Press Agency, London 131, 132 top, 132 bottom; Pakistan Air Force 146 bottom, 147 top, 147 bottom; Popperfoto, London 36, 76 top, 76 bottom; Radio Times Hulton Picture Library, London 16 top, 17; Hans Ring 104 bottom; Roger-Viollet, Paris 11, 14, 15 top; Frank F. Smith 75 bottom; Smithsonian Institution, Washington 2–3, 43, 46; Society for Cultural Relations with U.S.S.R. 103 top; Sotamuseo, Helsinki 91 top, 92 top; Stattsbibliothek, Berlin 47, 99 bottom, 107 top; Suddeutscher Verlag, Munich 13, 18, 22 top, 24 bottom, 29, 102 top, 104 top; Ullstein Bilderdienst, Berlin 1, 23, 100, 101, 105 top; U.S. Air Force 6, 45, 56, 57, 59 top, 65, 66 top, 136–137, 139 top, 141, 143, 144, 146 top, 148; U.S. Marine Corps 60, 61; U.S. Navy 68, 155.

Bibliography

E. C. R. Baker. *The Fighter Aces of the RAF, 1939–45*, 1962
T. J. Constable and R. F. Toliver. *Fighter Aces. Horrido!*, 1965
R. F. Futrell. *The United States Air Force in Korea, 1950–1953*, 1961
G. Gurney. *Five Down and Glory*, 1958
W. N. Hess. *The Allied Aces of World War II*, 1966. *The American Aces of World War II and Korea*, 1968
W. Musciano. *Eagles of the Black Cross*, 1965
H. J. Nowarra and K. S. Brown. *Von Richtofen and the 'Flying Circus'*, 1958
E. Obermaier. *Ritterkreuzträger der Luftwaffe, 1939–45*; *Band 1*; *Jagdflieger*, 1966
B. Robertson (ed.). *Air Aces of the 1914–18 War*, 1959
C. Shores and C. Williams. *Aces High; the fighter Aces of the British Commonwealth, Air Forces in World War II*, 1966
C. Shores and H. Ring. *Fighters over the Desert*, 1969
C. Shores, H. Ring and W. N. Hess. *Fighters over Tunisia*, 1975
E. H. Sims. *The Fighter Pilots*, 1967. *Greatest Fighter Missions*, 1962. *American Aces of World War II*, 1958
G. B. Stafford and W. N. Hess. *Aces of the Eighth*, 1974

In addition to these works, there are numerous biographies and autobiographies concerning various fighter aces of many countries, such as *Flying Fury* by J. T. B. McCudden, *Nine Lives* by A. C. Deere and *Fighter Over Finland* by Eino Luukkanen, together with a number of campaign, unit, or air force histories, such as Roger Freeman's *The Mighty Eighth*, which give much information of great interest regarding the aces involved.

Index